HOW RUSSIA BECAME A ZOMBIE STATE

"The greatest crimes are committed out of a desire for excess, not for necessities; thus, for example, one does not become a tyrant to escape the cold; therefore, great honors are given not to the one who kills the thief, but to the one who kills the tyrant."

Aristotle, "Politics"

ALEXEY MOLCHANOV

Dedicated to Putin and my ex-wife. Both of them know thing about law and morality.

Alexey Molchanov

Contents

PREFACE

M Y NAME IS ALEXEI MOLCHANOV. I have worked as a lawyer in Russia for over 15 years. I graduated from a law institute with honors and was twice a laureate of a presidential scholarship and one of the Moscow Government once. It was in the early 2000s, and although I had already seen the Russian legal system's shortcomings, I was optimistic and hoped for the best.

As time passed, I worked in different companies as a general practitioner, and I especially liked litigation. I also, occasionally, represented acquaintances in courts in this or that case.

However, over time, it became more and more challenging to do my job. The already chaotic legislation was changing rapidly, and at first, the concept of "law" disappeared from the courts, followed by logic. In 2012, I realized that the legal system had degraded almost completely, but to my amazement, after 2014, it got even worse.

At some point, when writing a statement of claim, realizing that the decision made by the court of the first instance directly contradicts the law, I referred to the Russian Constitution. It may seem strange, but it was rare in ordinary cases to refer to it—and I made a reference with a strange mixed feeling. As I remember now, paragraph 2 of Article 15 proudly states, "Government authorities, local self-government bodies, officials, citizens, and their associations are obliged to comply with the Constitution of the Russian Federation and its laws." Can you imagine? I had to remind the court to obey the laws! It was an appeal in the case of a friend of mine, and the court considered it had the right not to apply the law as it was written. However, my appeal was declined.

I had long suspected that, as such, the Constitution in Russia had not been working for a long time, but, obviously, I thought about it seriously for the first time.

Chaos grew, and I realized that it is impossible to be in a system with no rights and at the same time remain honest and sane. And so, I retired from law practice.

In 2018, due to rigged elections, V.V. Putin retained his office. It was his second term (after "castling" with his accomplice, D.A. Medvedev), which, according to the same Constitution, was supposed to be his last. Even then, I realized that Putin would look for ways to stay in power, and the Constitution would be changed. I turned out to be correct. In the summer of 2020, amid the epidemic, a shameful procedure was carried out, which I will talk about in this book, supposedly allowing Putin to be "elected" for other terms.

At that moment, I realized that the Constitution was dead. It has turned into a tangle of contradictory norms, not enforced by the courts or the authorities. But I still had a question: are all its articles not valid, or maybe something else remains?

This book is an attempt to clarify for me, and publicly disseminate, all significant contradictions between the Constitution, existing laws, and law enforcement practices in Russia to show that Russia is not at all the country that it wants to appear to be.

Legal language and terms are rather complex for laypeople to understand, so I will explain, simplify, and give examples of all the rules of law that I will quote. At the same time, I want to show the whole problem from a legal point of view so that I will cite the necessary laws and cases. I hope it will not be boring, and at least not unfounded.

Why do you need to know this at all?

The constitution is the framework for the functioning of the state. If it does not work, lawlessness and corruption begin to arise. Corruption is like cancer. If we accept the analogy that countries are organs, then cancer metastases will not be limited to one country. They always go beyond it.

So, corruption and dictatorship can manifest themselves outside countries:

- In aggression: A favorite trick of thieving politicians and dictators to justify their failures not by total theft but by the machinations of an "external enemy." Not surprisingly, sooner or later, brainwashing one's people is an attempt to justify one's incompetence. Often, the authorities try to provoke anger towards a specific group of people (foreigners, sexual and other minorities, etc.). And such a spread of hatred towards particular groups and countries often leads to wars, which we have proof of, having the most significant war in Europe in the 21st century.

- In exile: Few people want to live in extreme poverty and lack rights. Therefore, at every opportunity, citizens will begin to leave their country searching for a new life, increasing tension in the more prosperous countries where they aspire.

- In murders: When persecuting their enemies abroad, even if they are not citizens of another country, often, the victims are citizens of the land of refuge for such persons. It has happened several times already. Can you guarantee that you or your acquaintances will not be poisoned along with some refugee who said something 'wrong' in Russia?

- In corrupt officials in other countries: A corrupt official does not want to live in a situation of total lawlessness. Therefore, he uses his native country as a source of income while he seeks to settle all his money and his family in countries with rights where his property is protected. Is it necessary to say that in another country, his behavior will change little, which creates a significant burden on public institutions?

- In interference with trade relations: Sanctions are imposed for violation of human rights. It is challenging to deal with such countries because you never know when one will be banned from working with a particular enterprise or individual (regardless of who introduces such restrictions: the country that violates human rights or other countries as measures of deterrence and punishment).

- The possibility of imposing sanctions already implies an increase in market volatility: The same sanctions increase the uncertainty in the market—one does not know what foot Putin will stand on today and whether it will occur to him to shoot down a couple more planes to show the 'greatness' of Russia.

- Milking of foreign companies: Even if a company is located outside a specific country and does not have representative offices, it risks its money. For example, courts in Russia have already fined GOOGLE and META vast sums of money for, allegedly, violating Russian law.

The attitude towards Russia can be a litmus test for this or that leader: how informed, moral and honest they are, how much the rights of not only Russian citizens but also citizens of their country mean to them.

Let's assess how bad things are.

HOW TO READ THIS BOOK?

I HAVE MADE READING THIS BOOK as informative as it is entertaining. And even after reducing its volume significantly, it came out quite voluminous. However, I made it as easy to read as possible and created QR codes in the margins of materials that I consider worthy of your reading if a respected reader is interested in a particular topic and believes (not without reason) my comment to be unusually superficial or brief. In that case, such links will help them delve deeper into their subject of interest.

I cite most of the sources in Russian, so if this language is not your native language, I'm afraid you will have to use automatic translation tools. The good news is that this is relatively easy to do in today's world, and most browsers support this feature.

P.S. I started to write this book before February 2022, when Putin turned from an ordinary criminal into a military criminal. That confirmed its conclusions but deprived it of its predictive character.

Chapter 1

THE HISTORY OF THE EMERGENCE OF CONSTITUTIONS.

W HY DO WE NEED A constitution, and what is the history of their appearance? I will try to briefly outline the history of the coming to the idea of creating modern constitutions.

One of the main disputes in legal science is the dispute about what came first, the law (as a set of established norms and rules) or the state. Some scientists say that most ancient tribes already had the law, which, one way or another, made decisions about what one could do in the tribe and what one could not. Other scientists say that before the creation of the state, there was no law as such; the leader decided what would come to his mind at the current moment. Still, only the need to maintain order with a large population arose the need to create a unified system of law. That is, the state appeared at the beginning, and then it was already necessary to develop a system of law for the convenience and efficiency of management.

In my view, the state and law are sides of the same coin, and one cannot exist without the other.

Howbeit. The first states were despotic; that is, all power belonged to one person and his family. The source of such power was the myth that God appointed such a person. The Greek cities stood a little aside. There was a king too, who was elected in some cities through direct democracy (where the decision was made not by an elected body, but by all the inhabitants of the polis, with the exception, of course, of women, children, freedmen, and slaves). But even as democracies, the policies appointed themselves a king so that he could make quick decisions. As you might guess, the king, when his power was not limited, often ruled as he saw fit and changed the laws not only as needed but simply at will, so even then, people began to think about how to limit the absolute power of the king. At that time, they did not come to the idea of a constitution or the division of powers into 'branches'; instead, they adopted a system of two rulers (as in Sparta and Athens, there were two kings; in ancient Rome, two consuls). As we know, everything ended badly: Greece fell under the onslaught of Rome. And in Rome, the rivalry between the two consuls, Julius Caesar and Marcus Aurelius, ended in a civil war between them, as a result of which Julius Caesar defeated his rival and became the first Roman emperor, destroying the Roman Republic together with the second consul. For him, however, this ended badly. But the newborn Empire did not die with him on the steps of the forum by the hands of the Republican Brutus.

As the Roman emperors ruled, information has also come down to us well. The cruelty and lawlessness of many of them forever left an indelible mark on history. Over time, the gigantic Roman Empire habitually received two emperors, one of whom ruled in Rome and the other in Constantinople.

When the barbarians swept the heavy and clumsy Roman Empire off the earth, they set back the development of jurisprudence for centuries. Of the states that arose from the ruins, there was none with a system that somehow limited the king's power.

But were the subjects so powerless? As I noted above, if there is a state, there is a law. Of course, the inhabitants were not impotent. Moreover, the king's armed retinue initially had the same rights as the king, who was only the "first among equals." But the system was changing. The king could not keep his comrades near him. He gave them the lands from which they received income in exchange for a vassal oath—to be loyal and come to him at the first call with armed people. And if, in ancient Rome, all the troops were directly subordinate to the consuls and then to the emperors, the medieval system of army formation assumed that the king, even if he had an army, could not match the combined troops of his subordinates.

Of course, the king tried to rule as he wanted, but the situation was already different. His arbitrariness was limited to the interests of his vassals. Sooner or later, such interests were bound to collide.

And so it happened. As a result of the barons' uprising against the arbitrariness of the English king, John Lackland, in 1215, he had to sign the first document limiting the absolute power of the king, the Magna Carta. You will probably be surprised, but this document is still part of an unwritten (that is, not existing in a single document) constitution in the UK.

Did the Magna Carta save England from arbitrariness and rebellion? Of course not. No king's reign has passed without revolts. There were uprisings under Edward II and Edward III, under his grandson Richard II, then under Henry IV, etc. But now, the people and the nobility could say that they not only did not like the ruler's behavior but that he violated certain norms of law, which he undertook to observe when ascending the throne. And the educated Parliament made decisions on approving new taxes or raising old ones, which undoubtedly made the life of ordinary citizens not so gloomy.

A series of wars in Europe brought out all the shortcomings of the feudal army, and the entire command and power again began to concentrate in one hand, the hand of the ruler. Moreover, the monarchs took not only secular but also spiritual power, thus forming an absolute monarchy.

Everything seems to have returned from where it began. Still, already in the 17th century, the English philosopher John Locke outlined the theory of separation of powers, in which he proposed to divide power not by multiplying the number of rulers, as in ancient times, but into three branches of law we know today: legislative, executive and judicial; as well as the concept of natural rights. If earlier people believed that rights are granted to a person by the state, therefore it can take them away (including, of course, the right to life), then John Locke realized that a person's rights arise by his birth, and the state cannot limit them. And accordingly, the power source is the people, not God or the intercourse of the king with the queen.

Since absolute power was more concentrated, this could not but provoke a response from a society that did not control it. The struggle became even more severe and cruel with the increase of uncontrollability. Charles I in England in the 17th century, Louis XVI in France in the 18th century, and many nobles lost their heads, becoming a clear example of the minor shortcomings of unrestricted and uncontrolled power.

However, six years before the tragic death of Louis XVI, on the other side of the world, the world's first Constitution appeared, which included the most advanced ideas of separation of powers and their checks and balances. The founders managed to solve the serious problem of power—constant distortions—and break the endless circle of lawlessness and uprisings. Undoubtedly, the United States did not escape civil war after almost a century. Still, it was not an uprising in the former sense; that is, far from being a war of the impoverished population against the presumptuous and oppressive government. Instead, on the contrary, it was a war of the rich south against the rules of a more technologically advanced, but less wealthy north.

One of the problems of this war was the problem of slavery. At the beginning of the 18th century, Hegel, in his work 'The Philosophy of Law,' discovered the concept of 'wrongful law,' a law that, in its essence, contradicted the natural rights of man. It was what the Americans faced in their civil war;

15

slavery was legal. That was inherently contrary to natural rights. According to the same idea, neither slavery, the Holocaust, nor any other law that violates fundamental human rights can be applied since, although it has the form according to all the rules of the adopted law, it is illegal.

Let me explain a little about natural rights and wrongful laws. To live, a person needs to eat, breathe, sleep, and so on. Hypothetically, some states could try to ban their citizens from breathing. But can a person live without it? Therefore, such a law is wrongful; it should not be enforced nor applied. Its adoption is either a desire to deprive one's subjects of life or is specifically done so the person would violate it and receive benefits from it (for example, in the form of fines or the threat of punishment for its violation).

After World War II, just over a century after Hegel's death, countries finally accepted the concept of natural rights. It became clear that despotism feeds on hatred and goes beyond the borders of a single state. It was necessary to limit absolute power to avoid or at least significantly reduce the number of wars in the world. Countries signed the Universal Declaration of Human Rights in 1948, and European countries signed the Convention for the Protection of Human Rights and Fundamental Freedoms in 1950. These documents have become a kind of minimum, a set of rights that belong to absolutely any person in the world, which are natural and inalienable, and their violation is impossible. Any law that violates these rights will be illegal. I want to emphasize this separately because, in the future, we will refer to these documents more than once.

I hope I was able to show through a brief history what exactly constitutions are for. In a nutshell, by limiting his power, the ruler reduces the likelihood that his head will become an ornament to the throne of his successor. According to statistics, the average dictator has a significantly reduced chance of dying a natural death or in freedom. The same document has a 'side' effect. With specific, logical legislation that does not restrict but protects the rights of citizens, the well-being and happiness of the citizens of a given country grows.

Is it necessary to say that the most technologically advanced and wealthiest countries have legislation where human rights are respected? A citizen can be sure that he can invest in an enterprise and that his money will not be extorted. And they will not pass into the hands of the son of some close friend of the president, so the money is invested in the economy and not hidden or moved abroad.

Thus, constitutions began to appear all over the world. And even if the ruler did not particularly care about the well-being or happiness of his citizens, the prospect of not living to old age seemed not entirely fantastic to them.

Chapter 2

A BRIEF HISTORY OF LAW IN RUSSIA (UNTIL THE 1990S)

WHAT IS THE HISTORY OF human rights in Russia? In this chapter, I will briefly talk about the main milestones in developing human rights and freedoms in Russia until the collapse of the USSR. You should keep in mind that the information is very general, there were movements both in one direction and in the other, and I focus not on historical events but on human rights and their development. Therefore, such a retelling may seem superficial to many, which is not far from the truth.

Russia has always had problems with freedom. In the almost thousand-year history, there have been only three short periods of not ideal, but still freedom.

The Slavs came with other tribes to Central and Eastern Europe in the 2nd century. It was a massive group of tribes united by a common Proto-Slavic language. Naturally, at that time, the union was doomed to disintegrate without a state. Their general development went on the same wavelength as the Germanic and other 'barbarian' tribes of Europe. They first fought and served the Roman empires. Then they created their states (the Kingdom of Bulgaria,

Great Moravia, Kievan Rus, etc.). A group of Eastern Slavs formed a union of principalities, with the main seat of government (Grand Duke) in Kyiv. This association of tribes did not have special law; they used custom law. From the 9th to the 10th centuries, the feudal system began to strengthen, which, in general, corresponded to the development of other European countries and peoples of that time.

However, in the XIII century, the development changed. Kievan Rus was conquered by the Mongols, whose form of government was not feudal but rigidly despotic. It was impossible to resist such power with honest and noble methods. All resistance attempts were drowned in blood. Skillful Muscovite princes with Mongols' hands eliminated their less cunning but more noble competitors from other principalities. And when there were already enough forces, Moscow Prince Ivan III managed to free himself from the power of the Mongols.

But, as the English proverb says, "If you have a hammer in your hands, any problem seems to be a nail." The Moscow princes, having received a tool for absolute power, began to use it with all their might. Ivan IV, the grandson of Ivan III, who ruled in the XVI century, went on the counteroffensive. He captured the Mongolian Kazan, Novgorod, and Pskov principalities, which were always extraordinarily free, electing a prince for themselves and even included in the European commercial Hanseatic League.

However, in old age, Ivan IV began to go mad. He dissolved the parliament, the Verkhovna Rada, deciding that he would rule by himself. He established a particular order of his associates, who were supposed to monitor the implementation of his will, placing them above any law. They were called 'guardsmen' (or 'Kromeshniks') from the Russian word 'oprich,' 'krome' (except). All this resulted in such terrible lawlessness that he forever remained in the history of Russia as Ivan the Terrible, one of the cruelest rulers of Russia. Not that his atrocities were on a large scale (there were more), but they were ferocious even by the harsh standards of the Middle Ages. For example, when he sent guardsmen for his treasurer, whom he suspected of theft, they cut off his head and that of his entire family, including his 16-year-old daughter.

Another 'wonderful' principle introduced by Ivan the Terrible was the principle of 'word and deed,' where any person could point to another with these words, and that person was immediately dragged to prison to be tortured on the subject of a conspiracy against the sovereign. Is it necessary to say that under torture, any person, in most cases, slandered himself?

Naturally, this feast of lawlessness ended badly. Ivan IV started the Livonian War, in which his valiant guardsmen did not show such feats as in the field of executions of defenseless people, and they lost this war. When Ivan IV died, he had no living heirs, and the country, with its institutions destroyed, naturally plunged into chaos.

With difficulty getting out of the most challenging crisis, the boyars chose the new tsar, the first Romanov after decades of leapfrogging rulers.

It was evident that it was impossible to resist the European countries in military affairs, using an outdated system of troops and obsolete weapons. Therefore, Alexei Mikhailovich Romanov, then Peter I, his son, made many profound reforms to modernize the entire system, which had already become the Russian Empire under Peter I, as in the European model.

However, Peter was too carried away by state building and neglected his son's upbringing. He fell under the influence of revanchists, who did not like the reforms of Peter, for which he was imprisoned where he died. Peter had no male heirs left. Therefore, he issued a decree in which the Emperor had the right to appoint any person as the successor independently. However, in 1723, Peter became very ill and died in terrible agony. It is not known whether he managed to name a successor. However, for some reason, if he did call him, this name remained a secret.

Given that the Emperor was still a person with absolute power, the period of the struggle of different people for power began again; this period in Russian history is called the 'epoch of palace coups.' Is it necessary to clarify that none of the rulers even thought of trying to reduce their power in such instability? On the contrary, power was concentrated in one hand more and more. When Anna Ioannovna (niece of Peter I) was ascending the throne, the nobility attempted to force her to sign 'conditions' of accession that would limit her powers, but she tore them up.

Naturally, large peasant uprisings arose, but they were all brutally suppressed.

Under Alexander I, Russia joined the war with Napoleon. The returning victorious army brought with it the French ideas of freedom, equality, and fraternity. And when Alexander I died in 1825, the army revolted. The purpose of the uprising was to force the new emperor, not yet crowned, to accept the Constitution. Everything went wrong. The heir of Alexander I, Constantine, renounced the throne, and his brother, Nicholas, by the time the troops gathered on the square, had already assumed the kingdom. The rebellion was brutally suppressed, five organizers were executed, and the rest of the officers were exiled to Siberia.

Nicholas I remembered all his life about the Decembrist uprising. And so he was a reactionary. However, the situation with the economy and people in Russia was getting worse. There were huge problems with serfs — peasants who lived in the position of slaves (they could be sold, including separation from other family members, beaten, etc., but they had minimal rights and could own property). His father granted a constitution to Poland in 1815, which at that time was part of the Russian Empire, while not giving freedom to his citizens. But the Poles did not like the rule of Moscow in general. They revolted in the 1830s, for which they were criticized by everyone in Russia, including the most liberal representatives of the Russian Empire. 'They have a constitution, which the citizens of Russia did not have, and they were unhappy!' But the Poles wanted to rule their state on their own without a viceroy of the Russian king. Therefore, when Nikolai was given the draft of the Russian Constitution, he postponed it forever.

However, having lost the Crimean War (1853-1856) with a bang, it became clear that a lack of rights and a lousy economy greatly affected the military power of the Empire. Not surviving the defeat, Nicholas dies, leaving all the problems to his son, Alexander II, who received the nickname 'Liberator' among the people.

Alexander carried out many reforms, immediately freeing the peasants and buying them out from the landowners, for which they had to pay an annual fee to the banks, which made these payments to the landowners. He created a system of courts, with a jury, based on the parties' competitiveness and equality, so perfect that it became a model not only in Russia but even abroad.

At the same time, the protracted solution of the peasant question, its impact on the well-being of the peasants, and rooted Marxist ideas led to the revolutionaries killing Alexander II. Thus ended the second free stage in Russia.

His son, Alexander III, curtailed all progressive reforms, created a massive staff of political police, and everything returned to its usual lack of rights. By his death, the snowball of problems had grown to incredible proportions.

In 1904, to raise the authority of Nicholas II, the son of Alexander III, the advisers proposed to conduct a "small victorious war" against Japan, which interfered with the plans of the Empire to expand in China. As a result of the Russo-Japanese War, in which Russia did not win a single battle, Russia was forced to sign a humiliating peace, and a genuine general uprising began. Not only the peasants, who had already paid their value to the banks three times for their freedom, were dissatisfied, but the landlords and the laymen as well. Nobility forced the emperor to sign the Manifesto on October 17, 1905, which granted citizens fundamental rights, freedom of personality, faith, assembly and association, and speech. Still, the tangle of contradictions could not be resolved that quickly. And although a parliament — the State Duma — was created (even with an advisory voice only), it never suited the emperor, and he dissolved it five times during his reign.

And when the Russian Empire also entered World War I in 1914, this spring of unfreedom laid under the regime could not stand it and unclenched again. In 1917, the revolution was repeated, as a result of which Nicholas II was forced to resign. For almost a year, Russia was a republic, but the Provisional Government, appointed before the general elections, accepted all the obligations of Nicholas II, which caused the general displeasure of the people. In early December 1917, when, as a result of the elections, the Bolsheviks realized that they had lost the elections miserably, they just seized power in the country by force, unleashing a civil war.

The civil war lasted five years and ended in 1922 with the victory of the Bolsheviks.

The country, exhausted by wars, needed a respite. Having pursued a policy of 'war communism' (when property, including food, was forcibly confiscated from the population), the Bolsheviks were forced to introduce a new economic policy. In 1924, the first Soviet Constitution was adopted. I cannot say Lenin was such a great supporter of human rights and freedoms (in this Constitution, there was not a single word about human rights and liberties at all), but as a result of the wars, the Russian Empire collapsed: Poland, Finland, Lithuania, Latvia, Estonia were formed, and other republics stood in the balance of seceding as well. The only way to hold the territories non-violently was the adoption of this constitution. In addition, the Constitution even provided for the right of republics to secede from the state freely. Instead of communism, the NEP (the New Economic Policy) was proclaimed a liberal economic policy modeled on Western countries. The NEP boosted the development of banks, private enterprises, and general freedom. Thus began the third period of freedom in Russia. I believe Lenin had realized by that time that the building of communism was impossible and the NEP should become a permanent system of economics and law. However, we will never know. In 1924, he was killed.

After Lenin's death, the NEP did not last long until 1927, three years after Stalin came to power.

Stalin brutally curtailed all the ongoing economic policy. De facto depriving people of their rights and freedoms. Until now, the 30s of the 20th century are not perceived in Russia in any other way than as years of complete lack of rights, mass repressions, executions, and fear.

However, in 1936, Stalin approved a different constitution to show that people supposedly had any rights in the USSR. It was a very progressive document for the time. The problem is that it was dead, no one observed it. There were no other parties in USSR, except for the CPSU, there was no ownership of the real estate, there were no personal rights, and there were no courts (as well as the competition of the parties in them), which, moreover, could sentence anyone to death, regardless of guilt. Ongoing trials and executions of 'comrades' began, who were far from Stalin, then closer and closer to him. And there were special services, looking for 'enemies of the nation' everywhere.

On March 1, 1953, after several hours of lying on the floor, Stalin was hospitalized; he suffered paralysis of the entire right side of his body, but his guards were afraid to approach him. On March 5, he died.

The frightened elite no longer wanted such lawlessness. If, at first, under Stalin, they imprisoned and shot ordinary citizens, then they began to do the same with party members and the same representatives of the special services. Now the authorities became softer, and although the population no longer had rights as such, in any case, the number of arrests and executions decreased significantly, which seemed like an 'extraordinary thaw.' It seemed to the people that it was possible to live like this in general.

In 1977, Brezhnev approved another constitution. This constitution did not differ significantly from the previous one, except that it established a one-party power system.

By the 1980s, extreme poverty and lawlessness had reached another limit. It became evident that without significant reforms, the country would not exist. Mikhail Gorbachev, who was then the General Secretary, actually the ruler, announced 'perestroika.' As a result of the widely promoted 'glasnost,' when people were finally able to say and express what they wanted, it became clear that the legal system of the USSR did not suit practically anyone.

Gorbachev's attempts to modify the Constitution, making the Constitution of the RSFSR, as a result of which he became the first and last President of the USSR, did not produce results: this was not enough. The contradictions accumulated during the Soviet period, and compressed by the repressive apparatus, with its weakening, tore the country apart. Many republics left the union: Lithuania, Latvia, Estonia, Kazakhstan, Tajikistan, Turkmenistan, Ukraine, Belarus, Moldova, Georgia, Armenia, and Azerbaijan; realizing that, historically, they had more chances to become more successful being independent or that it was better to be the first in the village than second at court.

Thus the Russian Federation was born.

Before we continue, I would like to highlight the following points:

1. In Russia, the people were not free almost always, except for only a couple of short periods;

2. This does not mean that the population liked it, but any revolts were brutally suppressed;

3. Russia had no experience of real democracy (except Novgorod and Pskov principalities of the 11th-15th Century model);

4. By the time of the collapse of the USSR, a European-type legal school did not exist in Russia, and citizens did not have (and most do not even now) practically the slightest idea about how modern law and democracy work.

Chapter 3

THE HISTORY OF MODERN RUSSIA OR THE DEGRADATION OF THE RUSSIAN LEGAL SYSTEM UNDER PUTIN.

NEVERTHELESS, WHEN THE USSR FELL, the main fear was the possibility of revenge, a return to the USSR. The person at that time personifying liberal values was Yeltsin. The Congress of People's Deputies, Parliament, which had been formed back in the USSR, was still functioning. The creators of the Russian Constitution already faced a choice: to give all power to Yeltsin or to allow the reactionaries to influence his actions.

In 1993, the Russian Constitution was adopted.

In general, there are two main types of republics in the world; the Presidential, where the president has a lot of power, and the parliamentary, where the parliament rules everything. The founders of the 1993 Constitution, fearing the coming of revanchists to power, created not just a Presidential Constitution, but Superpresidential, in which the president controlled all government bodies, could dissolve parliament, nominate the prosecutor general, judges, form all ministries, submit bills to parliament, etc., etc., president can be removed, in fact, only as a result of elections or when he commits serious crimes.

While still a student in the early 2000s, I wrote an article about this and submitted it to the student journal of the institute where I studied. It was already Putin's reign. And for the first time, I encountered the fact that my reviewer, a respected professor of constitutional law, began to edit the article, changing, in fact, its entire meaning: an analysis of the distortions of the system of checks and balances towards presidential power. Having received corrections and comments, I did not publish the article in its corrected form.

However, let us return to the first draft of the Russian Constitution. Since 1990, since the fall of the USSR, the Constitutional Court has been operating, whose task was to check the legal acts and actions of officials for compliance with the Constitution of the RSFSR. Moreover, this right was initially active: the Constitutional Court itself, by its initiative, could check any act for compliance with the Constitution.

The most extended case in the history of that Constitutional Court, whose hearings lasted almost half a year, and the loudest and most massive was the case of checking the constitutionality of the decrees of the President of the Russian Federation, by which in August 1991, he suspended and then stopped the activities of the Communist Party and declared it outside the law. In the framework of the same case, the Constitutional Court checked the constitutionality of the parties themselves — the CPSU (Communists' Party of Soviet Union) and the CP (Communists' Party) of the RSFSR.

Many researchers believe that this case was the most underestimated and misunderstood. It probably happened because of the heat of political confrontation and a split in society.

The Constitutional Court made a controversial decision. It pointed out that there can be no ban on ideology in a democratic state; accordingly, a ban on the association of people with certain beliefs in an organization is also impossible. It also admitted that merging party structures with state power is unacceptable, while it brought ordinary party members out of the blow.

As a result, both those who defended the CPSU and the Communist Party of the RSFSR and those who wanted permission from the Constitutional Court for the lustration and punishment of all former communists were disappointed. Which, as we will see later, will have significant consequences.

And finally, the decision that entailed the most dramatic consequences was the one by which the Constitutional Court recognized Presidential Decree No. 1400 on the dissolution of the Congress of People's Deputies as inconsistent with the Constitution. On October 7, 1993, President Yeltsin suspended the activities of the Constitutional Court.

Taking into account such work of the Constitutional Court of the RSFSR, the founders of the new Constitution of Russia excluded from Article 125, the right of the Constitutional Court to independently check the legal acts for compliance with the Constitution. It was the first step towards its end. Not yet born, the Constitution, like a child with a genetic disease, was already under threat and subject to the president's will. Since then, the Constitutional Court began to consider the compliance of legal acts only by the application of the courts or state bodies. An ordinary person was already excluded from this process, like the Constitutional Court itself.

By 1996, Yeltsin had lost all his popularity this way; it was evident that he was clinging to power. He was getting old and had a big problem with alcohol. In addition, his team was very savvy not only in law but also in economics: they had to sort out the problems left as a legacy from the USSR (monopoly, massive inefficiency of enterprises, etc.), and the reforms were carried out indecisively, poorly and very slowly. The privatization of state assets was carried out in the way that allowed a limited number of people to use state money to obtain state assets in their ownership (the so-called 'loan auctions' — actually carried out on the principle of leverage buyout — the purchase of enterprises for state money for the promise to cover the loan from future income). Yeltsin believed that if he could get many wealthy owners, this would immediately solve the problems with the economy. As a result, all he managed to get was a circle of oligarchs close to the president's family, using all means possible to achieve their interests, including political pressure. Yeltsin and his family were no exception. One of the things that kept him in power was the fear that once he left office, he, his daughter, and his son-in-law would be prosecuted for corruption.

Yeltsin barely managed to win the 1996 elections. His main rival was the representative of the Communist Party of the Russian Federation, Zyuganov. And Yeltsin would never have won if it weren't for ordinary people's fear of the return of communism.

That did not help Yeltsin much. In 1998, Russia was forced to default on foreign obligations, and his rating fell unusually low. On December 31, 1999, in his New Year's speech, he announced that he was leaving his post. He already had a withdrawal plan ready; he appointed Putin as his successor.

Putin worked in the KGB in Soviet times. He still considers the collapse of the USSR 'the main geopolitical catastrophe of the 20th century' (obviously, because he never had any special skills or talents and dismissal from the KGB was the end of his career), in the mayor's office of St. Petersburg Mayor Sobchak. Putin took part in honest elections only once in his life, namely, in 1996, he helped Sobchak in his mayoral elections. However, they lost, and he ended up on the street. Putin did not like this experience very much and never took such a risk again.

Since his post in the mayor's office, Putin has left a criminal trail. "The Sovershenno Sekretno" newspaper of August 8, 2000, wrote: 'In 1992, Pyotr Aven, who is now commonly called an oligarch from the Alfa group, being the Minister of Foreign Economic Relations of Russia, transferred the functions of the MVEC representative in St. Petersburg to Vladimir Putin. Perhaps this appointment saved Putin from possible participation in a serious investigation into the issuance of export licenses for vast volumes of oil products, non-ferrous metals, and other grave goods by the Committee he leads. The Committee did not have the right to do so, and most of the firms with which it entered into contracts for importing food products into St. Petersburg turned out to be shell companies.'

Corruption scandals associated with him continued. The investigation regarding his participation in corruption cases during his service in the mayor's office in 1994 to 1996 was started in 1999. The case file received No. 144128. But it quickly hushed up, and investigator Zykin was fired after the forced closure of the case and almost imprisoned, accusing him of 'theft of documents,' but afterward, documents were 'found,' and he wasn't prosecuted.

Putin was introduced to Yeltsin, and in July 1998, Yeltsin appointed him the director of the Federal Security Service (FSB). He used the thoroughly corrupt Putin, who never respected the law and was not particularly ceremonious with methods, to remove Prosecutor General Skuratov, who had begun investigating the Yeltsin family. Yeltsin himself could not do this. The Parliament, then still beyond the control of the President, did not allow Yeltsin to fire Skuratov. Putin coped with the task by arranging a sex scandal for the prosecutor (more about the scandal here), and Skuratov was forced to leave. After Putin rendered such a service, Yeltsin agreed to transfer his powers to Putin if he could guarantee his safety and exemption from criminal prosecution for corruption.

And so it happened. Putin became Yeltsin's successor. He kept his word. While still president's deputy, Putin signed the Decree "On Guarantees to the President of the Russian Federation, who has terminated the exercise of his powers, and to members of his family." This Decree guaranteed not only the non-initiation of criminal cases but also the use, for example, of dachas at state expense and other maintenance for the former president. Should I say that such a decree contradicted not only the Constitution of Russia but also the Criminal Code (which in the hierarchy of normative acts is higher than the Decree of the President) and several other legal acts?

New elections were scheduled for the fall of 2000. But in 1999, Putin's rating was low; he did not show himself as prime minister and never possessed unique leadership qualities. However, in the fall of 1999, several terrorist attacks took place in Moscow, Buynaksk, and Volgodonsk—some residential buildings were blown up. As a result, 307 people died, and 1,700 were injured. Against this background, Putin, who promised to 'kill terrorists in the toilet' during his election campaign, and being the former KGBist, significantly improved his rating.

There are many black spots in this whole story. The strangest was the story of the so-called 'Ryazan sugar.' Against the backdrop of explosions of houses, the population mobilized and began to check all the basements of their residential buildings for suspicious objects and activities. On September 22, 1999, the bags with an unusual mixture were found in one of the houses in Ryazan. The initial express analysis showed the presence of an explosive - hexogen. A criminal case was initiated under Art. 205 part 1 of the Criminal Code of the Russian Federation (attempted terrorism). All the explosives were, of course, seized and handed over to the FSB laboratory.

Sometime later, the director of the FSB, Patrushev, announced that the bags contained not hexogen but sugar and that the training was being conducted in Ryazan.

This story smelt too bad. Many suspected that the FSB was behind all these explosions. Looking back, such catastrophes more than once raised Putin's rating 'on time.' Alexander Litvinenko, a lieutenant colonel of the Soviet and Russian state security (from 1988-1999, an employee of the KGB - FSB, where he specialized in the fight against terrorism and organized crime), spoke about this in detail. He wrote a book about it, 'The FSB Blows Up Russia' (ISBN 0-914481-63-0). In 2000, he was forced to flee from Russia to England, where in 2006, he was poisoned and killed by Russian FSB Officer Lugovoi (materials of the English investigation can be found here). It is the famous case where Litvinenko was poisoned with radioactive polonium, which traces were later recorded almost all over London. I will dwell on this episode in more detail later, but I cannot pass by these facts at the current stage. By the way, Lugovoy was not only not convicted of murder but he was rewarded. He became a senator of the State Duma, where he still is spouting, sometimes, one or another draft of wrongful law.

The first thing Putin started with when he came to power was to exercise control over the media. If, under Yeltsin, the media openly and freely criticized the government, which more than once went sideways, the situation began to change dramatically under Putin. Ironically, freedom of speech played a cruel joke on Yeltsin: during his reign, he (and his government) often became the object of criticism (which was not ungrounded); Putin, who took control of all the media, naturally, was no longer subjected to such criticism, which served beloved propaganda legend 'about the dashing 90s' and its lawlessness compared to the 'order' during Putin's reign. We will analyze this in detail when we speak of Article 29 of the Constitution.

In principle, the fight against freedom of speech was closely intertwined with the battle against oligarchs who disagreed with Putin, which often confused citizens who did not like oligarchs. Thus, one of the first independent television channels, NTV, which Putin took control of, belonged to the oligarch Gusinsky.

Putin ordered Khodorkovsky to be imprisoned as an example of what could happen to dissent oligarchs. Moreover, although in Russia, a legal entity cannot be subject to criminal law, Khodorkovsky's Yukos company was bankrupted and placed at the disposal of Putin's friend, Sechin. Until now, Yukos shareholders are challenging the illegality of this decision and seeking compensation in various international courts (case materials can be read here).

After another oligarch, Berezovsky, fled from Russia, the rest behaved submissively and did not contradict Putin openly.

On October 26, 2002, there was another major terrorist attack in Moscow. A group of 40 armed Chechen militants led by Movsar Baraev seized and held hostages for three days from among the workers, spectators, and the cast of the Nord-Ost musical — 916 people in the building of the Theater Center. The militants held the hostages for three days. On the third day, the decision to storm was made. Gas was released into the center through the vents, the formula of which was strictly classified. As a result of the actions of the gas, all the terrorists died or were killed during the assault. One hundred twenty-five of the hostages died from the action of this gas. The exact gas formula the special forces use was not disclosed even to the medical workers.

But it's not even about the cruelty of the authorities and the absolute indifference to the life of the hostages, the violation of their right to life, which we will discuss in detail later. This terrorist attack became another reason for restricting the freedom of not only the media but also laid down an 'interesting' concept, which 15 years later will hammer the last nail in the coffin of civil society in Russia.

If, at first, Putin vetoed these changes, then after the next terrorist attack, the amendments were adopted with a 'bonus.'

On September 1, 2004, in Beslan (North Ossetia), 32 terrorists seized a school and held 1,100 hostages in a mined building for three days. On September 3, the assault began with heavy weapons and flamethrowers. As a result, 314 people died, including 186 children, and 783 received injuries of varying severity.

This act of terrorism marked a significant turning point for Russia toward dictatorship. The authorities again showed complete indifference to people's lives. Moreover, it cynically used the attack to strengthen itself.

So, it was this terrorist attack on Dubrovka that caused changes in the legislation on the media. These changes were made slowly and carefully; two years have passed since the terrorist attack.

Watch the hands.

In Art. 4 of the Federal Law of December 27, 1991, N 2124-1 "On the Mass Media" were significantly amended (Federal Law of July 27, 2006 No. 153-FZ "On Amendments to Certain Legislative Acts of the Russian Federation in connection with the adoption Federal Law "On the Ratification of the Council of Europe Convention on the Prevention of Terrorism" and the Federal Law "On Combating Terrorism"). So, in part 1 of Art. 4 of the Mass Media Law, the list of goals for which it is not allowed to use the media added the goal of "dissemination of materials containing public calls for terrorist activities or publicly justifying terrorism, **other extremist materials** [highlighted by me - A.M.]". The first step has been taken to equate extremism with terrorism. Years later, the definition of 'extremism' will be so broad that any disagreement with the government can be understood as it. It turns out that if you do not agree with the authorities, then you are an extremist, which means you are a terrorist, and your activities cannot be covered by the media.

In addition, Art. 4 of the Mass Media Law was expanded by parts 4 and 5 with the following content: "The procedure for collecting information by journalists on the territory (object) of the counter-terrorist operation is determined by the head of the counter-terrorist operation.

When covering a counter-terrorist operation, it is prohibited to disseminate in the mass media information about special means, technical methods and tactics for conducting such an operation, if their dissemination may impede the conduct of the counter-terrorist operation or endanger the life and health of people. Information about employees of special units, persons assisting in conducting such an operation, identifying, preventing, suppressing, and disclosing a terrorist act, and family members of these persons may be made public in accordance with the legislative acts of the Russian Federation on state secrets and personal data."

Again, now I'm talking about the genesis of Putin's legal thought and the degradation of constitutional rights. More details on specific rights later.

In addition, after the terrorist attack in Beslan, Putin abolished the election of governors. Even though the system of authorities of the constituent entities of Russia, according to the Constitution, is formed by them independently (paragraph 1 of Article 77), Putin, by Decree of the President of the Russian Federation of December 27, 2004, N 1603 "On the procedure for considering candidates for the position of the highest official (the head of the highest executive body of state power) of a constituent entity of the Russian Federation," that is, in fact, by the Decree, he abolished the right of the states of Russia to form state authorities themselves (again, it is impossible not to see how the President changes the provisions of the Constitution just by his Decree).

The third 'effect' of the terrorist attack in Beslan resulted from a parliamentary investigation. On September 22, a parliamentary commission was formed to investigate the incident. It was held under the leadership of the Deputy Chairman of the Federation Council (upper house of Parliament), Torshin. The result of the investigation was a report where not a single official was called responsible for so many victims, and part of it was directly written off from the materials of the investigation of the Prosecutor General's Office. In this regard, the state refused to pay compensation, and the victims of the terrorist attack had to seek help from the ECtHR (European Court of Human Rights), where from 2004 to 2011, more than 400 people filed claims for damages and violation of their right to life. In 2017, the ECtHR upheld the majority of complaints.

However, the authorities did not even like the possibility of holding a parliamentary investigation in general. And this investigation became the last parliamentary investigation in the history of Russia. On December 7, 2005, the law "On the Parliamentary Investigation of the Federal Assembly of the Russian Federation" (Federal Law No. 196-FZ of December 27, 2005) was adopted, where paragraphs 2 and 3 of Article 4 stated:

"2. The following are not subject to the parliamentary investigation:

1) activities of the President of the Russian Federation;

2) activities of the court in the administration of justice;

3) the activities of bodies of inquiry and bodies of preliminary investigation carried out by them in accordance with the criminal procedure legislation.

3. The subject of a parliamentary investigation cannot be the establishment of the guilt of specific persons in the commission of a crime."

The Parliament has limited 'itself' to conducting investigations against, as we see, the president and, in general, establishing the guilt of specific individuals. Such checks and balances! Not surprisingly, Torshin's investigation into Beslan was the last parliamentary investigation in the history of Russia. However, the adoption of this law was not the only reason for this.

By that time, more and more people preferred to get information from the Internet rather than from TV. In the first half of the 2000s, the authorities did not pay too much attention to it, which gave great success in its development. Without the usual 'push and hold' laws passed by the authorities, aimed only at establishing obstacles in one area or another, Internet connection services developed unusually quickly, more and more improved, and became cheaper. In 2006, the authorities started to look closely and with concern at this phenomenon. Putin's coming to power began with an attack on freedom of speech, and the authorities could not help but pass by platforms where one can freely discuss something. In this regard, the Law "On Information, Information Technologies and Information Protection" of July 27, 2006, was adopted.

The law turned out to be almost repressive. So, paragraph 1 of Art. 9 stated that "Restriction of access to information is established by federal laws to protect the foundations of the constitutional order, **morality** [highlighted by me - A.M.], health, rights and legitimate interests of others, to ensure the defense of the country and the security of the state." And paragraph 2 of Art. 10 practically excluded the possibility of anonymous use of the Internet: "Information distributed outside of mass media must include reliable information about its owner or about another person distributing information, in a form and in an amount that is sufficient to identify such a person. The owner of a site on the Internet is obliged to place on his site information about his name, location and address, e-mail address for sending the application specified in Article 15.7 of this Federal Law, and also has the right to provide for the possibility of sending this application by filling out an electronic form on a website on the Internet."

At the time of its appearance, although it was the 'first sign' of the attack on the Internet, it did not yet have such a repressive character, which it would receive later. In particular, amendments to it in 2012 introduced additions on the 'protection of children from information' (sic!), leading to the creation of the Unified Register of Prohibited Sites, in which, among other justly prohibited sites (such as sites with child pornography, etc.), sites with "extremist content" as well as VPNs used to bypass these blockings, also were put.

The same changes, popularly known as the 'Yarovaya's Laws,' have obliged many companies to keep all information about Russian citizens on the territory of Russia. And the first company that refused to carry out this nonsense was LinkedIn, a large site and social network for recruitment. Finding out every time the citizenship of one person for regular business was not worth it to stay in Russia. Therefore, this site was one of the first to be included in the Register.

For five years of work (from 2012 to 2017), according to the official media (TASS), the Registry already contained more than 326,000 sites. It is quite natural that the dynamics are on the rise. So, in 2019, only from January to November 2021, **174,956** sites were added to the Registry. At the time of this writing, Instagram and Facebook were included in the Registry, both of which have been identified as 'extremist materials' as a whole! And any person is an 'extremist' only by the fact he uses them.

The amendments to this law of January 5, 2019, created the first steps to establish a 'sovereign Internet' by analogy to the Chinese model, Runet. Thus, the amendments set that:

- Telecom operators are required to install state-owned equipment at traffic exchange points for analyzing and filtering traffic (Deep Packet Inspection; DPI) within the country and communication lines crossing the border of Russia. That is, they were obliged to install a device at their own expense, which would be, in violation of Article 24 of the Constitution, engaged in surveillance of user activity;

- Telecom operators are obliged to enter the Register and use exclusively these exchange points (the Government determines the procedure);

- Roskomnadzor implements 'centralized management' of the Runet;

- Roskomnadzor implements restriction of access to sites prohibited in Russia;

- Exercises will be conducted to test the procedures; and

- A national domain name system is being created.

It was Putin's second term. In accordance with paragraph 3 of Art. 81 of the Constitution, "The same person cannot hold the office of the President of the Russian Federation for more than two terms." Putin was a lame duck, and power was slowly slipping out of his hands.

Then he still had the desire to give the appearance of legitimacy to his machinations. He chose Dmitry Medvedev as his successor, a man absolutely stupid, weak-willed, and lacking initiative. I believe that the choice fell on him because Putin understood that only such a person would not even try to show his ambitions and would 'return' the presidency to him after the expiration of his term. In return, Putin guaranteed Medvedev, during his presidency, the chair of the prime minister. They called it "castling." This plan was revealed by none other than Putin himself at the pre-election congress of the United Russia party on September 24, 2011.

In the 2008 elections, Medvedev won a landslide victory. Not surprising. You need to be able to lose in football to dummies neatly placed on the football field instead of the opposing team. He was opposed by the leader of the

Communist Party, Zyuganov, and the leader of the LDPR party Zhirinovsky (a complete populist and freak whom no one has ever perceived as a serious politician). The only opposition candidate, Kasyanov, was removed because there were 'too many errors' in the signatures he collected from voters. Note that this will be a favorite practice of the Central Election Committee (CEC): it came to oddities when an opposition candidate notarized all the signatures in his favor, but for the same reasons, he was removed—the CEC allegedly had a 'handwriting expert' and the Committee had determined that the signature was fake. Is it necessary to say that the candidates from the authorities have never faced such problems? We will discuss this in more detail when we analyze the violation of the electoral rights of citizens.

Be that as it may, since Medvedev was weak-willed and soft, two trends turned out at once: the first trend was towards liberalization, and the second was that the center of decision-making shifted towards the prime minister (and this is in a super-presidential republic!), i.e., Putin.

However, Medvedev's reign does not start off smoothly. Georgia, a former Soviet republic under Saakashvili, who came to power, began to move toward the West. Up to the point that he is applying for NATO membership. This made Russia very nervous. In August, as a result of a five-day war with Georgia, Moscow recognized the independence of Abkhazia and South Ossetia; Georgia, in response, severed diplomatic relations with Moscow. In this book, I cannot devote time to analyzing the causes of conflict. In a nutshell, Georgia claims that South Ossetia violated the ceasefire, while Russia called Georgia's actions a 'punitive operation.' In any case, Putin and Medvedev openly used their troops for the first time to separate part of another country's territory. According to Article 3 of the Definition of Aggression, approved by UN General Assembly resolution 3314 (XXIX) of 14 December 1974, such acts constitute aggression. However, Western countries reacted unusually passively to those actions. Although, at that time, it was already clear that lawlessness would not be contained within the borders of one country, and sooner or later, as in any dictatorship, it would spill out beyond its borders. Such a passive position will become the basis for a subsequent attack on the territory of another state, which Russia considers 'a zone of its interests,' namely Ukraine in 2014.

Medvedev carried out some insignificant reforms. The most famous is the renaming of the militia to the police. The Russians felt that the stranglehold of despotism had slightly loosened its grip. However, Putin's plans were different. With Medvedev's hands, he dragged through parliament the first changes to the Constitution; namely, he increased the term of the presidency from four to six years. Of course, not for Medvedev; according to the changes, the increase concerned the terms of the next president only. The funny thing is that having come to power, Putin will cancel Medvedev's timid, semi-liberal laws. It will even reach the point of absurdity: he will cancel the law on transferring clock hands to winter-summer time, which Medvedev introduced.

In 2010, Medvedev signed the Law "On the Protection of Children from Information Harmful to Their Health and Development" (Federal Law of the Russian Federation of December 29, 2010, N 436-FZ "On the Protection of Children from Information Harmful to Their Health and Development"). It is the typical rule of the Putin regime: if you want to get something, hide behind the children. The law is written very poorly (which is common for Russian legislative techniques). He introduced mandatory marking for all sites to indicate the age for which this or that content was intended. It's funny that in Europe and the USA, labeling is required to protect content producers from possible harm that a specific work can cause to a child but does not prohibit parents from showing a child, say, a movie, outside these restrictions. In Russia, the only beneficiary of the bans, of course, was a government that introduced fines for labeling violations.

But this was not the only, albeit curious, a flaw in the law. Its main drawback was the actual discrimination of sexual minorities. Due to the introduction of the term 'family values,' which are incredibly dear to a divorced, having several mistresses and illegitimate children and calling his daughters 'these women' Putin. The term turned out to be extremely vague, and paragraphs

4 p. 2 Art. 5 of the said law, which determines that "Information prohibited for dissemination among children includes information that denies family values, **promotes non-traditional sexual relations** [highlighted by me - A.M.] and forms disrespect for parents and (or) other family members." Subsequently, this will hit hard on sexual minorities and centers that provide psychological assistance to young gays and lesbians in their difficult life in an already homophobic country. Pay attention to how, once again, the principle of equality is violated; the state divides people into 'right' and 'wrong,' who cannot even be helped.

Putin started to understand that control of the traditional media does not mean that he controls all information. The number of people using the Internet was growing, while the number of people using TV was falling and continues to fall. Therefore, in 2011, amendments were made to the Law "On Information, Information Technologies, and Information Protection." It was a legislative establishment of censorship on the Internet. In particular, the law allows deleting articles included in the list of extremist materials (which we will also discuss later) or simply deleting this or that information for disagreement with authorities.

In 2011, Putin, at the same pre-election congress of his United Russia party, announced his intention to run for president and spoke about his 'cunning' plan. Medvedev did not even put forward his candidacy for the elections. The prospect of getting Putin again for the presidency, the exclusion of many parties from participating in the elections, and even outrage at the numerous falsifications in the 2012 (State Duma) and March 2013 (presidential) elections resulted in mass demonstrations, the largest of which were rallies on Bolotnaya Square and Sakharov Avenue in Moscow.

Putin brutally suppressed the protests. Being a vengeful man, he ordered that the protesters be roughly punished. About 100,000 people gathered in a small area of Bolotnaya Square. There was nowhere to go, and special forces blocked all exits. At some point, the riot police began brutally beating protesters, trying to defend themselves. About 400 people were detained, and absurd criminal cases were initiated against 30. So, Ilya Gushchin was sentenced to 2.5 years for grabbing a police officer by a helmet and body armor. Maxim Luzyanin received 4.5 years in jail for causing minor bodily harm to a riot police officer, the most serious of which was damage to tooth enamel. Vladimir Akimenkov threw a flagpole at the police (he missed). He was in prison from June 10, 2012, to December 19, 2013, with constantly deteriorating vision. He was lucky to get out only as a result of an amnesty. 'Funny' were the evidence in the courts. The court fully accepted the position of the 'victims' — the police — and did not see any contradictions in the lawyer's video testimony. The ECtHR recognized this case as a political one, violating "the right to liberty and security of person, the right to a fair trial, the right to freedom of assembly and association, and the limits on the use of restrictions on the rights of citizens."

In February 2012, another unusually high-profile story happened. The Pussy Riot case. On February 19, 2012, in the Epiphany aisle of the Epiphany Cathedral in Yelokhovo (Moscow) and on February 21 of the same year in the Cathedral of Christ the Savior, members of the Pussy Riot group held an action, designated by the group as 'Punk prayer' 'Mother of God, drive Putin away!' They added sound to the video footage in the studio and posted it on YouTube. Naturally, Putin did not like this very much. Therefore, they were tried under the article 'hooliganism' simply for dancing in the church and put in jail for two years.

But it matters to us now that this case was the impetus for the adoption in June 2013 of the law "On Insulting the Feelings of Believers" (Federal Law No. 136-FZ of June 29, 2013, Moscow "On Amendments to Article 148 of the Criminal Code of the Russian Federation and certain legislative acts of the Russian Federation to counteract insulting religious beliefs and feelings of citizens"). Putin accepted criminal punishment for insulting some unique, inherent only to 'believers' feelings. The state continued to divide its people into separate groups. With one law, Putin violated two Articles of the Constitution. We will discuss this in detail when analyzing Articles 14 and 19 of the Constitution.

In 2012, amendments to the law on non-profit organizations were adopted. The term 'foreign agent' was introduced. At that time, this rule was 'sleeping'; it did not work. But it will 'bloom' in all its glory much later, in 2020. Again, I mention this fact in order to see the genesis of the degradation of law. I will also analyze this in detail in the analysis of individual articles of the Constitution.

Also, in December 2012, the American Congress adopted the so-called Magnitsky Act (Russia and Moldova Jackson-Vanik Repeal and Sergei Magnitsky Rule of Law Accountability Act of 2012), introduced to punish those involved in the death of lawyer William Browder, Sergei Magnitsky. He investigated the theft committed in 2007 from the Russian budget of 5.4 billion rubles (roughly $174 million). Magnitsky found several officials who committed the crime, but he was accused of helping William Browder in tax evasion. After 11 months of pre-trial detention, Magnitsky died in the hospital of Detention Facility No. 1 in Moscow. The initiators of his arrest and the investigator in his case turned out to be persons accused by Magnitsky and his colleagues of embezzlement of budget funds.

The bill forbade entry into the United States and the seizure of funds of persons, more than 60 officials who took part in the death of lawyer Magnitsky in one way or another.

This act hit the sorest spot of a Russian official, if possible, not to live in Russia, which they are robbing. Again, I will dwell on this later, but for now, it is essential to understand that in Russia, corruption is not a flaw in the system; it is an integral part of it. At that time, the authorities were still trying to hide it. Accordingly, on December 28, 2012, in response to the Magnitsky Act, the Russian parliament adopted the "Law of scoundrels" or, as the authorities themselves call it, the "Law of Dima Yakovlev" (Federal Law of December 28, 2012, No. 272-FZ "On measures to influence persons who involved in violations of fundamental human rights and freedoms, rights and freedoms of citizens of the Russian Federation"). The law prohibits the adoption of Russian orphans by citizens of the United States and any countries that 'violated the rights of Russians,' as well as banning the activities in Russia of Non-commercial organizations (NCOs) funded by the United States and posing a threat to Russian interests.

For American readers, I will explain in terms of orphans. It is not the case in America, but in Russia, children left without parents are sent to the so-called 'orphanages.' As a rule, the conditions of their detention there are close to those of a prison. And it is not surprising that the main desire of children who have lost the most precious thing in life — their parents — is the desire to find a family. In addition, according to Russian law, citizens of Russia have priority in adopting a child. Since, for the most part, adoptive parents do not have a lot of money, sick children and disabled children, as a rule, were adopted by foreign citizens who were ready to spend a lot of money on the rehabilitation and treatment of a child. As you understand, the 'Law of scoundrels,' as the opposition called it, dealt a crushing blow exclusively to such children. Moreover, according to official figures, more than 200 children throughout Russia had already found American families, and a court hearing on their adoption were to be held in 2013. Honestly, I can't even imagine what exactly the children who were denied adoption by the court on the basis of this monstrous act felt.

Once again, Putin showed not only his vindictiveness and pettiness but, unable to really influence other countries' decisions, he took revenge on his own population, even worse, on defenseless and already unfortunate children.

However, it was clear that Putin was frightened by the protests and was forced to give at least some concessions. In particular, he returned the election of governors and reduced the number of signatures required to nominate candidates for the presidential elections in the Russian Federation. In addition, in April 2013, the Federal Law "On the contract system in the field of procurement of goods, works, services for state and municipal needs" of 05.04.2013 N 44-FZ, which obliged to publish information on all public procurement on the Internet (clause 1, Article 24.1 of this law). It was a lever that Navalny and his team used effectively in their investigations into the corruption of Russian officials.

At the same time, Putin decided to hedge against future fears. He significantly tightened the administrative responsibility for rallies through a puppet parliament (elected, as we remember, with huge falsifications). Fines were increased, for example, for participants in protests (individuals), the minimum penalty will be from 20 to 300 thousand rubles (from about $640 to $9,600). For organizations (legal entities), up to 1 million rubles (about $32,000), and compulsory work was introduced as a punishment for violations. It was forbidden to wear masks at rallies. It was forbidden to organize 'simultaneous mass stay of citizens in public places' if it threatened to violate public order, the rules for holding single pickets were tightened, it was forbidden to organize rallies for citizens who had an outstanding conviction for crimes against the state and public security, or who were held administratively liable for violations carrying public actions. He introduced the concept of "a specially designated place for the mass presence of citizens for the public expression of public opinion on topical issues." The court received the right to recognize several pickets, united by one theme, as a mass event (Part 1.1, Article 7 of the Law "On Public Events").

In addition, the government received the right to refuse to hold rallies if the organizer of the planned rally had previously committed administrative offenses regarding holding public events. Thus, a significant part of the opposition activists was deprived of the opportunity to declare mass events.

Another blow to civil society was the decision to liquidate the Supreme Arbitration Court of the Russian Federation. In Russia, initially, there were three highest Russian courts; the Constitutional Court (whose powers were significantly curtailed back in 1993); the Supreme Arbitration Court (SAC), which resolved disputes between commercial enterprises, as well as disputes involving them; and the Supreme Court, which resolved disputes between ordinary citizens.

The powers of the Supreme Arbitration Court were provided for by Article 127 of the Constitution of the Russian Federation.

Why was it necessary to liquidate the Supreme Arbitration Court in general?

The legislation in Russia was already terrible then (however, as always). Since the authorities did not like popular politicians—successful people who are loved by the population or people, and who generally understand the law and to increase popularity—it was necessary to attract famous people. United Russia (president's party) did not find anything better than to invite singers, athletes, and artists who have never read a single legal act in their lives, including the Constitution (Elena Isinbayeva's confession that she did not read the Constitution). Naturally, the number of lawyers in parliament was minimal, and the legislative technique suffered greatly: numerous contradictions, vague formulations, and illogical law enforcement, a minor consequence of the ruling party's attempt to retain power.

The SAC did what a typical court in its position should have done. He tried to normalize the practice. With his explanations of the legislation, he tried to make clear rules of the game, to clarify how and when this or that law should be applied, particularly the Tax Code. That is, the SAC tried to remove arbitrariness from the relations between the authorities and entrepreneurs. Needless to say, Putin did not like such behavior. Vague wording and uncertainty made it possible to squeeze additional taxes and fines out of enterprises. Putin always spoke disparagingly about companies and entrepreneurs in general, calling them "crooks by definition" and "hucksters", so he did not care about their condition. In addition, the judicial branch of power could, in general, prevent Putin from continuing to usurp power. As a result, Article 127 was excluded under the Law of the Russian Federation on the amendment to the Constitution of the Russian Federation of February 5, 2014 N 2-FKZ "On the Supreme Court of the Russian Federation and the Prosecutor's Office of the Russian Federation", which entered into force on the day of its official publication on February 6, 2014 г., and the Supreme Arbitration Court was abolished.

However, at the beginning of 2014, there was another turning point in the history of Russia, namely the seizure of another territory of a neighboring state. This time Ukraine.

In the fall of 2013, pro-Kremlin President Yanukovych, spurred on by multibillion-dollar payments from the Kremlin, refused to sign an association agreement between Ukraine and the European Union, which caused great discontent among Ukrainian youth, who organized indefinite protests in one of Kyiv's central squares, Maidan. Everything went peacefully for a long time until, according to some reports, after consultation with the Kremlin, authorities tried to disperse the protest. More than 100 protesters were killed in clashes in January. The Ukrainians did not tolerate the death of their youth and began to seize administrative buildings in Kyiv. Yanukovych fled to Russia. But, as we already know, the petty and vengeful Putin could not forget the humiliation that his protege was driven away. At that time, there were Russian troops under an agreement between the states in Crimea. Putin used them to effectively seize Crimea and hold a sham referendum on separating Crimea from Ukraine. And a couple of days later, the annexation of Crimea to Russia.

By UN General Assembly Resolution 68/262 of March 27, 2014, such 'attachment' by an absolute majority of votes was declared illegal. And so far, only a handful of countries agree with the Kremlin's position on Crimea's belonging to Russia.

Perhaps, realizing the annexation's illegality, Putin decided to shut up all those who disagreed. On December 28, 2013, Putin introduced criminal liability for "Public calls for actions aimed at violating the territorial integrity of the Russian Federation" (Federal Law of December 28, 2013, N 433-FZ "On Amendments to the Criminal Code of the Russian Federation"). Naturally, only a few would later tell the truth—that Crimea, which Russia claimed as its own, was, in fact, Ukrainian.

We also note that in this conflict, Putin showed himself to be an unusually cowardly and deceitful person. Initially, he stated that the 'little green men' who suddenly appeared were 'Crimean self-defense forces' who had bought uniforms from the local 'voentorg' (military and uniform shop). However, later, having understood that there would be no severe consequences, on the "direct line" on April 4, 2014, he admitted that they were Russian military.

In March 2015, a documentary film was shown on state television featuring Putin, who once again talked about the intention to seize Crimea after Yanukovych lost power: it unfolded in such a way in Ukraine that we were forced to begin work on the return of Crimea to Russia.

Unfortunately, no matter how illegal the annexation of Crimea was, Putin did not stop there.

Putin sent his troops to the Donbas, the territory of Ukraine in the east of the country. Most likely, he hoped for the same success as in Crimea: that the weakened Ukrainian government would not put up much resistance. Again, Putin tried to pass off the invasion as a 'civil war.' However, Strelkov (real name Girkin) — a former FSB colonel — admitted that he, at the head of other Russian combatants, invaded the Donbas to unleash a war (timecode at 1:35).

It always seemed to Putin that if he told a lie and did not back down from it, then everyone would believe in it. Therefore, he denied the presence of Russian troops in the Donbas. The 'curtain of secrecy'—and, in fact, the secret of the Open—was so transparent that few people believed in this lie then, and probably no one believes now. So much so that the courts of Russia are already openly admitting this. So, on November 10, 2021, the judge of the Kirovsky District Court of the city of Rostov-on-Don Sholokhov L.V. in criminal case No. 1-82/2021, sentenced Mr. Zabaluev to five years in a penal colony for bribing the chief sanitary doctor of the Southern Military District. The court states in the case file:

"During his career, his duties included the organization and fulfillment of obligations for purchasing and selling food and creating the necessary stock in the warehouse. This food was intended to be sent to the military units of the Armed Forces of the Russian Federation stationed on the territory of the DPR and LPR."

The Court's decision was soon removed from its official website, and Peskov (Putin's spokesman) said it was a mistake. However, the case materials have been saved; you can read them here: http://судебныерешения.рф/64073623.

In any case, fighting continued between Ukrainian military forces and Russian mercenaries in the spring of 2014. Aviation significantly interfered with the mercenaries, and Putin did not come up with anything better than secretly delivering an air defense system, BUK, to the mercenaries, as if the mercenaries found this air defense system in an old Ukrainian warehouse. It all ended very tragically. On July 17, 2014, mercenaries shot down a Malaysia Airlines Boeing 777 on scheduled flight MH17 on the Amsterdam-Kuala Lumpur route. All 298 people on board were killed (283 passengers, including 80 minors, and 15 crew members). Only recently, the trial of the defendants in the case ended in

The Hague (you can find all the materials here). At the same time, Alexander Borodai, Chairman of the Council of Ministers of the self-proclaimed DPR, a person with a Russian passport, and since 2021 also a member of the State

Duma, posts photos of himself posing with toys of children from a downed Boeing.

Again, I do not want to dwell on this process in detail; you can see all the parties' evidence and arguments in the links above. I want to highlight the critical points of degradation of Putin and his system.

Only after the death of about 300 EU citizens has Europe finally begun to think about the threat posed by Putin (and this is six years after the war with Georgia!) and introduced sanctions on Russia.

Note that, in response, Putin introduced an additional punishment for his population—the so-called 'anti-sanctions'—a ban on his population from buying food products from EU countries (Decree of the President of the Russian Federation of 08/06/2014 N 560 "On the application of certain special economic measures to ensure security Russian Federation"). Putin argued that it was necessary to punish European countries for imposing sanctions by depriving their farmers of a prominent Russian market. That would allegedly spur Russia's own farms' development. This only led to an increase in food prices and the inaccessibility of high-quality European goods for Russians. Initially, this argument seemed rather weak: the Russian farmer's market for European farmers did not exceed 6%, and the decrease in competition could in no way contribute to the emergence in Russia of what had previously worked poorly under more greenhouse conditions. In fact, this measure was aimed at increasing the benefits of Putin's oligarchs involved in agriculture. Restricting competition allowed them to raise prices and compensate for losses from European sanctions. What about ordinary citizens? Well, as always, Putin didn't care about them.

Obviously, not seeing any subjectivity in his own people, Putin thinks that if someone disagrees with him, at least in some way, then such a person is bribed by the 'hostile West.' This is probably why, on November 25, 2014, Putin signed a law prohibiting Russian parties from making deals with foreign states, international organizations and social movements, non-profit organizations that act as foreign agents, as well as Russian legal entities, more than 30% of the authorized capital of which is owned by foreigners.

Also, Putin wanted to shut the mouth of everyone who did not agree with the annexation of Crimea and the unleashing of aggression in the Donbas— Federal Law of May 5, 2014, N 128-FZ "On Amendments to Certain Legislative Acts of the Russian Federation," a special article was introduced into the Criminal code — 'rehabilitation of Nazism'. The reader may ask, what does the war unleashed by Putin in Ukraine have to do with the 'rehabilitation of Nazism'? Being entirely deceitful, Putin adopted the 'best practices' of Goebbels' propaganda. Russian propaganda was engaged in the 'dehumanization' of

Ukrainians. They did not call (and still do not call) them anything other than 'Nazis,' 'nationalists.' Accordingly, any support of the people of Ukraine could already then be considered a criminal offense.

In 2015, Putin amended the very Law of Scoundrels (introduced by the Federal Law of May 23, 2015, N 129-FZ). Now the term 'undesirable organization' appears there. "The activity of a foreign or international non-governmental organization that poses a threat to the foundations of the constitutional order of the Russian Federation, the country's defense capability or the security of the state, may be recognized as undesirable on the territory of the Russian Federation." Recognizing an organization as 'undesirable' eradicates it from Russia's legal field. And we'll talk about this again a little later. At the moment, we note that the court decides on such severe consequences, but by the decision of the Prosecutor General (paragraphs 4 and 5 of Article 3.1 of the said Federal Law).

For such an abundance of unlawful, unconstitutional, raw, and frankly repressive laws, the people began to call the State Duma of the VI and VII convocations the 'mad printer.'

As a result of the 'castling,' Putin rolled the entire civil society under the asphalt. Having seized Crimea, he caused a short period of euphoria among the illiterate population, drugged by propaganda. Everyone who disagreed was silenced.

For a while, the mad printer calmed down. But in 2018, the next 'elections' of the president were approaching.

European sanctions and Putin's own 'anti-sanctions' slowly began to affect the population's well-being. Putin, having neither charisma nor at least some intelligence, did not find anything better than abolishing the program of voluntary pension accumulation for the already impoverished population (and, of course, taking the money for himself), raising the retirement age by five years, and raising VAT. The euphoria from the annexation of Crimea had already faded away at that moment. As a result, even according to official polls, he approached the next 'elections' with a rating of 40% (and this is with complete control over all information and with all political repressions!).

In addition, even with the 'castling,' Putin's fourth term should have been his last. As much as he wanted to, he remained a lame duck. At that time, it was evident that Putin would do something about this. He no longer trusted his placeholder Medvedev: even though Medvedev was stupid, weak, and ridiculous ('pathetic,' as the people nicknamed him), even his rule, compared to Putin's, was perceived as an example of liberalism and well-being. Putin did not dare to take such risks for the second time. Remaining just as stupid, he nevertheless understood that as soon as he lost power, he would immediately go to prison (if not killed). This understanding still keeps him in power. In addition, he, nevertheless, inevitably grew old, and his senile boobs already little excited even the pro-Kremlin-minded audience. So he went straight ahead.

As always, he began by cleaning up the media. On November 25, 2017, as a response to the requirement of the US Department of Justice to register Russia Today and Sputnik as foreign agents, Law No. 327-FZ was adopted, introducing the concept of the foreign media agent. Now, almost all media that were not directly controlled by the government were required to designate themselves, not even by a court decision, as a 'foreign media agent.' Before each (sic!) publication, cite a special, popularly called 'ebala' (rude Russian word for something puzzling and nasty) inscription. For readers to appreciate all the insanity and farce, I quote it in full. At the same time, it was obliged to appear near each post, including (in the case of one of the oppositionists) even congratulating his daughter on her birthday (for the absence of which he was fined in this regards)!

"This message (material) was created and (or) distributed by a foreign media outlet acting as a foreign agent and (or) a Russian legal entity acting as a foreign agent."

The funny fact is that 'agency' is a concept in American law, and Russian law does not have it. Therefore, the meaning of this term is lost even for lawyers. I will also talk about this later.

Having carried out the next falsifications (the mathematician, Sergey Shpilkin, proved them; you can watch his reasoning here), which Putin, for some reason calls 'elections,' he (oddly enough, right?) stayed in his office for the fourth term. Carefully selected opponents, imprisonment of the oppositionists, total administrative control and stuffing, and Russia has a 'new' but old and somewhat battered by time president.

The lame duck began its next step — changing the Constitution so that the two-term clause would disappear or stop working.

It should be noted that the Federal Law of March 4, 1998, N 33-FZ, "On the procedure for the adoption and entry into force of amendments to the Constitution of the Russian Federation" (with amendments and additions), does not provide for the procedure for changing the Constitution of the Russian Federation by referendum. But Putin is a cowardly and irresponsible man; according to the old KGB habit, he decided to mess everyone up in this next crime so that later he could shrug his shoulders and say, 'Well, it's not my fault; they asked themselves.' What about the law? Well, this is Russia...

Suspecting that his botox-infused charisma might not endure the approval of amendments to remove the new term limit, Putin turned the Constitution into a trash can of conflicting rules. In addition, under Article 141 of the Decree of the State Duma of the Federal Assembly of the Russian

Federation of January 22, 1998, N 2134-II GD "On the Regulations of the State Duma of the Federal Assembly of the Russian Federation" (with amendments and additions), each amendment to the Constitution must be considered and discussed separately from the others. We will talk about this in a separate chapter of this book. For now, I will say that more than 339 (!) Amendments were proposed, of which 206 (!) were selected for adoption.

If you think that the farce is over, then you are wrong. The amendments were voted in car trunks and on stumps, and I'm not kidding. Again, we will talk about this in a separate chapter.

Looking back, it is clear that Putin began to shrink the legal field of Russia from the moment he came to power. As a state, Russia no longer functioned. Like a zombie, out of habit, it still tried to work, walk, and breathe. Like a zombie virus invented by science fiction writers, it penetrated the country's brain and began to destroy it, affecting all its parts. And at some point, Russia turned into a real zombie, which rushed at healthy people, trying to kill them. It was only a matter of time before Russia attacked its neighbors.

Chapter 4

ARTICLE-BY-ARTICLE ANALYSIS OF THE CONSTITUTION OF RUSSIA

S O, WE BRIEFLY ANALYZED THE degradation of the legal in chronological order in the last chapter. Some relatively minor violations were left out of our attention to avoid turning this book into a kind of opus for several volumes in the best traditions of Leo Tolstoy's War and Peace.

It is time to move on to this work's primary goal: to analyze the Constitution article by article operation to see which rules remain working and which do not. I'm not interested now in the chapters devoted to the formation and activities of state bodies; this is an important thing, but it is mainly artificial. I am primarily interested in articles relating to the rights and freedoms of citizens. If we understand how bad the situation is with them, we will be much less interested in how long the president or parliament is elected.

And some more of the theory

I deliberately posted the history of the development of law in modern Russia before assessing these changes.

Indeed, even the most distant from jurisprudence reader can see how much the legal system has degraded under Putin. Note that the changes began immediately. There was no period when the law would be preserved at least at the same level — it started the process of degradation immediately, from the moment of Putin's first presidency. This closes the question of whether Putin is supposedly democratic or that he was forced to tighten his policy due to some external circumstances or pressure. The only thing that can be clarified is that, most likely, Putin was initially more cautious in his totalitarian aspirations. However, as he dismantled the state bodies, he naturally became bolder and bolder until he could completely ignore the law.

In the theory of state and law, there are the following principles of government. In a democratic state, the guide is 'everything that is not prohibited by law is allowed'; in authoritarian states, 'everything related to political activity is strictly regulated by the authorities'; and in totalitarian states, 'everything that is not directly permitted by law is prohibited.'

The democratic principle disappears when so many laws bury the main democratic principle under them. Therefore, the main idea is to regulate only the most necessary. Russia has gone from democracy under Yeltsin (with significant flaws, but still democracy) to Putin's totalitarianism. Initially, Putin tried to maintain at least some semblance of legality. Even if the laws were wrongful and contradicted the Constitution, they were still some rules of conduct. Over time, the laws stopped working: law enforcement practice completely separated from them. It doesn't matter what was written in any law or even in the Constitution, they have ceased restricting authorities even to a minimal extent. Further, when analyzing individual articles, I will focus the reader's attention on this. So, from an authoritarian, Russia turned into a totalitarian state. There are no clear rules by which society can live, nor any rights for citizens or organizations that the state cannot violate in general.

The Constitution of Russia consists of 9 chapters. The first chapter is devoted to the state structure. The second is human rights and freedoms, and the ninth is the procedure for adopting amendments to the Constitution. The rest regulates the rights of various state authorities. The creators of the Constitution, as we remember, were very afraid of communist revenge. Therefore, Article 135 of Chapter 9 explicitly states that Chapters 1, 2, and 9 cannot be changed. If 'there is a need' to change them, another Constitution must be adopted. The prohibition on changing Chapter 9 prevents one from first making corrections to the procedure for changing the Constitution and then changing the state structure or the rights of citizens. How Putin tried to get around this in 2020 will be discussed later in Chapter 5.

The constitution is the basis of the foundations on what the state is built and by what very basic rules it lives. No law, decree, or action shall be contrary to the constitution. Of course, it is impossible to write every rule in one document or establish the procedure for implementing an individual right. Still, it is the foundation on which the entire legal system is built. Ideally, this system is rigid — from the rules written in the constitution, the rules for implementing these rights are logically created — laws and by-laws describe them (in the case of the common law system, also in court decisions). The legislative branch adopts laws that should not contradict this very essence of the state; the executive branch must not violate the constitution but also execute it and force any citizen to comply. The judiciary, again ideally, monitors the consistency of the laws and actions of the authorities of the constitution. Moreover, this should concern not only the Constitutional Court (or another court that has the right to cancel the adopted legal act) but also any court in principle, such is the logic of law.

In the section on the history of Russia, I mentioned the Stalin Constitution of 1936, which was one of the most progressive in the world. Still, the reality was completely different, and any assertion that the USSR was a democratic state since it had such an excellent constitution is, at its best case, contradictory. Therefore, to understand if a state is democratic or, conversely, totalitarian, it is necessary not only to study the constitution of this state but also to look at other laws and the practice of their application.

It should be noted that legal acts that, in theory, should not contradict the constitution but only supplement and clarify it, as well as law enforcement practice on how exactly this or that law is applied.

In the case of legal acts, my task is a little easier. I give a link to the law and explain precisely how it contradicts the Constitution. In the case of law enforcement practice, I will have to refer to indirect evidence that this or that rule of the Constitution does not work—these can be the words of the officials themselves, the verdicts of the courts, and other documents, even if they are not laws. In the end, Putin also pretended to understand at least something about the law and tried to hide behind rules, albeit not legal ones. However, over time, even this fig leaf was discarded by Putin.

ARTICLES 1 AND 2 OF
THE CONSTITUTION

The logic of the arrangement of the articles of the Constitution can be confusing. It goes from the most vital and general things to specific and not very significant ones. Therefore, Chapter 1 of the Constitution is devoted to the Fundamentals of the constitutional system, Chapter 2 to human rights and freedoms, and then goes to the state structure and the highest authorities.

In theory, this should create a hierarchy of rules, clearly showing the most critical priority for the state, that is, at the beginning. So, in the same Stalin Constitution of 1936, the Basic rights and freedoms of citizens were given only in the 10th chapter.

Article 1 of the Constitution describes as:

"1. The Russian Federation - Russia is a democratic federative legal state with a republican form of government.

2. The names Russian Federation and Russia are equivalent."

Though I don't have any remarks and questions about paragraph 2, we can only confirm or refute the statement in the first paragraph after analyzing the articles on human rights. It would be logical to place the analysis of this article at the end of our research.

The same applies to the content of Article 2 of the Russian Constitution: "Man, his rights and freedoms shall be the supreme value. The recognition, observance, and protection of human and civil rights and freedoms shall be an obligation of the State."

Anticipating our analysis, and thus putting a big spoiler at the beginning of the article-by-article research, it can be argued that Russia is neither a democratic state nor a republican form of government. And the rights and freedoms of a person (not even his life) is of no value to the State.

In practice, we will prove the above statement throughout the complete further analysis.

I'm not fond of historical analogies too much. Still, in Russian history, there was a character who already ruled feudal Russia, separated his friends from the law by creating guardsmen, and ruled with the cruelest and terrorist methods—Ivan the Terrible. The situation is very similar. At that time, the mad king's reign ended in defeat in the war and a 'troubled time' for several decades. In this situation, as if by a textbook, Putin repeats his actions and fate; he has even unleashed another war, which he definitely cannot win. How will it all end? Probably with another troubled time.

If we take 14 signs of fascism by the famous writer and philosopher Umberto Eco, then Russia in its current state is a fascist state.

Briefly, these features are:

1. **The cult of tradition** is the very 'spiritual bonds' that Putin and top officials love so much. Umberto Eco notes that the proposition 'there is no place for the development of knowledge' follows from this. The closed archives

of the 2nd World War, numerous cases against famous scientists, and the persecution of journalists — as a result of the technological backwardness of Russia — are direct confirmations of this.

2. **Rejection of modernism.** Umberto Eco writes, "Both the Italian fascists and the German Nazis seemed to love technology, while traditionalist thinkers usually stigmatized technology, seeing it as a denial of traditional spiritual values. But Nazism enjoyed only the external aspect of its industrialization. In the depths of his ideology, the theory of Blut und Boden—'Blood and Soil' dominated. The denial of the modern world was carried out under the sauce of the denial of capitalist modernity. It is essentially a negation of the spirit of 1789 (and also, of course, 1776)—the spirit of the Enlightenment. The Age of Rationalism was perceived as the beginning of modern depravity. Therefore, eternal fascism can be defined as irrationalism." I would add that if you look at the interviews of officials or the propaganda channels of Russia, an average person may develop that this is a collection of foolish people who were accidentally released from a mental hospital; you will not see so much stupidity anywhere else. Irrationalism is the main feature of modern official Russian politics. The madness of one king affects his entire entourage, who, physically, cannot say 'no' to him.

3. **The cult of action for the sake of action** thinking is considered an unmanly thing. You can't talk; you have to act! This is suspicion of the new culture (for example, a ban on all artists who spoke out against Putin, such as Oxxximiron, Shevchuk, Pusi Riot, Serebrennikov, etc.) and of universities and schools, where lessons of 'patriotism' are already being introduced to form children and teenagers of the necessary state of mind. For the same reason, the state pushes out of the country or represses all dissenting and thinking people and journalists, investigators and labels them as 'foreign agents.'

4. **Disagreement is treason.** This criterion has become particularly pronounced lately. The label I have already mentioned of 'foreign agent'—almost like the star of David on the clothes of Jews during Nazi Germany—is gladly

hung on any person who publicly disagrees with the words or actions of the Russian authorities. Moreover, this does not even require evidence or a court decision. It is, therefore, almost impossible to dispute it. I will elaborate on this later.

5. **Racism**. It is expressed in hatred for everything foreign. The average Russian promotes hatred for everyone: Americans, Europeans, Blacks, Asians, Caucasians, Ukrainians, Poles, gays and lesbians, the opposition, liberals, and so on. On federal channels, 'people' are happy to tell how they will 'wipe America into nuclear ashes' or destroy Great Britain. This is even happening at the highest level, with Putin showing third-rate cartoons in his message about a new super-rocket hitting Florida.

6. Fascism is born out of individual or social **frustration**. All historical fascisms have relied on frustrated middle classes that have suffered from some economic or political crisis and are afraid of the threat from the irritated lower classes. Putin did not have to work on this point for long: he deprived the Russians of their rights and freedoms, and the corrupt system of distributing money from natural resources and the budget he built drove them into permanent poverty and frustration.

7. **Nationalism**. The constant attitude that 'Russians are the most spiritual people, and the rest are not like that,' 'We are Russians, God is with us' (like German's 'Gott mit uns') is a common thing in the speeches of senior officials. It also implies the assertion that the country is surrounded by enemies, and it is necessary to unite in order to fight them.

8. Members should feel **offended** by the fact that the enemies flaunt their wealth and strength. As in point 6, the unusually low standard of living of Russians makes most of them the envy of the entire Western world. They do not understand that in their poverty, they owe solely to the corrupt regime of Putin, and they splash out their hatred on other people who live better. Even the word 'liberal' in the lexicon of the average Russian has a negative and even abusive meaning. The same hatred applies to people who, for one reason or another, left Russia. You are mistaken if you think the remaining

compatriots help or support them. Most of those who left are accused of 'betrayal' and become the object of hatred from their fellow citizens who remained in Russia.

9. For eternal fascism, there is no struggle for life, but there is **life for the sake of battle**. Therefore, pacifism means fraternization with the enemy. It is especially true since the outbreak of Putin's aggressive war with Ukraine, where the police arrest people for the poster 'no to war'.

10. **Elitarism**. Namely, the very "new oprichnina"—the presence of people unreachable to law, who receive colossal funds from the budget, and who, before a clash with some closer president's friend—cannot be subjected to any persecution by the 'law enforcement' bodies.

11. Each and everyone is brought up to be a hero. In myths, the hero embodies a rare, extraordinary being; however, in the ideology of eternal fascism, heroism is the norm. This manifests itself from the procession of the 'immortal regiment' (an event organized by the state, when relatives march with portraits of their ancestors who participated in World War II) to the design of prams in the form of tanks or decorating the interior of schools and kindergartens with military symbols.

12. **The cult of masculinity**. That is the disdain for women and the ruthless pursuit of any non-conformist sexual habits: from chastity to homosexuality. This is a significant and painful topic. In legislation, it is expressed from direct discrimination against gays and lesbians to vetoing the law 'on domestic violence' and decriminalizing domestic beatings (beating by a husband of his wife). And the favorite propaganda phrase is: 'If you didn't serve [in the army], you're not a man.' As usual, we will discuss this later when analyzing several articles of the Constitution at once.

13. **Qualitative populism**. In the eyes of eternal fascism, according to Umberto Eco, the individual does not have individual rights. The people appear as a quality, a monolithic unity, expressing the total will. This is expressed in the almost complete lack of rights of ordinary Russians, their removal

from influence, and the formation of authorities. And the will of everyone is 'expressed' by Putin.

14. **Newspeak**. The term from Orwell's novel "1984" is a new language designed to change attitudes towards certain phenomena and facts. Navoiaz is rapidly gaining momentum in modern Russia. So, instead of the word 'explosion,' the official media and propagandists use the word 'clap' instead of 'decrease,' 'negative growth' instead of 'dictatorship,' 'sovereign democracy,' instead of 'war,' 'special military operation,' etc.

In our analysis, all these features will be touched upon in one way or another. For now, I recommend bookmarking this page so you can revise it from time to time.

ARTICLE 3 OF THE CONSTITUTION

"1. The bearer of sovereignty and the sole source of power in the Russian Federation shall be its multinational people.

2. The people shall exercise its power directly, as well as through State government bodies and local self-government bodies.

3. The supreme direct expression of the power of the people shall be referendum and free elections.

4. Nobody may usurp power in the Russian Federation. The seizure of power or usurpation of State authority shall be prosecuted under federal law."

At the time of writing this book, this article is also wholly non-working.

The people of Russia are almost completely excluded from making any political decisions. The state persistently and scrupulously eliminates all vertical and horizontal ties, destroying any attempts at self-organization.

The most obvious example is, of course, elections.

In order not to be unfounded, I present to you a list of documents that made changes to the legislation on elections to the State Duma after 2014 (Federal Law of February 22, 2014 N 20-FZ "On Elections of Deputies of the State Duma of the Federal Assembly of the Russian Federation"):

Amendments were made by Federal Laws No. 355-FZ of November 24, 2014, No. 231-FZ of July 13, 2015, No. 272-FZ of July 14, 2015, No. 287-FZ of October 5, 2015, No. 29-FZ of 03/09/2016 N 65-FZ, dated 03/09/2016 N 66-FZ, dated 04/05/2016 N 92-FZ, dated 12/28/2016 N 474-FZ, dated 12/28/2016 N 505-FZ, dated 06/18/2017 N 127 -FZ, dated 02/05/2018 N 1-FZ, dated 02/19/2018 N 30-FZ, dated 06/04/2018 N 150-FZ, dated 12/11/2018 N 464-FZ, dated 12/27/2018 N 528-FZ, dated 05/29 .2019 N 104-FZ, dated 02/27/2020 N 27-FZ, dated 05/23/2020 N 153-FZ, dated 05/23/2020 N 154-FZ, dated 07/31/2020 N 267-FZ, dated 03/09/2021 N 43- FZ, dated 04/05/2021 N 89-FZ, dated 04/20/2021 N 91-FZ, dated 04/20/2021 N 96-FZ, dated 04/30/2021 N 115-FZ, dated 06/04/2021 N 157-FZ, dated 14.03. 2022 N 60-FZ, dated 04/01/2022 N 90-FZ, dated 06/28/2022 N 220-FZ, with amendments by the Resolution of the Constitutional Court of the Russian Federation dated 04/13/2017 N 11-P).

If you think that in 2014 the legislation on parliamentary elections did not change so much, then you are mistaken. Before the Law of 2014, the Federal Law of May 18, 2005, N 51-FZ "On the Election of Deputies of the State Duma of the Federal Assembly of the Russian Federation" was used, which was amended by the following legislative acts:

Amendments were made by Federal Laws No. 106-FZ of 12.07.2006, No. 107-FZ of 12.07.2006, No. 128-FZ of 25.07.2006, No. 274-FZ of 30.12.2006, No. 64-FZ of 26.04.2007, 07/21/2007 N 188-FZ, dated 07/24/2007 N 211-FZ, dated 07/24/2007 N 214-FZ, dated 02/09/2009 N 3-FZ, dated 05/12/2009 N 94-FZ, dated 06/03/2009 N 108 -FZ, dated 19.07.2009 N 196-FZ, dated 19.07.2009 N 203-FZ, dated 22.04.2010 N 63-FZ, dated 27.07.2010 N 222-FZ, dated 04.10.2010 N 263-FZ, dated 29.11 .2010 N 325-FZ, dated 12/23/2010 N 384-FZ, dated 12/28/2010 N 404-FZ, dated 02/23/2011 N 17-FZ, dated 06/14/2011 N 143-FZ, dated 07/11/2011 N

200- Federal Law, dated 23.07.2011 N 259-FZ, dated 25.07.2011 N 262-FZ, dated 25.07.2011 N 263-FZ, dated 20.10.2011 N 287-FZ (as amended on 02.05.2012), dated 02.05.2012 N 41-FZ, dated 02.07.2013 N 147-FZ, dated 10.21.2013 N 283-FZ, dated 12.28.2013 N 396-FZ, dated 02.04.2014 N 51-FZ, dated 01.12.2014 N 419-FZ, dated 10/05/2015 N 287-FZ, with amendments by the Resolutions of the Constitutional Court of the Russian Federation t 04/22/2013 N 8-P, dated 12/16/2014 N 33-P).

And before the law of 2005, the Federal Law of December 20, 2002, N 175-FZ "On Elections of Deputies of the State Duma of the Federal Assembly of the Russian Federation," was in force. The funny thing is that in its short life, this law also changed every year: amendments were made by Federal Laws of December 20, 2002, N 175-FZ, of June 23, 2003, N 82-FZ, of June 23, 2003, N 83-FZ, of June 23, 2003, N 84-FZ, dated 06/23/2003 N 85-FZ, dated 05/18/2005 N 51-FZ, dated 02/02/2006 N 19-FZ, dated 07/25/2006 N 128-FZ, with amendments by the Resolution of the Constitutional Court of the Russian Federation dated 11/14/2005 No. 10-P.

Why did I bring almost a whole page of changes to laws that establish rules for elections only (sic!) to the Russian parliament, not counting presidential elections and municipals? This suggests that there was not at least one pair of elections that would be held according to the same rules. Each time, the rules were changed in a way that was beneficial to the authorities.

It got to the point that the parliament ceased to be representative at some point. I will explain here: The representative is elected to the country's parliament to represent the interests of the people who elected them. And people are all different (only in a totalitarian state are they trying to fit them into a particular ideal of a 'true Aryan,' acting and thinking the same way, naturally, in accordance with the leader's will). There are rich people, poor people, business people, civil servants, men and women, believers and non-believers, and so on. Ideally, each group should be represented in parliament. Naturally, this or that group often has different desires and interests, the realization of which leads to a clash of such interests. Hence, disputes arise in a normal functioning and living parliament. They are unavoidable.

In the Russian parliament, however, disputes ceased to such an extent that Speaker Gryzlov directly stated that 'parliament is not a place for discussions.'

The same happened with presidential and municipal elections, which, according to the Constitution, are not part of the state authorities.

This is from a formal point of view.

There have been no free elections in Russia for a long time. President's administration removes the candidates. Recently, a special 'municipal filter' has been introduced. That is, a candidate must obtain the approval of a certain number of municipal deputies to participate in elections (again, we note that formally, local governments are not state authorities and why their authorization is required, from a legal point of view, is unclear). The elections are held with numerous violations, from stuffing (dropping several ballots into the ballot box for one — always pro-government — candidate) to outright forgery. As proof, I can cite the mathematician, Sergey Shpilkin's, studies. Now electronic voting has also been added — a unique technological miracle where the electronic vote you enter does not correlate with what the system will eventually give out.

At the same time, despite the presence in the Criminal Code of several articles on violations of electoral procedures: obstruction of the exercise of voting rights or the work of election commissions (141 of the Criminal Code of the Russian Federation), falsification of election documents (142 of the Criminal Code of the Russian Federation), falsification of voting results (142.1 of the Criminal Code of the Russian Federation), illegal the issuance and receipt of a ballot, a ballot for voting in a referendum, a poll for an all-Russian vote (142.2 of the Criminal Code of the Russian Federation), not a single high-profile case was even initiated. Of those claims filed at different times by the opposition and the candidates who lost as a result of violations, not a single one was satisfied, and the court never changed the results of the vote in the history of Russia.

We will discuss elections in more detail when analyzing Article 32 of the Constitution. So far, in a nutshell.

The same goes for referendums. Russia has not held a single referendum since 1993, which approved the first version of the Constitution. The rules for its implementation make even its organization a task almost impossible.

The same applies to paragraph 4 of the commented article. Putin has long seized and is holding power. Only the 'castling' with Medvedev, about which Putin directly announced on September 24, 2011, has all the signs of an illegal seizure of power: it was not Medvedev and Putin who had to decide twice who would be president, but, according to the Constitution, the people of Russia. Despite this, Putin and Medvedev did not end up in the dock but are still in power.

It should be noted that 'castling' is just the tip of the iceberg. Let's carefully look at all the changes in the electoral legislation (listed by me above). We will see that the electoral system was changed step by step only so that there was not the slightest chance as a result of which Putin would lose power. The whole system built by Putin is tailored only for him alone, precisely as Article 278 of the Criminal Code of Russia says.

ARTICLE 4 OF THE CONSTITUTION

The full text of the article looks like this:

"1. The sovereignty of the Russian Federation shall extend to the entirety of its territory.

2. The Constitution of the Russian Federation and federal laws shall have supremacy on the entire territory of the Russian Federation.

3. The Russian Federation shall ensure the integrity and inviolability of its territory."

The first point is rather abstract and does not cause any special remarks. What raises many questions is how Putin himself and his attendants understand the concept of 'sovereignty.' In their understanding, this is complete freedom in the most negative sense: freedom from law, rules, obligations, and morality. Every time Putin is reminded of the agreements he (or Russia before him) signed, he refers to sovereignty in his rhetoric. For this, he even came up with a particular term, 'sovereign democracy,' the essence of which boils down to the fact that "we do what we want, but call us democracy." Naturally, there is no legal definition of this newspeak in Russian legislation. It was said by Putin in 2008, formulating it as: "Russia is a country that has chosen democracy for itself by the will of its people. It has embarked on this path and, observing all generally accepted democratic norms, will decide for itself how, taking into account its historical, geopolitical, and other specifics, it is possible to ensure the implementation of the principles of freedom and democracy. As a sovereign country, Russia can and will independently determine the terms and conditions for moving along this path." As we can see, this definition fits perfectly under the first point of the signs of fascism, which we cited above.

What is the catch? I have also already mentioned the rights and freedoms of a person arising from the moment of birth. They are as natural as the need to breathe, sleep, eat and drink. The very attempt to establish some kind of unique democracy, different from other democracies and 'based on geopolitical and other specifics,' is not an expansion but a severe defeat in the political rights of its citizens. It is hilarious to listen to this pseudo-historian in the context that there was some genuine democracy in the history of Rus, the Russian Empire, and the USSR (as mentioned, except for a short period of democracies of Novgorod and Pskov principalities before their destruction by Ivan the Terrible). There is no particular democratic tradition in Russia. There has always been a prince, tsar, emperor, or chairman, whose orders were unquestioningly carried out, and there was a disenfranchised and impoverished people (except for a thin layer of a class close to the ruler) whose right was only to bow as low as possible and pay taxes.

In this regard, the term has no other meaning than the opposite of the very word 'democracy.'

Paragraph 2 of the commented article indicates that the Constitution and federal laws have supremacy throughout the entire territory of the Russian Federation.

Again, we anticipate our article-by-article analysis of Chapter 2 of the Russian Constitution, dedicated to the rights and freedoms of man and citizen. I will conclude that the Russian Constitution does not work almost entirely.

And although, in theory, no law or legal act should contradict it, practically all Russian legislation is a massive contradiction of the Constitution. This is also facilitated by the numerous internal provisions of the Constitution, multiplied a hundredfold by Putin's amendments introduced in 2020, which completely paralyzed the already somewhat contradictory Constitution.

Paragraph 3 says, "The Russian Federation ensures the integrity and inviolability of its territory." That is an unusually ironic point.

First, Putin is constantly engaged in the transfer of land to other countries. So:

In 2005, 337 square kilometers of land were transferred to China — the islands of Bolshoy, Tarabarov, and half of the island of Bolshoi Ussuriysky.

In 2010, then 'Vice-President' Medvedev, as a result of the signing by him and Norwegian Prime Minister Jens Stoltenberg of an agreement on maritime boundaries in the Barents Sea and the Arctic Ocean, transferred half of the water area of the Barents Sea and the Arctic Ocean with a total area of 175,000 km^2.

Also, in 2010, Medvedev handed over to Azerbaijan, after signing an agreement on the demarcation of the Russian-Azerbaijani borders, the villages of Uryan-Uba (Uryanoba) (1,480 km^2) and the village of Khrakh-Uba (Palydly) (2,150 km^2) in the Republic of Dagestan, as well as about half catchment area of the Samur River (approximately 3,665 km^2).

In 2013, Putin, on his behalf, transferred to Azerbaijan two Dagestan villages and half of the local Semur River, with a total area of 30,000 square kilometers.

At the same time, in 2013, a special article 280.1 was introduced into the Criminal code, not even for "Violation of the territorial integrity of Russia" (although there is such an article—280.2), but just for 'calls' for this.

Secondly, while there are criminal prosecutions for "violating the integrity of Russia's borders" and active leadership in their distribution, Putin does not hesitate to organize "referendums" in other countries on joining Russia or separating certain territories from another state. This happened in 2008 in Abkhazia, South Ossetia in 2008, Crimea in 2014, LPR and DPR in 2014, and Transnistria in 2016. In 2022, Russia also attempted to organize a "referendum" in the recently captured other territories of Ukraine—Zaporizhzhya, Kherson, and Kharkiv regions. In particular, Andrei Turchak, Secretary of the General Council of United Russia Andrei Turchak, stated this when visiting Kherson.

At the same time, as we remember, there is criminal liability even for calls to change the territory of Russia (in particular, to give Ukraine the illegally occupied Crimea). It looks funny, however, that Russia allows citizens of other countries to do more than their citizens. Such hypocrisy.

Thus, we see that 1) Russia does not comply with this paragraph of the Constitution, neither about its lands nor to lands belonging to other states; 2) This is one of the first times we see the principle 'quad licet Jovi non licet bovi' (what is allowed to Jupiter, not allowed to the bull - Lat.) in regards to the head of the Russian state, he can freely do for what an ordinary citizen is subject to criminal prosecution. Looking ahead again, I will make a reservation that there are a lot of such cases, and we will analyze them; and 3) I also draw your attention to the inconsistency in the application of legal principles expressly stated in the Constitution and the hypocrisy of Putin, who in other countries is satisfied with what in his own country falls under several criminal offenses.

Consequently, Article 4 of the Russian Constitution is also inoperative.

ARTICLE 5 OF THE CONSTITUTION

The full text of the article looks like this:

"1. The Russian Federation shall consist of republics, krays, oblasts, cities of federal significance, an autonomous oblast and autonomous okrugs, which shall have equal rights as constituent entities of the Russian Federation.

2. A republic (state) shall have its own constitution and legislation. A kray, oblast, city of federal significance, autonomous oblast and autonomous okrug shall have its own charter and legislation.

3. The federal structure of the Russian Federation shall be based on its State integrity, the unity of the system of State power, the division of matters of authority and powers between State government bodies of the Russian Federation and State government bodies of constituent entities of the Russian Federation, the equality and self-determination of peoples in the Russian Federation.

4. All constituent entities of the Russian Federation shall be equal with one another in relations with federal State government bodies."

The article establishes the federal principle of territorial administration. It is assumed that the subjects have their laws, they have the right to choose their leader—the governor—and are equal among themselves.

However, Putin has always, from the very beginning of coming to power, been irritated by the relatively independent status of governors. In addition, the governors formed the Federation Council, the upper house of parliament.

In 2000, Putin created an unconstitutional institution of 'presidential plenipotentiaries.' He divided the country first into seven and later into twelve districts and appointed his overseer for each of them. Five of the seven first representatives were associated with law enforcement agencies; in 2003-2009, half of them (six out of twelve) were associated with law enforcement bodies.

Note that the president's representatives are employees of the presidential administration. The institution itself was not even created by law but by the Decree of the President (The Regulation "on the Plenipotentiary Representative of the President of the Russian Federation in the Federal District" approved by Decree of the President of the Russian Federation dated May 13, 2000 N 849).

Nevertheless, among the powers specified in Article 6 of the said Regulations, their functions were to control the activities of the bodies of the constituent entities of the Federation. Without being established in the constitution, these 'officials' could, among other things:

- take part in the work of state authorities of the subjects of the Russian Federation, as well as local governments located within the federal district; and

- represent in the legislative (representative) body of state power of a subject of the Russian Federation a temporary acting senior official (head of the highest executive body of state power) of a subject of the Russian Federation within a month from the date of his appointment.

In 2004, Putin abolished the direct election of governors. Until 2012, they were now elected in the Kremlin, and the legislative body formally approved their powers. This change was slightly adjusted after the enormous unrest of 2012, which I wrote about earlier.

However, Putin found another way to control subjects' heads—money. The tax legislation has changed in such a way that the regions have, in fact, only two types of taxes that they could leave for their own needs (Article 14 of the Tax Code of the Russian Federation):

- corporate property tax;

- gambling business tax (however, taking into account the fact that gambling business has been banned in Russia since 2009, except for five entities— the 'Republic of Crimea,' Altai Territory, Krasnodar Territory, Primorsky Territory, and Kaliningrad Region—this tax is not available for the vast majority of other subjects); and

- transport tax.

And that's it. All other taxes are collected by the subjects and sent to the federal budget, which distributes them back to the subjects in exchange for loyalty. Even if some independent governor appeared, he simply would not receive enough money for the functioning of his subject. One way or another, he will have to negotiate with the Kremlin.

It comes to the point of absurdity. So, for example, Yakutia, with vast reserves of oil, gas, diamonds (90% of Russian diamonds are mined in Yakutia), and gold, with a small population, is formally a subsidized region (that is, a region that requires money from the federal budget). Moreover, it stands in second (sic!) place regarding the volume of subsidies allocated by the center. As of 2022, only 23 out of 85 regions in Russia are donor regions. And as I mentioned above, this is explicitly done to control them.

In general, money is Putin's favorite tool. He turned the same scheme first with the media, then with the Courts, then with state employees and political parties. Again, we'll talk about this later.

Also, several waves of "bringing the legislation of the constituent entities into conformity with the federal legislation" took place, in 1999, 2002 (Federal Law "On the principles and procedure for delimiting the subjects of jurisdiction and powers between the state authorities of the Russian Federation and the state authorities of the constituent entities of the Russian Federation" of June 24, 1999, N 119-FZ), 2017, 2021.

As a result, the legislation of individual subjects ceased to differ in any way from the federal one. There were some pretty funny moments. The head of the Republic of Tatarstan bore the formal title of President of the Republic of Tatarstan. Still, this title was also taken away from him under the pretext that there could only be one president in Russia.

Summarizing what has been written, at the moment, the subject of the Russian Federation does not have the usual rights of subjects of other federations. So, for example, the State in the United States has the right to make a wide variety of laws in entirely different areas: from corporate law to gun laws. The same goes for taxes; change or remove the entire state tax to attract people and businesses, stimulate activity, etc. In general, there is nothing similar in Russia and close.

As a result, local authorities cannot solve any local issue independently without order or funding from the center.

Instead, we see how every year, Putin despondently throughout the country tries to manually solve the minor problems of phoned (and carefully pre-screened) citizens. This shameful stand-up show of total incompetence is called 'Direct Line with the President' and probably seems to him as an exit to

the people of the king in white clothes, distributing gifts (see, for example, here).

Summing up, it can be noted that, formally, Article 5 is valid. But in fact, Russia is not a federal state, and its subjects, if equal, are equal in their lack of rights.

ARTICLE 6 OF THE CONSTITUTION

The full text looks like this:

"1. Citizenship of the Russian Federation shall be acquired and terminated in accordance with federal law, and shall be one and equal, irrespective of the grounds on which it is acquired.

2. Every citizen of the Russian Federation shall enjoy all rights and freedoms on its territory and shall bear equal responsibilities as envisaged in the Constitution of the Russian Federation.

3. A citizen of the Russian Federation may not be deprived of his (her) citizenship or of the right to change it."

Although paragraphs 1 and 3 are really in force, and there are no violations yet (or they are not present in a systematic way), proposals are already being heard in the rhetoric of authorities to deprive the citizenship of 'traitors.' In particular, the speaker of the State Duma, the lower house of parliament, Volodin spoke about this. And even a corresponding bill has been introduced. Whether such a procedure will actually be adopted is unknown. But given the trend of degradation of legislation, this may happen.

However, I consider the second paragraph of the commented article to be the most important, which proclaims the equality of all citizens in freedoms and responsibilities. Nothing is further from the truth than this statement. On the contrary, I would say that society in Russia has become feudal-class, where each class has completely different rights and obligations.

I would single out the following groups:

Conditional 'New guardsmen.' A privileged class, standing above the law, freely violating it, and having immunity from criminal prosecution in whole or partially. It can be attributed to the following:

- Officials and members of their families;

- Siloviki - FSB officers, prosecutors, judges, Russian Guard ('Rosgvardia'), the investigative officers ('Sledstvenny committee), police officers; and

- 'Useful idiots': propagandists and employees of 'PMCs' ('private military companies').

I will discuss each class in more detail below. Naturally, they have their invisible hierarchy, which usually manifests itself when representatives of certain groups conflict with each other.

- The 'middle class' are:

- Veterans

- Believers

They do not have any special rights compared to other classes, but they have several privileges that allow them to be distinguished into separate groups. Such benefits immediately call into question the operation of paragraph 2 of Article 6 of the Constitution, which is why I determine this group.

- The class of 'serfs.' These are ordinary people — anyone who does not fit into any other group. At the same time, their civil rights and freedoms are still questioned, so I designated them as 'serfs,' disenfranchised servants.

- A class of outcasts and 'enemies of the nation.' If the rights and freedoms of the previous class can be both violated and respected depending on the circumstances and the other side of the conflict, then this class is heavily repressed regardless of anything. The execution of their rights is complicated precisely because they belong to their group. These groups are:

  - Oppositionists (and, in principle, all those who disagree with the authorities for any reason);

  - 'Foreign Agents';

  - oddly enough, journalists;

  - gays and lesbians; and

  - prisoners.

Now let's go through the classes in detail.

Class 'New Oprichniki' ('New guardsmen').

Officials. As of 2021, according to official data, the number of officials in Russia is 3.5 million people. Also, according to official figures, there are only 83.2 million labor-fit people in Russia. That is, the total number of officials reaches almost 4.5% employed. Naturally, given such a large number of people, there is a classification among them; from the highest (President, members of parliament, ministers) to petty clerks. And their main feature is that they all do not earn money, but on the contrary, they spend money from the budget.

Like any other massive system, it is shockingly costly and monstrously inefficient. And even this is not the most important thing; it is unparalleled corrupt. Corruption is not a crime in Russia, it is a loyalty system built by Putin. He allows his vassals to enrich themselves at the expense of the budget, and, in return, he receives compromising evidence. At the slightest disloyalty, he can initiate a criminal case against any of the officials. For details, you can refer to Navalny's investigations, for which the authorities are frantically trying to destroy him by all available means — he and his team's investigations undermine the very essence of Putin's system — personal enrichment in exchange for loyalty.

To be fair, it should be noted that such a system is not without signs of reliability. Any of Putin's billionaires is absolutely nothing. They have no unique mind, no education, and no talent. Coming from security and officials (and even Putin's bodyguards like Zolotov), they became dollar billionaires solely thanks to Putin, and without him, they are nobody. This is one of the reasons why the personal sanctions of the West, although they displease them, do not lead to their rebellion, without being burdened with intelligence, and they are not able to save their money without Putin (even if they remain free and with money); therefore, firmly clamped between the hammer and the anvil.

At the same time, corruption is formally a criminal offense under Russian law. There is a wide range of articles that, in one way or another, deal with corruption (as an unusually capacious term):

- abuse of official powers (Article 285 of the Criminal Code of the Russian Federation);

- abuse of office (Article 286 of the Criminal Code of the Russian Federation);

- illegal participation in entrepreneurial activity (Article 289 of the Criminal Code of the Russian Federation);

- receiving a bribe (Article 290 of the Criminal Code of the Russian Federation);

- giving a bribe (Article 291 of the Criminal Code of the Russian Federation);

- provocation of a bribe (Article 304 of the Criminal Code of the Russian Federation);

- official forgery and the introduction of deliberately false information (Article 292 of the Criminal Code of the Russian Federation and Article 285.3 of the Criminal Code of the Russian Federation);

- misappropriation or embezzlement (Article 160 of the Criminal Code of the Russian Federation);

- fraud with use of official powers (Article 159 of the Criminal Code of the Russian Federation);

- obstruction of legitimate business activities (Article 169 of the Criminal Code of the Russian Federation);

- misappropriation or other misuses of budgetary funds (Article 285.1 of the Criminal Code of the Russian Federation and Article 285.2 of the Criminal Code of the Russian Federation);

- registration of illegal transactions with land (Article 170 of the Criminal Code of the Russian Federation); and

- negligence (Article 293 of the Criminal Code of the Russian Federation).

But these articles operate in Russia selectively, depending on the official's loyalty, the official who protects him, and the official who has the opportunity to initiate this or that case.

So, in 2016, the then Minister of Economic Development, Alexei Ulyukaev, came into conflict with Putin's close friend, Igor Sechin. The Ministry of Economic Development did not consent to the acquisition of OJSC ANK Bashneft by PJSC NK Rosneft, which Sechin led. After one of the meetings, Ulyukayev was accused of taking a bribe and sentenced to eight years in prison and a fine of 130 million rubles. Is it necessary to say that the deal to acquire the assets of Bashneft soon took place? (a summary can be found here).

The impunity of officials is sometimes simply amazing. So, on January 9, 2009, in Altai, in the area of Mount Chernaya, a Mi-171 helicopter of the Tomsk branch of Gazpromavia crashed with high-ranking officials on board. As a result of the crash, seven people died, including the permanent representative of the President of the Russian Federation in the State Duma, Alexander Kosopkin. Four, including Anatoly Bannykh, deputy head of the government of the Altai Republic, were injured. After that, it turned out that officials during the incident were hunting Altai mountain goats, which are also called argali, and which are endangered species and placed in the so-called 'red book.'

However, on May 23, 2011, the Kosh-Agachsky Court of the Altai Republic acquitted all the helicopter crash survivors. The 'funniest' thing is that such a sentence is an infrequent exception. In Russia, a tiny number of acquittals is less than 1%. The court prefers to give a 'probationary term'—that is, a sentence without actually serving a sentence in a colony—to an acquittal. This 1% of acquittals falls on the security forces and officials, emphasizing their special status.

In general, you can read more about the hunting of officials and their hunting estates here. I would like to pay special attention to how vast lands belong to people who have never been in business and are officials.

It is also common practice for officials to fence off plots of land contrary to the requirements of the law (for example, paragraph 8 of Article 11 of the Forest Code prohibits preventing citizens from accessing the forest, and Article 6 of the Water Code to water bodies; and paragraph 6 and paragraph 8 of Article 6 of the Water of the Code of the Russian Federation, establishing a sanitary zone in which buildings should not be located at all). However, the authorities not only do not prosecute officials for such violations but, on the contrary, protect their lawlessness. So, the governor of the Krasnodar Territory, Tkachev, illegally fenced off a 5.3 hectare forest plot. At the end of 2011, Suren Ghazaryan, a member of the Ecological Watch Council, wrote an official letter to the Forestry Department in which he demanded that action be taken against the illegally installed fence. Curiously, this letter was later attached to the materials of the criminal case on the 'damage' of the governor's fence.

As a result, the ecologist was sentenced to three years in prison for 'damaging the fence'; he wrote on it that the forest was for public use (details here).

The above cases are not the only ones and are no exception. From time to time, the prosecutor's office jails some officials who, most likely, have overstepped some invisible red lines or maintain the illusion that the state is trying to fight corruption. For example, during the search in FSB Colonel Cherkalin's flat 12 billion (sic!) Rubles ($184 mil at that time) were found, or in the case against another slightly more modest FSB Colonel Zakharchenko with its modest 7.5 billion rubles ($117 mil at that time).

Separate, explicitly emphasizing the status of an official, his importance and disregard for the rules is 'a car with a flashing light (a light signal giving the right to violate specific traffic rules).' Typically, such devices are provided to emergency vehicles: ambulances, firefighters, gas services, and police. In Russia, the 'flashing light' is an indication of status. Any high official is entitled to it by their position. In total, officials have no more than 1,000 of them, and they are distributed among 18 departments. Still, they are associated not only with a deliberate demonstration of the lack of rights of citizens who are forced to stand in a traffic jam while some finance minister rushes along a separate lane or even an oncoming lane to the dacha but also with numerous excesses associated with their use: from fatal accidents to the death of patients in ambulances, forced to wait until such an official car passes. On Kutuzovsky Prospekt in Moscow, special concrete barriers for oncoming traffic lanes were even dismantled to make a dedicated lane for such officials to drive. Even if we disregard the costs (first for the installation of barriers and then for their removal), after the barriers were removed, the number of accidents increased several times!

I do not even mention the enormous fortunes of all the top officials in Russia, amounting to billions of dollars.

Impunity and 'status' are so ingrained in officials that they don't give a damn about ordinary people. Here, for example, a deputy from United Russia knocks down a child, gets out of the car, checks for damage, and leaves. He was tried before the court on December 23th, 2022 and, of course, acquitted. Pay attention to his complete disregard for even a child's life; how do you think they are treating the rights of people if they don't care about their life? If you believe this is an exception, then look at more examples of the attitude of officials towards ordinary people, which I cite when analyzing Article 21 of the Constitution.

The situation with the second group, the **security forces**, is about the same. After all, they are officials too. Only one exception allows them to be singled out in a separate class; they do not have the right to travel outside Russia. Contrary to paragraph 2 of Article 27 of the Constitution, they are prohibited from leaving by order of the Ministry of Internal Affairs (sic!) dated September 12, 2013, No. 705-dsp "On Certain Issues of Departure of Police Officers, Federal State Civil Servants and Employees of the Ministry of Internal Affairs of Russia on Private Affairs Outside the Territory of the Russian Federation." I can't provide the text of the order since the mark in its number is 'dsp,' 'for inner use,' that is. It does not formally have the status of a secret; its test is hidden from the public. Given its unconstitutionality, its 'secrecy' is logically justified. At the same time, the Supreme Court dismissed the complaint about the illegality of this order. That is, again, the order of the Ministry, which is even lower in legal force than the Law, cancels the provision of the Constitution. However, when analyzing this article, we are more interested in the legal status of the security forces; they are kept close, not allowing them to scatter and see for themselves the falsity of what the propaganda tells them about the 'decaying West.'

And the last group in this class is '**propagandists and employees of 'PMCs'** (private military campaigns).'

Not being formal officials, they receive money directly from the budget and, like the same officials, are immune to several criminal code articles. Being, in essence, the same highly paid bandits but with a different 'bouquet of articles.'

If you have never watched talk shows on official Russian channels, you are lucky. Trying to shut down each other, unusually deceitful and stupid people are trying to argue about who should be shot today and how beautiful Putin is in his kingdom. I recommend the YouTube channel of blogger, Alexander Balu, who has the nerve and firmness to listen and calmly comment on this nonsense.

Propaganda is the primary weapon of the Kremlin. Its goal is not to convey some news or explain it but to throw in so much nonsense that any person has doubts about their knowledge. He begins to doubt. 'There is no smoke without fire,' 'Everything is not that simple,' the words of those infected with the zombie virus of Russian propaganda. These people don't even remember what those same propagandists told them a week ago, just like in Orwell's 1984, "Ostasia never went to war with Oceania," remember?

However, for the current analysis, the immunity of propagandists to several articles of the Russian criminal code is more important for us. In particular, Article 282 of the Criminal Code of the Russian Federation "Inciting hatred or enmity, as well as humiliation of human dignity," given the Russian attack on Ukraine, also Article 354 of the Criminal Code of the Russian Federation "Public calls to unleash an aggressive war."

Even though propagandists are constantly calling for 'shooting all oppositionists,' 'turning America into radioactive ashes,' 'wipe England off the face of the earth,' 'smear the liver of the protesters on the asphalt,' 'castrate gays' and 'do not stand on ceremony with 2% of the shit [dissatisfied with Putin],' moreover, live from the screens of official television. That is, with the aggravating circumstances provided for by Articles 282, 354 of the Criminal Code of the Russian Federation, they have never been accused or prosecuted. This is because the authorities are deliberately building a fascist state and generating hatred for any minority (and not only). An external enemy is a crucial element of distraction from internal problems. To be more precise, these are immediate points 4, 5, 6, and 8 in the "14 signs of fascism" by Umberto Eco, cited above. Therefore, propaganda, like corruption, is the backbone of the Russian state.

I want to emphasize that the state's unwillingness to initiate criminal cases against all these persons speaks of their direct support and of the state policy in these areas—propaganda and actual terrorism. International law enforcement agencies and organizations should closely monitor this situation. The imposition of sanctions against propagandists is a correct measure but not sufficient. They should be subject to international arrest. In general, the status of a propagandist requires a severe rethinking in international law; their destructive activities bring even more damage than terrorist ones.

Members of the 'PMC' (short for 'private military company') stand not much differently. Russian legislation has no law on private military companies or anything like that. Moreover, Russian legislation is stringent and nervous about everything related to the possession of weapons by individuals. In particular, the Law "On Weapons" generally excludes the circulation of military weapons and their possession by ordinary citizens.

Therefore, by enrolling in such a PMC, in theory, a citizen can immediately be prosecuted under several articles of the Russian Criminal Code (moreover, with aggravating signs, in particular, "committed by a group of persons"):

- Article 210. "Organization of a criminal community (criminal organization) or participation in it";

- Article 222. "Illegal acquisition, transfer, sale, storage, transportation, transfer or carrying of weapons, main parts of firearms, ammunition";

- Article 222.1. "Illegal acquisition, transfer, sale, storage, transportation, transfer or carrying of explosives or explosive devices";

- Articles 222.2. "Illegal acquisition, transfer, sale, storage, transportation, transfer or carrying of large-caliber firearms, their main parts and ammunition";

- Article 359. "Mercenary"; and

- And as soon as they cross the border, the article "322. Illegal crossing of the state border of the Russian Federation" kicks in.

They engaged in extrajudicial ISIS-style executions participation (and here), which they not only do not deny but are even proud of.

The rest of the articles are 'added' depending on what such people will do while abroad.

What are they needed for? This is an expendable material of the army and the FSB. They do the dirty work so that the FSB and Putin, bulging their eyes like a child, can babble that 'It's not us,' 'We're not there.' They think it's a genius move. In fact, they are de facto sponsors of an inherently terrorist organization.

I classified them as a separate group since the members of PMCs do not have official status. They are simple bandits in the service of the state. Still, they have immunity to a large set of Criminal Code articles that allows them to be classified as 'guardsmen,' albeit its lowest layer.

'**Middle class.**' This name has nothing to do with the globally accepted definition of the middle class concerning wealth. I mean their legal status in relation to other social classes in Russia.

On the one hand, they do not have specific immunity from some articles of Criminal law; on the other hand, the state recognizes their special status, highlighting certain 'special feelings' that believers have and the 'special status of veterans' for the protection of which part 1 article 148 of the Criminal Code of the Russian Federation "Violation of the right to freedom of conscience and religion" and article 354.1 of the Criminal Code of the Russian Federation "Rehabilitation of Nazism" was written.

Let's go into a little more detail.

Both of these rules are purely reflexive. The article about 'insulting the feelings of believers' arose after the performance of Pussy Riot in the Cathedral of Christ the Savior in 2013. The band filmed a short video using their dances filmed at the temple, which they overdubbed with music. This song was called "Mother of God, drive Putin away." Naturally, Putin, who considers himself a believer, did not like this. Officials, in the best traditions of the manners of the XIX century, rushed to 'hold and not let go' mode. However, it turned out that the group did not violate any legal rules; there was no corpus delicti. If you think that the girls were just released, you are mistaken; they were given a 'dvushechka' (in the vile expression of Putin himself) — "a little twos" — that is, two years in prison. And they made appropriate changes to the Criminal Code of the Russian Federation.

These amendments endowed believers with those very 'special feelings,' violating two articles of the Constitution at once. The very one that we are commenting on, Article 6 and Article 28, which implies freedom of conscience (that is, whether to believe in a higher being (God) or not to believe at all). It presupposes the equality of both believers among themselves and believers and unbelievers.

The same thing happened with article 354.1 of the Criminal Code of the Russian Federation, "Rehabilitation of Nazism," in terms of 'special dignity of the personality of a veteran.' So, part 3 of Article 354.1 reads:

"The dissemination of information expressing clear disrespect for society about the days of military glory and memorable dates of Russia related to the defense of the Fatherland, as well as the desecration of the symbols of Russia's military glory, insulting the memory of the defenders of the Fatherland, or humiliating the honor and dignity of a veteran of the Great Patriotic War, committed publicly…"

The article was introduced in 2021 after the measures taken by the authorities to amend the Constitution. The state, in support of the amendments, which were supposed to turn a lame almost 70-year-old duck into a beautiful swan, made several commercials that starred, among others, a veteran of the Second World War. Navalny called the participants in the video 'corrupt lackeys,' but did not specifically mention the veteran. As a result, Navalny was accused of slandering a veteran who, along with several well-known Russians, appeared in an RT campaign video for amendments to the Constitution.

And again, the authorities are faced with the fact that there is no corpus delicti. I also want to note that slander is determined as "... the dissemination of knowingly false information that discredits the honor and dignity of another person or undermines his reputation." It is assumed that you cannot discredit the reputation of a person who is not even mentioned. Also, I draw your attention to the fact that slander was already in the Criminal code—this is article 128, which was once decriminalized (removed from the Criminal code). When Putin returned, it was reintroduced back. Therefore, in 2021, an amendment was made to protect veterans' honor and dignity. As we remember, the Russian state, in the best traditions of fascism, is trying to instill a cult of tradition, and therefore the cult of the Great Patriotic War is far from the last place.

However, here, I will make a reservation. During the analysis, I found two people to whom the Russian Constitution does not apply in general: Putin and Navalny. You understand that the veteran was used by the authorities only as a tool to put pressure on Navalny. In ordinary times, veterans are not only very elderly but also unusually poor people whom the authorities take out of the closet like a dusty uniform on Victory Day on May 9, uttering empty promises and the eternal false 'let the war be never again' (while saying, 'We can do it again' on all other days).

You can be convinced of the present deplorable state of veterans by going to the site https://мечтаветерана.рф, where funds are collected and directed to the fulfillment of their cherished desires. You can very well assess their standard of living simply by what they dream of.

That is, it turns out that the state formally puts the "honor and dignity of a veteran" higher than the honor and dignity of any other person, in violation of Article 6 of the Constitution, but does not want to spend money on veterans.

The class of '**serfs**.' Technically, these are ordinary people, those who do not belong to the privileged classes or whom the propaganda has not chosen as its target for hatred.

In a sense, they are equal (in their lack of rights) and can even defend their interests in state bodies and courts. This is especially true if two class representatives are suing or arguing among themselves. At the same time, their legal status lies in their lack of rights — this will be revealed when analyzing Chapter 2 of the Constitution. At the moment, it makes no sense for me to say where and in what way they are infringed and limited; there will be a detailed analysis further.

However, in most cases, they serve as a source of income for the upper class: from extortion of bribes to the banal initiation of criminal cases against them to receive 'stars '— promotion (the number of stars on shoulder straps in Russia indicate ranks).

It comes to absolutely monstrous cases. So, one married couple from Kaliningrad was convicted for 'revealing an FSB officer' at a wedding, who himself did not hide this; he was photographed and talked about his career. The couple was sentenced to 12 and 13 years in prison.

Such stories are no exception. The security forces have put on stream extortion from the business. Putin himself acknowledged the seriousness of the problem. 45% of cases brought against entrepreneurs do not reach court. In 90% of cases, the court determines the duration of the investigation for entrepreneurs, not house arrest or a written undertaking not to leave the country, but placement in a pre-trial detention center. However, while recognizing the scale and even labeling it as a 'threat to the country's economy,' Putin considers entrepreneurs to be 'hucksters' and 'crooks by definition', so they are not worthy of state protection and from the state.

Of course, with such a hypocritical approach, Putin did not solve the problem of seizure and destruction of business by the security forces. In addition, as we said earlier, corruption is the backbone of Putin's system. By allowing the security forces to get rich at the expense of business, he maintains his rotten system afloat to the detriment of the country's economy.

Officials extort bribes at any level: from medicine to the courts. Your humble servant, being a professional lawyer, for a whole year (sic!) was removing the arrest imposed by the bailiffs on the car, although the enforcement proceedings were already closed by the same bailiff (a small fine was paid). Given the consistency, this is done consciously and intentionally to squeeze money out of the population for fines and bribes to maintain a corrupt system. In such conditions, anyone who acts within the framework of the legislation in Russia is in a significantly worse position than someone who violates the legislation.

 In particular, this is why the GDP in Russia remained practically unchanged from 2010 to 2020. There was no economic growth for ten years, despite the enormous prices for oil and gas. Economists have called it the 'lost decade.'

A class of outcasts and 'enemies of the nation.' In the best traditions of fascism (point 4 according to Umberto Eco) and of any dictatorship, anyone who doubts the leader's decisions becomes an 'enemy of the nation' and a traitor and is persecuted by all supporters of such a tyrant.

And if, in the days of Nazi Germany, badges were used on clothes for different groups (Jews, Gypsies, gays, and lesbians, etc.), and Jews were required to indicate their nationality in documents, the practice of calling dissenting people 'foreign agents' spread in Russia. This label is used to emphasize that these people do not express their opinion (how can it possibly be other than one of such a brilliant Putin?) but act at the expense and on the orders of foreign states (which, of course, are only busy with intrigues against Russia).

In Russian law, the term 'agent' existed only as a particular type of contract in the Civil Code of Russia, where one person, at the expense and on behalf of another person, undertakes to perform specific actions. In American law, agency relations can be contractual and based on actual circumstances. For example, teachers who take children on a camping trip are agents of their parents. Be that as it may, in both of these cases, the agent has a will of his own and only has a specific commission or permission to act on behalf of another person. Let's break these rules into elements: (1) An agent has the authority to act on behalf of another person. Separately, I want to note that it is 'on behalf of,' that is, for someone; therefore (2) He does not acquire the rights and obligations of the person on behalf of whom he acts (Principal), on the contrary, if he appropriates something, he will be obliged to return everything; (3) The Agent acts at the expense of the Principal, that is, the Principal pays all his actions, not in his interests.

However, except in civil law, the term 'agent' has never been used.

What is the definition of 'foreign agent' contained in the amendments to the law "On non-commercial organizations"?

Paragraph 6 of Article 2 of the Law on Non-Profit Organizations reads: "Under this Federal Law, a non-profit organization performing the functions of a foreign agent is understood to be a Russian non-profit organization that receives funds and (or) other property from foreign states, their state bodies, international and foreign organizations, foreign citizens, stateless persons or persons authorized by them, and (or) from citizens of the Russian Federation or Russian legal entities receiving funds and (or) other property from these sources or acting as intermediaries in receiving such funds and (or) other property (with the exception of open joint-stock companies with state participation and their subsidiaries), and (or) from Russian legal entities, the beneficial owners of which in the meaning defined by paragraph 8 of Article 6.1 of the Federal

Law of August 7, 2001 N 115- Federal Law "On counteraction to legalization (laundering) proceeds from crime and financing of terrorism" are foreign citizens or stateless persons (hereinafter referred to as 'foreign sources') and which participates, including in the interests of foreign sources, in political activities carried out on the territory of the Russian Federation."

To simplify this word salad, let's highlight the elements of the article again:

1. It must be a non-profit organization;

2. It must receive income from foreign organizations; and

3. It participates in political activities in Russia.

At the same time, political activity is understood by law in an unusually broad way. For clarity, here is another quote from the 'law' (I have italicized the most outrageous ones):

1. Participation in the organization and conduct of public events in the form of meetings, rallies, demonstrations, processions, *pickets*, or various combinations of these forms, organization, and *taking part in public debates, discussions, and speeches*;

2. Participation in activities aimed at obtaining a certain result in elections, a referendum, in **monitoring** *the conduct of elections, a referendum, the formation of election commissions, referendum commissions, in the activities of political parties*;

3. *Public appeals to state bodies, local self-government bodies, and their officials, as well as other actions that affect the activities of these bodies, including those aimed at the adoption, amendment, repeal of laws or other regulatory legal acts*;

4. *Dissemination*, including with the use of modern information technologies, *of opinions* on decisions made by state bodies and their policies;

5. Formation of socio-political views and beliefs, including by *conducting public opinion polls and publishing their results or conducting other sociological research*;

6. Involvement of citizens, including minors, in these activities; and

7.   Financing of the specified action.

Should I comment on these points? Their non-legal nature is quite apparent.

On November 25, 2017, Law No. 327-FZ was adopted, introducing the concept of a 'foreign media agent.' In fact, the same as the usual 'foreign agent.' According to these amendments, the Ministry of Justice (MOJ) received the right to recognize as a 'foreign agent,' any foreign media outlet that receives funding or property from foreign bodies or citizens directly or through Russian legal entities. In terms of their duties, these definitions are identical.

And in 2018, the State Duma adopted amendments to recognize an individual as a 'foreign agent' when he distributes materials to an unlimited number of people and receives foreign funding. The amendments to the second reading made it possible to include in this category those who distribute messages and media materials—foreign agents or participate in creating these materials and at the same time receive funding from abroad. Thus, individuals, foreign agents, could be recognized, for example, as journalists who work in the media, already recognized as such in Russia.

Not even a court, but state bodies, the Ministry of Justice and the Ministry of Foreign Affairs, were appointed to award these 'Nazi badges.' In addition, an individual can be recognized not just as a 'foreign agent' but as a 'foreign mass media outlet acting as a foreign agent.' Within a month, such an individual, contrary to Article 30 of the Constitution, is obliged to establish a Russian legal entity and notify the authorities about this. As a result, journalists who worked in the media-foreign agents, citizens working in companies with foreign funding, or scientists who received foreign grants fell into the risk zone.

Three UN special rapporteurs (on the right to peaceful assembly, on the situation of human rights defenders, and the protection of the right to freedom of expression) criticized the law at the draft stage. They called the law "a direct challenge to exercise their right to freedom of association," emphasizing that "civil society organizations have the right to receive funding from abroad, just as governments have the right to receive international assistance," and restrictions on such a right are 'unfair.' According to UN experts, the new rules allow human rights defenders to be subjected to special control, regardless of whether they receive support from abroad or not, which "will prevent them from carrying out their significant activities." They pointed out that an extremely broad definition of 'political activity' would allow any advocacy activities of NGOs to be included under it, which would violate "the right of human rights defenders to raise human rights issues in society." The labeling of a 'foreign agent' reveals, in their view, "the clear intent to stigmatize any activity of civil society that receives support from abroad." It also notes that the statutory fines are disproportionate and shift the burden of proof to non-profit organizations engaged in legitimate human rights activities.

When Putin was approached with the question of "why the court does not even take the decision [on recognition as a foreign agent], but by the executive bodies," Putin, either due to his inherent ignorance or inability to read or, as always, lied: "Well, this imposes no obligations on them."

According to the same criterion, participation in 'political activity' (as understood by its authorities) is persecuted by any persons who do not agree with this authority or even 'express their [other than official] opinion.' The authorities use all methods to fight not only with politicians who disagree with it but also with journalists who are simply doing their job: reporting on the crimes of government officials and corruption. Moreover, the methods of struggle against civil society are not limited by anything—up to direct murder. The most striking example is the poisoning of former FSB colonel Litvinenko (I provided a link to the investigation materials earlier, but I will take this opportunity to leave it here again); Boris Nemtsov, who was killed right in front of the Kremlin (collection of publications on the topic) and Navalny (his colleagues collected all the documents on this case here). I will elaborate on this later. While I want to stop, Putin does not disregard any methods, eliminating everyone who uncovers his criminal activities.

The same is with journalists. During Putin's rule, these journalists were killed:

- Abashilov, Gadzhi Akhmedovich

- Akhmedilov, Malik

- Bogomolov, Lev Viktorovich

- Magomed Uspaev

- Evloev, Magomed Yahyaevich

- Ivanov, Valery Evgenievich

- Kalinovsky, Sergey Arturovich

- Kamalov Khadzhimurad Magomedovich

- Karimov, Farhad Asker

- Kuashev, Timur Khambievich

- Napiorkovskiy, Anton Yulianovich

- Popkov, Viktor Alekseevich

- Sidorov, Alexey Vladimirovich

- Skryl, Natalya Vladimirovna

- Tsilikin, Dmitry Vladimirovich

- Chaikova, Nadezhda Vladimirovna

- Shevchenko, Leonid Vitalievich

- Estemirova, Natalia Khusainovna

- Yudina, Larisa Alekseevna

Also, recently, the court sentenced Ivan Safronov to 22 years in prison for his open-source publications about corruption in the Ministry of Defense.

Again, we intersect with the topic of further articles of the Constitution, particularly with the right to life. However, here I just want to note that the 'right to life,' the basic human right, is not just about the state shall not kill anyone (which, by itself, is the very, very minimum), but also the duty of the state to investigate crimes against citizens and take preventive measures so that they never happen again. In the exercise of this right, hypothetically, a whole complex of state bodies is involved: from the Ministry of Internal Affairs to the FSB and the Federal Penitentiary Service (FSIN). The problem is that they do not work with journalists — not a single case has been investigated to the end. At best, the executors have been convicted, and the customer has not been found and convicted in any of them. Regarding Navalny's poisoning, the investigative committee refused to initiate a criminal case and conduct any investigation in general.

The next group in the class is **Gays and Lesbians**. The Russian state harbors a particular irrational hatred towards this group.

I am not a sociologist, but I assume two reasons here: the great conservatism of Russian society, fueled at one time by the USSR legislation on gays (there was a criminal punishment for 'sodomy' (Article 121 of the Criminal Code of the RSFSR)), and after the collapse, by the Orthodox Church. The second reason is the need to find something alien, inherent in other countries, to say, "Look how sinful and fallen they are, but we are just so holy and right."

Formally, hatred towards this group is not expressed. In words, the authorities say that their rights are protected routinely. But there is Article 6.21 of the Code of Administrative Offenses of the Russian Federation, "Propaganda of non-traditional sexual relations among minors." It sounds like this:

"Propaganda of non-traditional sexual relations among minors, expressed in the dissemination of information aimed at the formation of non-traditional sexual attitudes among minors, the attractiveness of non-traditional sexual relations, *a distorted idea of the social equivalence of traditional and non-traditional sexual relations* [highlighted by me - A.M.], or the imposition of information about non-traditional sexual relations, causing interest in such relations, if these actions do not contain a criminal offense."

100

I ask you to pay attention to the highlighted fragment, which indicates that the legislator is convinced that 'traditional relations' are not at all equal to 'non-traditional,' indicating that not only the scope of their rights is different (which contradicts the commented Article 6 of the Constitution), but even to say that they are equal is already an administrative offense. It's funny, in the light of this logic, anyone who quotes Article 6 or Clause 1 of Article 19 of the Constitution ('everyone is equal before the law and the court') is subject to administrative liability under Article 6.21 of the Code of Administrative Offenses of the Russian Federation due to an apparent logical contradiction.

Also, the article refers only to 'propaganda' among children. However, this does not only apply to 'propaganda.' The prosecutor's office has never yet had to prove actual harm (which is impossible), and the criterion for referring to this composition is the sufficiency of the fact that 'children could see it.'

Please note that even though there is only administrative punishment, its harm is colossal. Remember that Russian society has had a conservative and negative attitude towards gays and lesbians from the beginning. And instead of trying to extinguish hostility (and even hatred), the state is doing everything to kindle it. This is usually done by propagandists. However, sometimes the government is connected directly. The loudest and most shameful case was banning the psychological help center for young gays and lesbians.

In addition, usually in crimes, aggravating circumstances are the commission of crimes motivated by hatred. At the same time, no court in Russia has yet considered a case where hatred of gays was named as an aggravating circumstance (p. 9), and the prosecutor's office repeatedly refused to initiate a criminal case on the fact of hatred of gays.

The following supposedly state-guaranteed rights do not apply to gays and lesbians:

- The right to life, personal dignity, and security;

- The right to privacy;

- The right to a fair trial;

- The right to freedom of expression;

- The right to associations and associations;

- The right to peaceful assembly and procession;

- The right to health care;

- The right to education;

- The right to work;

- The right to motherhood, childhood, and marriage; and

- The right to change gender and name.

We will analyze each of the points later when analyzing the corresponding articles. In the meantime, here is a list to emphasize the special status of individual Russian citizens.

And the last group, in every sense, is the '**prisoners**.' In theory, the purpose of imprisonment is to re-educate the criminal to reintegrate him back into society. And the only punishment for him is what the court sentenced — imprisonment. He must retain the rest of his rights.

In reality, the situation of prisoners is somewhere in the middle between slavery and torture.

 If you want to delve into this topic in more detail, I advise you to read these books by Olga Romanova, the founder of the non-profit organization "Imprisoned Rus."

 I want to emphasize the inhuman conditions in which the prisoners are. The FSB and other law enforcement agencies have put on stream, a torture conveyor to extort money from prisoners or knock them out of testimony (more information here). This link contains videos with torture directly (CAUTION, VERY VIOLENT CONTENT 18+).

I also want to remind you that only 1% of acquittals take place in Russia, mainly in the upper classes. Therefore, for all other classes, the perspective of going to prison is not just a real prospect but rather an inevitable one. This is especially true of other outcasts and 'enemies of the nation' class groups.

As you can see, Article 6 of the Constitution is not something that does not work; it does not correspond to reality at all. My analysis is only the briefest and most incomplete reflection of the facts. But even from it, it is enough to understand that society in Russia is a class society. If not even according to the feudal model, then precisely according to the model of fascism; the elitism of certain groups, the lack of rights for others, and perfect hatred for some are very clearly seen.

One way or another, we will touch upon the problem of classes in the analysis of other Articles, but now the reader, I hope, has a clearer impression of the legal status of citizens in Russia.

ARTICLE 7 OF THE CONSTITUTION

The full text of the article reads as follows:

"1. The Russian Federation shall be a social state whose policy is aimed at creating conditions ensuring a worthy life and a free development of Man.

2. In the Russian Federation, the labor and health of people shall be protected, a guaranteed minimum wage shall be established, State support shall be provided for the family, maternity, fatherhood, and childhood, to the disabled and to elderly citizens, the system of social services shall be developed, and State pensions, allowances, and other social security guarantees shall be established."

In a nutshell, we are talking about the fact that the Russian state is obliged to support people who need help and cannot feed themselves due to temporary or permanent circumstances. In a broader sense, it provides economic equality among citizens.

At the same time, Russia, being a class state, has a vast social inequality.

Not being an economist, here I am quoting an article by Ivan Aleksandrov, "Russia: causes and consequences of extreme stratification into rich and poor."

The five hundred richest Russians have concentrated in their hands 40% of the country's financial assets, or 47 trillion rubles ($640 billion), according to a report by the Boston Consulting Group, that is, the property stratification in the Russian Federation is three times higher than on the planet as a whole. On average, super-rich people control 13% of global finance.

According to the World Inequality Database (WID), in 2019, 10% of Russians with the highest incomes (on average, 600 thousand rubles (roughly $10,000 per month)) accumulated 46.5 % of national income. At the same time, they share the poorest half of the population, earning an average of 46 thousand rubles a month, accounting for only 17%.

According to Credit Suisse's 2020 Global Wealth Report, the top 1% of Russia's population accounts for 58% of national wealth (that is, financial and non-financial assets), which is twice as much as in Germany, and one and a half times as much as in the United States.

Inequality is not synonymous with low living standards. Substantial inequality is combined with high or rapidly growing wealth in some countries, like the US, China, or Saudi Arabia. In Russia, however, wealth stratification and poverty go hand in hand.

According to the official version, 70% of Russians are middle class. However, even such commentators as billionaire Oleg Deripaska doubt the reliability of such declarations.

The authorities classify as the middle-class, everyone who receives more than one and a half times the minimum wage. Consequently, people with a monthly income of 20-30 thousand rubles (about $350 - $500) a month also fall into it (even though, according to polls, Russians need at least 50 thousand rubles (about $850) a month for a decent life).

Four-fifths of consumer spending falls on payment for goods and services; one-sixth on mandatory fees; and only a few percent on savings, HSE (High School of Economics) experts stated.

According to polls, about half of Russians can buy food and clothes, not a washing machine or refrigerator. About 20% are even poorer, and about the same number are a little richer (they can afford expensive purchases, but not a car). Thus, most citizens may belong to the poor in the broadest sense of the word.

Endemic poverty results from inequality in the distribution of funds, limited due to stagnation and low productivity of the Russian economy, says Matveev. First of all, we are talking about low salaries.

"The average salary [of a salesperson] at Magnit (a large chain of retail stores) is 25,000 rubles (about $400) per month. [Company founder] Sergei Galitsky sold his share in Magnit for 138 billion rubles ($2.3 billion). Where did this number come from? The assets of the oligarchs are the shares of their companies. Why are they worth so much? Because these are enterprises where workers are paid a penny (which increases their profitability)," the expert illustrates his point.

Another link between inequality and poverty is a monopoly and related corruption.

About 80% of banking assets are concentrated in fifteen credit institutions, half of which are state-owned. The "Big Three" mobile operators control the mobile communications market. Eleven companies hold 85% of oil production, and 60-70% of pork produced falls on the twenty largest agricultural holdings.

Cartels are widespread in all sectors of the economy, especially those related to public procurement, construction, transportation, medicines, and food, states the Federal Antimonopoly Service (FAS) report on the state of competition in Russia.

"The largest private and state companies have concentrated monopoly rents in their hands. They arbitrarily set prices ... And although economists tell us that there is such a thing as a trickle-down ("leakage" of wealth from the upper floors of the social pyramid to the lower ones), nothing like this happens in Russia. The tide does not lift all boats. He raises only expensive yachts, and fragile boats sink," emphasizes the Eurasianet.org interlocutor.

Alexandrov says, "The redistribution of budgetary funds in favor of the rich is another cause of poverty and inequality, Matveev believes.

"Money that could be spent on social programs is spent on enriching the oligarchs with the help of state orders [or in other ways]. The state creates rich 'political capitalists,'" the researcher is convinced.

The Kremlin publicly denies the very existence of the oligarchs.

"The oligarchs are those who use their proximity to power for super-profits. We have large companies... But I don't know of any large company that would enjoy preferences from proximity to power," Vladimir Putin said in an interview with the Financial Times.

The population is convinced otherwise. The fact that Putin failed to curb the oligarchs is said by 34% of the Levada Center respondents, 10% more than in 2010. Thirty-eight percent are sure that the president expresses the interests of "oligarchs, bankers and big businessmen."

Social inequality was named the most acute problem in Russian society by 26% of respondents surveyed by Levada in March of this year [2021 - A.M.]. The stratification into rich and poor has left behind topics such as the poor quality of medicine, the economic crisis, the environment, and the arbitrariness of officials. More Russians are concerned only with rising prices, poverty, corruption, and unemployment, that is, problems that are closely related to inequality."

As a result, in Russia, there is a massive number of the so-called "working poor." Although they have permanent jobs, they receive so little that they are below the poverty line.

According to the Analytical Center for the Government of Russia, the working poor in Russia in 2016 was 12.1 million people or 16.8% of the employed population.

This does not mean that these people do not have an education. On the contrary, many of them have a good education (in particular, thanks to free higher education). Oddly enough, these categories include professions that are very highly paid in other countries: medical workers, teachers, accountants, laboratory assistants, and scientists (more about working poverty in Russia can be found here).

I want to add my considerations as a lawyer, not an economist (which I am not). There has long been a dispute in legal science: what comes before the rights of people or their well-being. There are two points of view: one says that people first become wealthy and start fighting for their rights, and the second, that at first, people have some rights, and using them, people slowly accumulate wealth. A sort of legal chicken-and-egg issue. In this dispute, Putin put an end to it: without rights, it is impossible to become wealthy. At any moment, a person can be imprisoned, and money extorted. Note that the crazy wealth of people close to Putin comes from here; they have many times more rights than most Russian citizens.

Thus, Russia is not a social state. The monstrous stratification and uneven distribution of benefits make the country not social but additionally point to its class character.

ARTICLE 8 OF THE CONSTITUTION

The full text reads as follows:

"1. The Russian Federation guarantees the unity of the economic space, free movement of goods, services, and financial resources, support for competition, and freedom of economic activity.

2. In the Russian Federation, private, state, municipal, and other forms of ownership are recognized and protected in the same way."

I will not analyze the second point. In general, it is difficult to imagine different types of protection for different types of property. The main thing is the rights of the owner (which, as we remember, vary greatly depending on the class), and the object is deeply secondary.

But with the first point in Russia, there are significant problems.

Putin does not like the independence of anyone; while believing that he is more intelligent than the rest, he prefers to manage the economy manually. Consequently, creating monopolies in Russia is an inevitable process because that way, it is easier to manage them manually.

Thus, the Bank of Russia, for example, pursuing a strict policy on almost all fronts, cannot fail to notice a steady increase in the banking sector's monopolization level. If back in 2013, the largest five banks accounted for about 50% of the banking system's assets, which was then considered an extremely high level, now it is already about 60%, despite the fact that four out of five of these banks are state-owned.

By the beginning of 2020, 17 subjects of the Russian Federation did not have credit institutions (only branches). And this is entirely consistent with the data that in 2019, three regions accounted for 68.4% of all loans issued in the country, while the entire Siberian Federal District accounted for only 4.4% and the Far East for 2.4%. However, by reducing the number of credit institutions in the country, the Bank of Russia does not show that it is really concerned about how healthy the banking market environment remains due to these actions.

The same situation in Russia exists in the following areas:

- RZD (Russian Railways) has a monopoly on rail transportation;

- Aeroflot (Russian Airlines) - practically a monopoly in air transportation;

- GAZPROM is a monopoly in the field of gas transportation through pipelines and the sale of natural gas;

- Transneft - (transports of more than 90% of the oil produced in Russia) and others (these are the brightest).

Such monopolies are called 'natural.' Paradoxically, there is even a particular Federal Law, "On Natural Monopolies," dated August 17, 1995, N 147-FZ.

This law provides for as many as 14 areas where 'natural monopolies' operate; in fact, there are many more monopolies.

That is, instead of getting rid of monopolies and breaking them in accordance with this article of the Constitution, the state took them under its control.

In 2017, the FAS estimated that state-owned enterprises contribute to Russia's GDP by 70 percent. Monopolization is growing, and with it, the inefficiency of enterprises and corruption.

More information on the situation with monopolies (as of 2017) can be found here.

As a result, it is clear that Article 8 also does not have legal force.

ARTICLE 9 OF THE CONSTITUTION

"1. Land and other natural resources shall be utilized and protected in the Russian Federation as the basis of the life and activity of the peoples living on the territories concerned.

2. Land and other natural resources may be subject to private, State, municipal and other forms of ownership."

Several completely different legal terms and concepts are mixed here.

First is the concept of 'land' as a land plot—a formal piece of land that may or may not contain resources. Secondly, 'land' as a place of residence, environment, and habitat (including animals and plants). Thirdly, natural resources, both living and non-living (minerals).

I want to note that not all natural resources can have different forms of ownership. In particular, according to clause 1.2 of the Law of the Russian Federation of February 21, 1992, N 2395-1 "On Subsoil," "subsoil within the boundaries of the territory of the Russian Federation, including underground space and minerals, energy and other resources contained in the subsoil, are state property." Unlike English and American legislation, where the subsoil belongs to those who can extract it. So, formally, this article is no longer valid.

We have already discussed in the analysis of Article 5 of the Constitution that the income from minerals also goes to the federal budget, leaving the regions rich in valuable resources (subjects of the Russian Federation) and, therefore, their population in a practically impoverished state.

The remaining resources are living resources: flora and fauna. In varying degrees, there are indeed laws regarding their protection, including the Forest Code, a whole section of environmental legislation, and hunting rules.

However, is this protection that effective?

China has severely restricted commercial logging in its natural forests for over 20 years. The government assessed the pollution of rivers and floods due to reservoirs clogged with floating timber and decided to correct the ecological situation urgently.

"The ban was introduced, but the demand remained. **China is the world market's largest exporter of plywood and wooden furniture** [highlighted by me - A.M.]. It had to look in the direction of its neighbors. Moreover, Russia began to sell logging tickets much cheaper than in other countries: the price in 2019 was about two dollars per hectare or 80 cents per acre per year, wrote The New York Times.

"In 2017 alone, China exported almost 200 million cubic meters of wood from Russia. Many believe that corruption, crime, and the lack of economic development in forest regions contributed to such predatory appetites of neighbors. After all, a considerable part of the country's natural wealth was cut down and smuggled out."

In quarries, a similar situation occurs with coal, mined by the so-called open-pit method. Such prey threatens not just animals but even people themselves. In particular, the indigenous peoples of Southern Siberia suffer from it: Khakasses, Shors, and Teleuts. (More details on the problem here).

Separately, there is a big problem with fires in Russia. From one million to three million (sic!) hectares of forests are burned annually.

At the same time, the authorities do not want to deal with them because: "according to these fires, there is no threat to settlements and economic facilities, and the projected costs of extinguishing them exceed the predicted harm they can cause."

The constant rupture of pipelines causes great harm to the environment. So, in 2021 alone, Greenpeace counted more than 10,000 (sic!) such breaks, most of which did not even become known to the mainstream media. Fines for environmental damage are so minimal that it is easier for companies to pay a fine than to upgrade equipment. In addition, as mentioned above, most oil and gas companies are owned by the state. And the state is engaged in control over its activities, which does not add efficiency: in the event of an accident, money is only transferred from one state pocket to another.

Also, one should remember the class nature of society. If these laws can work for the lower class, then the upper class calmly violates them (recall the case of officials hunting Red Book animals, which we talked about when analyzing the class nature of Russian society).

I think the above examples are enough to show that Article 9 of the Constitution also does not work as it was intended. Even if you do not take ownership of the subsoil, the state takes care of natural resources not as a prudent owner, but as a temporary worker, whose only goal is to get rich as quickly as possible by selling them, without regard of harm to the environment and even people.

ARTICLE 10 OF THE CONSTITUTION

"State power in the Russian Federation shall be exercised on the basis of its division into legislative, executive and judicial authority. Bodies of legislative, executive and judicial authority shall be independent."

Like the provision on the equality of everyone in the face of the law and the courts, the application of this article is the exact opposite of what it is.

The ideal system of separation of powers looks like this: the legislature makes laws and rules by which society lives. Since, ideally, the legislature is representative and (ideally) represents the interests of all groups in society, the law must be balanced and consider the interests of all members of the community. It is clear that this rarely happens, but the likelihood of adopting completely biased and odious laws is significantly reduced.

The executive branch implements these laws: it collects the budget, takes measures to enforce the rules, and controls their implementation. And that's all. The executive power should not do as it pleases and as it sees fit; in theory, it only executes the laws (hence the principle of 'the rule of law'—the subordination of power to the law).

The judiciary branch, on the other hand, monitors the legislative branch in terms of how laws are adopted, whether they comply with the Constitution and other adopted laws, and the executive branch, over how the laws are enforced and whether the implementation violates someone's interests outside the meaning of the adopted law.

In Russia, the executive branch has subjugated the legislative and judicial branches.

Earlier, I touched on the process itself and how exactly this happened. In a nutshell, the executive branch has financial leverage over the judiciary (thus, the Ministry of Justice, being the administrative body, provides for all judges in Russia) and control over elections in the case of the legislature. Like in the USSR. Where did such a strange title for the head of state come from— 'Secretary General'? A secretary is only someone who must fix the decisions made by some collective body and does not have additional powers. But at one time, Stalin, being the secretary of the Central Committee of the RCP (b) (communist party), and having all the flows of documents and decisions, slowly subjugated the entire government of the country and became its leader.

The situation with Putin is the same. It follows from the very essence of the Russian Constitution of 1993: its creators were very afraid of communist revenge and, in fact, wrote it for one person — Yeltsin — making it 'super-presidential.' As a result, there was a clear bias towards presidential powers (that is, the executive branch of power). And if Yeltsin, while still a man of liberal views, for the time being, did not usurp and subjugate power for himself, then Putin immediately took advantage of this opportunity.

All the threads of influence were in his hands: through the powers to form and finance election commissions, in conjunction with ever-increasing propaganda, he subjugated the entire legislative power. Since 2012, the parliament has become a 'mad printer,' quickly, without discussion and resistance, accepting all the laws the presidential administration passed. In the 1990s, many parliamentarians insisted on banning the state from owning television companies. Still, during the Yeltsin period, the proposal did not pass because "it is for the evil communists that the state media serve bad purposes, and for a liberal president they will serve good purposes." Again, although he did not like criticism, Yeltsin never interfered in the work of the media. Naturally, Putin, as soon as he came to power, immediately began to take control of them.

At the same time, Putin began to break the judicial system. He did not like that the court could cancel one or another of his decisions. The most striking decision was the Supreme Arbitration Court (SAC) liquidation, which I also spoke about earlier. The court dealt with disputes of legal entities, including with the state (in particular, with the tax authorities). Formally, the Supreme Arbitration Court could not give instructions to lower courts, but since it was the highest appellate body, naturally, its opinion was listened to. The SAC regularly held general meetings—plenums—and decisions were issued based on their results. Such resolutions of the plenums of the Supreme Arbitration Court had significantly streamlined the chaotic practice of applying laws (again, especially concerning taxes). The laws themselves, adopted by absolutely incompetent people who came to the Duma due to the most careful selection by the presidential administration, even then were monuments of legal illiteracy, inconsistency, and ambiguity. They hardly succumbed to legal analysis and almost did not succumb to logic. This situation was highly beneficial for the authorities; the more incomprehensible the law, the easier it is to collect a fine for its violation. The SAC has begun to significantly hinder Putin's vertical from getting rich. The logical fate of the court was its complete liquidation in 2010.

By appointing Zorkin (who had already been the chairman of the Constitutional Court, and it was he who refused to lustrate members of the CPSU) to head the Constitutional Court in 2003 instead of Tumanov, Putin turned the Constitutional Court into a servile body. Despite the increase in applications to the Constitutional Court with a request to check this or that law for compliance with the Constitution, practically very few laws has been repealed or changed. Among the most odious decisions of the Constitutional Court are the following:

- 2005 - The Constitutional Court confirmed the constitutionality of the law adopted at the initiative of the President of the Russian Federation on a new procedure for appointing senior officials of the constituent entities of the Russian Federation by legislative bodies at the proposal of the President of Russia (that is, on the actual abolition of the election of heads of subjects of the Federation we discussed earlier).

- 2014 - The Constitutional Court confirmed the legality of the procedure for the entry of Crimea and Sevastopol into the Russian Federation and the formation of two new subjects of the Federation, the Republic of Crimea and the Federal city of Sevastopol. This decision became the basis for the withdrawal of the Constitutional Court from the Conference of European Constitutional Courts (CECC).

- 2015 - The Constitutional Court established the procedure for implementing the legal positions expressed in the European Court of Human Rights (ECtHR) decisions into Russian national legislation. The procedure is as follows: after the decision of the ECtHR, in which it is established that a certain provision of the legislation of the Russian Federation, applied in the case, violates the rights of the applicant, the latter submits to the court of the first instance to review his case. The court of the first instance is obliged to suspend the proceedings and apply to the Constitutional Court with a request to check whether the disputed provision of Russian legislation complies with the Constitution of the Russian Federation. If the Constitutional Court of the Russian Federation recognizes that this interpretation of the ECtHR is contrary to the Constitution of the Russian Federation, then this decision is not subject to execution (which violated Article 15 of the Constitution).

- 2016 - The Constitutional Court allowed the courts to reduce compensation for violation of exclusive rights below the minimum legal limit of 10,000 rubles (in case of a breach of rights to several intellectual property objects by one action).

- 2017 - For the first time in the history of Europe, the Constitutional Court decided to prohibit the national government from paying compensation following the international court's decision in the Yukos case. Execution of the decision of the ECtHR on compensation to the former shareholders of Yukos of €1.8 billion was considered impossible by the Constitutional Court since such a payment would violate the constitutional principles of the "welfare state, equality and justice." In a dissenting opinion, Judge Vladimir Yaroslavtsev opposed the consideration of the case: the Ministry of Justice, which applied to the court, should have filed an appeal with international instances and not sought a "simplified" way out in a Russian court.

- 2018 - The Constitutional Court confirmed the constitutionality of the Agreement on establishing borders between the Republic of Ingushetia and the Chechen Republic, signed by the heads of these regions. The court concluded that the borders between the subjects of the Russian Federation could be established without holding a referendum and taking into account the opinion of the population of municipalities and recognized the Agreement and the Law of the Republic of Ingushetia on its approval as subject to application contrary to the earlier decision of the Constitutional Court of the Republic of Ingushetia.

- 2020 - Conclusion on compliance with chapters 1, 2, and 9 of the Constitution of the amendments introduced by the president.

- 2022 - the Constitutional Court recognized all four agreements on annexing the territories of Luhansk, Donetsk, Zaporizhia, and Kherson regions as per the Constitution of the Russian Federation.

At the grassroots level, the situation is the same. This is especially true for criminal prosecution. As we discussed earlier, only 1% of acquittals are in Russian courts. The courts do not work as they should, and there is no fair trial: it is easier for the courts to reprint the prosecutor's indictment, inserting it into the decision, than to try to make some other decision. It comes to the fact that in the court's decision, the same grammatical mistakes are present in the indictment. On this occasion, the lawyers applied to the Supreme Court, but it considered such a practice 'corresponding to the law.'

A similar system was formed in the legislature. None of the formal parties object to the bills being passed. Thus, in connection with the war in Ukraine and the planned mobilization, a package of amendments to the Criminal Code was submitted to the State Duma. There were 16 amendments in total (once again, 16 acts became criminal offenses or the punishment for them increased significantly), which were adopted in half an hour, that is, 2 minutes per amendment.

It should be noted that party dues from their members do not fund political parties as they should. They are financed from the federal budget (sic!) (Article 33 of Federal Law No. 95-FZ of July 11, 2001, "On Political Parties"). Is it necessary to say that the budget is managed by the Ministry of Finance, the executive branch?

Thus, the executive branch controls all stages of elections: financing of election commissions, propaganda, holding elections, changing the rules for which elections are held, counting votes, and funding parties in the future. In such a situation, adopting amendments to the law in 2 minutes already seems like a model of prudence and professionalism.

However, if you think there are some checks and balances within the executive branch, you are mistaken. The last official who said that Putin was wrong was Alexei Kudrin in 2010. After that, he ceased to be the Minister of Finance. No more officials wanted to say, 'Volodya, you are wrong.' At best, such a person would be fired. At worst, go to prison. Given that Putin is unusually stupid, the system has become a collection of even more ridiculous, dishonest, and unprofessional people, not limited to some control mechanisms in the form of separation of powers.

As a result, as in any feudal state, Russia does not have a separation of powers. All the fullness of power is concentrated in the hands of one person, not limited, at the moment, by absolutely nothing.

ARTICLE 12 OF THE CONSTITUTION

I skipped Article 11 of the Constitution. It simply indicates, separated by commas, the bodies through which state power is exercised. I quote the full text for verification:

"1. State power in the Russian Federation shall be exercised by the President of the Russian Federation, the Federal Assembly (the Council of Federation and the State Duma), the Government of the Russian Federation, and the courts of the Russian Federation.

2. State power in constituent entities of the Russian Federation shall be exercised by bodies of State government formed by those constituent entities.

3. The division of authorities and powers among State government bodies of the Russian Federation and State government bodies of constituent entities of the Russian Federation shall be established by this Constitution, the Federation Treaty and other treaties on the division of authorities and powers."

I don't have much of an objection. We can say that most authorities do not perform the functions they should theoretically perform (representations, discussions of laws, etc.), which we discussed when analyzing Article 10. However, formally, such bodies still exist for some reason.

Therefore, let us turn to the following article, Article 12 of the Constitution.

The full text goes like this:

"Local self-government shall be recognized and guaranteed in the Russian Federation. Local self-government shall be independent within the limits of its competence. Bodies of local self-government shall not form part of the system of State government bodies."

The idea is profound, indeed. Who, other than the local authorities, knows better whether it is worth repairing the bridge over the Stinky river or building a new building for the store?

However, Putin does not like and does not tolerate any independence and self-organization. He implicitly realizes that the effectiveness of almost any self-organizing structure will be many times higher than the effectiveness of the authorities created by him (or rather, destroyed by him), and therefore, at some point, there may be a replacement of functionality: effective organs will take over the functions of inefficient ones. We have already seen this in the case of the SAC, which has almost succeeded in streamlining the formulation and application of many laws.

The logical (for Putin) step was to gain control over local self-government.

As always, Putin's favorite lever is financial leverage. Local governments have only three taxes left (Article 15 of the Tax Code of the Russian Federation):

1) land tax;

2) tax on the property of individuals; and

3) trading fee.

Local authorities cannot change the rate or add any other sources. As a result, they have a catastrophic lack of money, and they are forced to ask for help from the authorities of the constituent entities of the Russian Federation or the central government. Accordingly, the regions are in significant decline. Take photos of any settlement (outside the district center), and you will see broken roads, rickety houses, broken power lines, and destroyed architectural monuments. Moreover, we can also talk about pretty large cities—Kostroma, Rostov the Great, Nizhny Novgorod, Makhachkala, Samara, etc. (you can see here: глубинка россии).

For further control (not only of local authorities but also of the heads of regions), Putin introduced the so-called 'municipal filter.' This filter allows him to select the necessary candidates for the election of heads of subjects. At the same time, it integrates municipal deputies into the system of state authorities. The most surprising thing is that this filter contradicts the commented article and is absent in federal law on electing the heads of the subjects. More details can be found here.

With Putin's amendments to the Constitution of 2020 (more on this in a separate chapter below), Part 3 of Article 132 was generally introduced, which contains a direct contradiction to the commented Article: "local governments and state authorities are part of a single system of public power and interact for the most effective solution of problems in the interests of the population living in the relevant territory"; and Part 1.1 of Article 131: "State authorities may participate in the formation of local government bodies, the appointment, and dismissal of local government officials in the manner and cases established by federal law."

In general, almost all the amendments of 2020 have turned the Constitution into a tangle of insoluble contradictions. Still, these two have a direct contradiction that makes the provisions of Article 12 inoperative; in which case, the authorities will always refer to these new provisions of Articles 131 and 132 of the Constitution (if it would care about at least the semblance of legitimacy).

ARTICLE 13 OF THE CONSTITUTION

The full text of the article reads as follows:

"1. Ideological diversity shall be recognized in the Russian Federation.

2. No ideology shall be proclaimed as State ideology or as obligatory.

3. Political diversity and the multi-party system shall be recognized in the Russian Federation.

4. Public associations shall be equal before the law.

5. The establishment and activities of public associations whose goals and activities are aimed at the forcible changing of the basis of the constitutional order and at violating the integrity of the Russian Federation, at undermining its security, at creating armed units, and at instigating social, racial, national and religious strife shall be prohibited."

This is a somewhat non-obvious article in terms of its violation (except for the last two paragraphs).

Formally, there is no state ideology in Russia. However, it cannot be said that Putin did not try to find at least some idea that would rally people around him. He, having no concept of morality or any principles in general, himself ranged from 'a real liberal' to "the fall of the Soviet Union - the main geopolitical catastrophe of the 20th century." At one time, he was very fond of demonstrating his piety while being divorced and having mistresses and illegitimate children and crossing himself in the wrong direction. That indicates the complete unusualness of the gesture (in Orthodox — the primary religious faith in Russia — crossing is made from right to left, while in Catholics is from left to right), which a true believer does several times a day. I suppose he would have dug up his mother and sold her corpse if it had done him any good.

In such a situation, no ideology could be used. It all came down to the fact that the main thing is what Putin wants. As the speaker of the lower house of parliament, the State Duma, Volodin put it: "There is Putin—there is Russia, there is no Putin—there is no Russia," almost repeating the Goebbels formula, "Ein Volk, Ein Reich, Ein Führer," "one people, one state, one leader."

Now, let's turn to the third point: "3. Political diversity and multi-party system are recognized in the Russian Federation."

We have already discussed how independent and representative the Russian parliament is. And although, formally, there are several political parties in it, in theory, having their programs and ideals, they are only a formal screen for the adoption of laws issued by the presidential administration. Any dissent is suppressed.

Thus, Deputy Rashkin criticized the "elections" of municipal districts in Moscow held in 2021 and, in particular, electronic voting. He was quickly removed from the State Duma. He was caught with a dead moose in his car trunk, and a criminal case was initiated against him under Part 1, Clause "a" of Art. 258 of the Criminal Code of the Russian Federation "Illegal hunting." The Prosecutor General's Office demanded to remove the parliamentary immunity, which was granted.

It is a somewhat murky story; how did the moose end up in Rashkin's car trunk? Did he break the rules of the hunt, indeed? However, the speed of the whole case is more reminiscent of a special operation, especially considering how other officials hunt endangered animal species with impunity (which we talked about earlier).

Here, you can also see how quickly disloyalty in the Putin system leads to overthrowing a person from one class to another.

 Any dissent in Russia at the time of writing this book is severely suppressed. Russia has more than 420 political prisoners, which is even more than during the Brezhnev's era.

At one time, when Russia was at least trying to seem like a state of law, Navalny and his team tried to register their political party, 'Russia of the Future' (at different times, it had different names). The Ministry of Justice refused to register them about 13 times under various pretexts. The funniest moment was when Alexei's associates got tired of unreasonable refusals. They copied the charter of the United Russia party (Putin's main party), changed all the names to new ones, and applied for registration again. However, the party was not registered under the pretext that the charter did not comply with the legislation of the Russian Federation. More details here.

Authoritarian regimes are characterized by the fact that they do not restrict or slightly restrict the fundamental rights of citizens but sharply suppress all attempts at political action. For a while, it was like that in Russia. However, Russia has ceased to be an authoritarian country; it has become a full-fledged dictatorship, where any disagreement is severely suppressed. We will talk about the right to rallies and peaceful marches later, but for now, I want to emphasize that the authorities are arresting even for pickets (which are formally allowed not only by the Constitution but also by law) and arresting for an expanded poster with abbreviations, 'asterisks' and even for blank sheet.

Accordingly, there is no political diversity in Russia, and even the slightest signs of disagreement are severely suppressed. There are no legal methods to influence the state's formation and adoption of decisions.

So, item 4, "Public associations are equal before the law."

Let us immediately define that 'public associations' are very diverse: from religious organizations to non-profit organizations and enterprises.

Again, we will talk separately about religious organizations regarding freedom of conscience. But even within this framework, there are already discrepancies: different religions are perceived by the state in different ways; from granting tax benefits to the Russian Orthodox Church (ROC) to a complete ban on the activities of Jehovah's Witnesses and Krishnaites.

We also touched on the topic of 'foreign agents.' In fact, any organization that dares to express thoughts or information that differs from the official one. I also remind you that if a person is recognized as a foreign person, he is obliged to create a legal entity so that it would be easier for the state to control and fine him. There is no need to say that foreign media has a completely different status than regular media, and even more so propaganda channels that receive huge funds from the federal budget (in particular, the Russian Today (RT) holding, which receives almost 20 billion (sic!) Rubles (approx. $350 mil) a year? At the same time, many media outlets were closed, which at least somehow tried to sit on two chairs: to comply with the numerous 'red lines' dictated by the state, and at the same time truthfully cover the course of the war unleashed by Putin. Thus, Novaya Gazeta (laureate of the Nobel Peace Prize in 2021), Memorial (laureate of the Nobel Peace Prize in 2021), and Echo Moskvy, one of the oldest radio stations existed since 1990.

The same situation occurs in business. It is one thing to be a state- owned enterprise and quite another to be an ordinary business. The whole army of officials is a feeding trough for a private business. Thus, the number of inspections by various state bodies depends on the enterprise's owner. You can find out about the scope of checks here. Under the condition of a non-working judicial system, this results in the fact that when an inspector comes to your enterprise, he can offer to indicate the violation yourself, for which he will take a fine or bribe, since 'there is no enterprise where there would be no violations of the law at all.' Technically, this phrase is accurate: so many restrictions are imposed on the business that it is physically impossible to fulfill all of them. Often, these restrictions can conflict, and the company has to choose which violation has the least significant impact on its activities or for which one it will have to pay less. This, of course, often leads to great tragedies. Businesses are forced to give bribes, and the inspector, receiving them, 'turns a blind eye even to significant violations.' Thus, as a result of a fire in the Zimnyaia Vishnia Shopping Center, 60 people died (including 41 children) or a fire in the Khromaya loshad club, where 151 people died.

In state-owned enterprises, the situation is diametrically opposite. The irony is that this leads to the same results: they are practically not checked by the regulatory authorities, which often leads to accidents. When analyzing Article 9 of the Constitution, I already cited that Greenpeace counted more than 10,000 pipeline ruptures in 2021 alone. In such a system, the fine does not matter—this is a transfer from one state pocket to another; under the same condition, the bribe also does not make sense: why give the fine if it turns out to be minimal?

A similar situation exists with non-profit associations. Thus, representatives of sexual minorities are generally denied their right to public associations.

The list can be continued for a long time. Still, they, like the images of Plato, reflect the class structure of Russian society: The upper class stands above the law and feeds at the expense of the lower classes, including their associations and organizations.

And then point "5. The establishment and activities of public associations whose goals and activities are aimed at the forcible changing of the basis of the constitutional order and at violating the integrity of the Russian Federation, at undermining its security, at creating armed units, and at instigating social, racial, national and religious strife shall be prohibited."

I have already mentioned the vast concept of 'extremist activity.' In fact, any disagreement and criticism of the Russian authorities is 'extremism.' Also, one should not forget that propagandists quite calmly incite discord on all the indicated grounds: social, racial, national, and religious, which we spoke about earlier, and which is, in principle, characteristic of fascist regimes.

Pay attention also to the ban on the creation of 'armed formations.' While we have already talked about the PMC "Wagner" - an armed group created by the former (well, to be honest, current) criminal, Prigozhin. These scumbags do all the dirtiest and most monstrous work in numerous conflicts led by Russia (more details here).

Thus, Article 13 also does not work for many reasons.

ARTICLE 14 OF THE CONSTITUTION

Its full text reads as follows:

"1. The Russian Federation shall be a secular state. No religion may be established as the State religion or as obligatory.

2. Religious associations shall be separate from the State and shall be equal before the law."

And again, we are faced with many problems.

To date, 803 religious organizations are officially registered in Russia. According to the meaning of the commented article, the state's attitude towards them should be the same: complete non-intervention and equal taxation.

However, we have already mentioned Putin's idea to use the ROC as the main idea to rally people around him. Naturally, such a desire inevitably leads to favoritism to the ROC.

Firstly, the state was directly engaged in planting and spreading Orthodoxy in 2011; a whole program was invented with the unofficial name of '200 churches,' the purpose of which was to "correct the plight of the lack of churches" in Moscow. Moreover, the Moscow government allocated super-expensive capital land for these new churches for free. Is it necessary to say that neither mosques nor synagogues were built in such a quantity, and even the land plots for them were never provided for them free of charge?

I want to note that Orthodoxy (before the revolution of 1918) was the dominant religion in the Russian Empire. And there are unusually many churches in Russia, especially in Russian cities. There is absolutely no shortage of them. According to the Russian Orthodox Church's official data, there are 1218 churches and chapels in Moscow. Therefore, the decision to build these "200 temples" is controversial for many reasons. Note that Buddhists have only one temple in Moscow, built in 2015. Before that, they were simply denied opening it.

In addition, the state directly allocates huge funds (about 1 billion rubles ($16 mil)) to the ROC allegedly for the restoration of historic churches and monasteries.

In general, more details about the income of the ROC can be found here. There are also special 'military priests' who receive a salary from the budget of the Ministry of Defense.

It all comes down to rather curious cases when priests consecrate space and even nuclear rockets (the funniest case was with the sanctifing of the nuclear rocket 'Satan') (for more information about the coverage of nuclear weapons, see Dmitry Adamsky's book *"Russian Nuclear Orthodoxy"* (Dmitry Adamsky. Russian). Nuclear Orthodoxy: Religion, Politics, and Strategy Stanford, CA: Stanford University Press, 2019).

The Ministry of Defense, on the other hand, built a monstrous temple, popularly nicknamed the "temple of war" with steps made of melted weapons, frescoes depicting Putin and Shoigu (Minister of Defense) and even Hitler's cap (sic!) as a shrine.

In addition to use, there are also minor but status-indicative signs. In particular, the government provided Patriarch, a 'flashing light' car as for any high official (see commentary on Article 6 of the Constitution).

The ROC, accordingly, is doing everything possible to agitate for power. Among other things, he welcomed Putin's victory in the "elections," and called for voting for 'amendments to the Constitution' (read its abolition), openly spoke out for the war with Ukraine, and supported Putin.

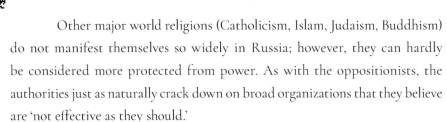

Other major world religions (Catholicism, Islam, Judaism, Buddhism) do not manifest themselves so widely in Russia; however, they can hardly be considered more protected from power. As with the oppositionists, the authorities just as naturally crack down on broad organizations that they believe are 'not effective as they should.'

In particular, in Russia, the activities of the churches of Jehovah's Witnesses were prosecuted and banned. The Church was recognized as extremist and liquidated by formally recognizing inconsistency with its charter (sic!).

As a result, any religious activities of its members (including reading the Bible to a group of parishioners in their apartment) were severely suppressed. Thus, as of June 9, 2020, the list of 'prisoners of conscience' on the website of the Russian Jehovah's Witnesses lists 327 people who are being persecuted in Russia.

During 2019-2020, Russian courts passed judgments on Jehovah's Witnesses:

- April 2020, Yakutia: Igor Ivashin to six years of probation;

- January 2020, Primorsky Krai: Grigory Bubnov to five years of probation;

- December 2019, Penza: Vladimir Alushkin to six years in prison, five more received suspended sentences;

- November 2019, Tomsk: Sergey Klimov to six years in prison;

- September 2019, Saratov: six Jehovah's Witnesses sentenced to terms ranging from two to three and a half years in prison;

- September 2019, Khabarovsk: Valery Moskalenko to two years and two months of forced labor and six months of restriction of liberty; and

- July 2019, Perm: Alexander Solovyov fined 300 thousand rubles.

On June 9, 2020, the Pskov City Court sentenced 61-year-old Gennady Shpakovsky to six and a half years in a penal colony. This is the longest known sentence of all Jehovah's Witnesses convicted in Russia (part 1 of article 282.2 of the Criminal Code of the Russian Federation and part 1 of article 282.3 of the Criminal Code of the Russian Federation, organizing and financing an extremist organization). On August 3, 2020, the sentence was changed to a suspended sentence (with a two-year probationary period).

I note that Jehovah's Witnesses have never posed a particular threat. Yes, among the banned religious organizations, there are indeed those who fully deserve it (like Al-Qaeda), but even here, the Russian authorities are showing a fair amount of flexibility.

In particular, this applies to the Taliban movement. Although it is recognized as a terrorist movement by the UN and even by Russia itself, this does not prevent them from officially dealing with them and even inviting them to an economic (sic!) forum in Russia. It is hilarious to observe how the official Russian media, under the law, put after each mention of the word 'Taliban' that its activities are prohibited in Russia in the articles about their visits to Moscow and Kazan, as well as their meetings with Lavrov.

I hope the reader understands that religious organizations have no equality, both between permitted and forbidden ones.

You can read more about the problem of religion in Russia here.

ARTICLE 15 OF THE CONSTITUTION

The full text of the article reads as follows:

"1. The Constitution of the Russian Federation shall have supreme legal force, direct effect and shall be applicable on the entire territory of the Russian Federation. Laws and other legal acts, which are adopted in the Russian Federation, must not contradict the Constitution of the Russian Federation.

2. State government bodies, local self-government bodies, officials, citizens and their associations shall be obliged to observe the Constitution of the Russian Federation and laws.

3. Laws must be officially published. Unpublished laws shall not have force. Any normative legal acts concerning human and civil rights, freedoms and obligations shall not have force unless they have been officially published for the information of the general public.

4. Universally recognized principles and norms of international law as well as international agreements of the Russian Federation should be an integral

part of its legal system. If an international agreement of the Russian Federation establishes rules, which differ from those stipulated by law, then the rules of the international agreement shall be applied."

This article was critical. It describes the very pyramid of legal norms, frameworks, and restrictions for the rules in force in Russia. The entire book is an analysis of this particular article. Its last point is significant for us. But let's start from the beginning.

The first point says that the Constitution is the very foundation of the legal system, and nothing in the state can contradict its provisions. This is what I am trying to demonstrate in this book: Russia has a dead Constitution and a lot of laws and legal acts that directly contradict it. That makes it a zombie country, an openly fascist state, and a dictatorship.

As we said earlier, in theory, any law, if it was found to conflict with the Constitution, could not be applied: it would be possible to declare a contradiction in court, which would be enough. The practice has shown that, for a start, if such a contradiction was discovered, the issue was sent to the Constitutional Court for consideration. Then the courts simply forgot about the Constitution and its provisions, applying any law or legal act as they are. In principle, given the pro-government position of the Constitutional Court (which we spoke about earlier when analyzing Article 10 of the Constitution), such a position of the courts logically makes sense: the Constitutional Court would still leave such a law in force.

The same applies to paragraph two of the commented article—only if the first paragraph refers to the formal side of the issue: laws and legal acts, then the second paragraph concerns the direct actions of all persons and organizations on the territory of Russia. Again, I think there is no need for me to dwell on this point in more detail, since almost all of this work is devoted to analyzing how much the government, in principle, respects the Constitution.

The third point is somewhat trickier. It should be noted that it is unusually ancient and originates in Roman law, where sometimes laws passed by the senate were hung so high that it was impossible to read them and therefore avoid their violation. Thus, in the modern world, all laws and legal acts are subject to official publication. In the US, you can even view the discussions of a particular law in Parliament to help determine the exact meaning of the adopted bill and present this discussion to the court in case of discrepancies. However, in Russia, there are many secret regulations. Of course, in any country, there is information that constitutes a state secret. But this does not apply to rules but secret and vital state information. And the difference here is significant.

Often, in Russia, they cover up specific unconstitutional rules, attributing them to 'secret acts.' So, we have already mentioned the order of the Ministry of Internal Affairs of September 12, 2013 No. 705-dsp "On certain issues of departures of police officers, federal state civil servants and employees of the Russian Ministry of Internal Affairs system on private matters outside the territory of the Russian Federation," which prohibits ordinary police officers from leaving Russia. Why care about the order's constitutionality if you can classify its text?

From the recent one, we can cite the Decree of the President of the Russian Federation of September 21, 2022, No. 647 "On the announcement of partial mobilization in the Russian Federation." If you study the document's text, you will find that paragraph 7 is 'for inner use.' Such a mark means that although the document may not be formally secret, it may be closed from public viewing. Which directly contradicts the commented article 15.

You can read more about the problem here and here.

Thus, paragraph 3 of Article 15 does not apply either.

Let's move on to the next point, 4. It was one of the most important up to a certain point (or rather, until Putin's "amendments to the Constitution" of 2020). And it was a bone in the throat of the Russian authorities, which, on the one hand, wanted arbitrariness and impunity, and on the other, to be part of the Western community, where its representatives could receive guarantees for their stolen money and get a 'reserve airfield' and a cloudless future for their children, wives and mistresses.

I'll quote the paragraph in full:

"Universally recognized principles and norms of international law as well as international agreements of the Russian Federation should be an integral part of its legal system. If an international agreement of the Russian Federation establishes rules, which differ from those stipulated by law, then the rules of the international agreement shall be applied."

In theory, by analogy with the fact that nothing in the law of Russia and the actions of its authorities can contradict the Constitution, precisely the same provision exists for international treaties Russia has signed and accepted. This is logical because, otherwise, the point of forming the only source of international law — an international treaty — is lost, which would take Russia out of the international legal field altogether.

In fact, this is exactly what has happened.

Russia is formally not only a member of the UN but even, for some reason, a member of its Security Council (I will explain why this is wrong later after analyzing the articles). Accordingly, it must abide by the UN Charter and the Universal Declaration of Human Rights in 1948. Being invited to the Council of Europe, Russia signed the Convention for the Protection of Human Rights and Fundamental Freedoms at one time.

However, like its Constitution, these documents have been violated by Russia and are constantly broken now. The body that monitored the implementation of the Convention for the Protection of Human Rights and Fundamental Freedoms until the shameful expulsion of Russia from PACE was the European Court of Human Rights (ECtHR or ECHR). Russian lawyers joked sadly: "What is the best Russian court? ECtHR!" It was exactly like that. Only through the ECtHR could an ordinary Russian get at least some justice in the absence of Russian courts. In 2021 alone, the ECtHR had 9,432 cases from Russia pending, slightly behind Turkey with its 9,548 cases and well ahead of Ukraine, which had 3,721 cases.

Moreover, Russia was the primary violator of the Convention. In the vast majority of court rulings in 2021, 986 out of 1105, the ECtHR found at least one violation of the Convention. The Strasbourg Court issued most of its rulings concerning Russia; 219. For example, in regards to Turkey, only 78.

Moreover, if initially, Russia tried to take measures to correct the situation with violations of the Convention, then it limited itself to simply paying compensation to the victims according to the decisions of the ECtHR. Then the State Duma adopted a law to which it could not pay these compensations. In 2022, Russia, due to gross violations of international law, was expelled from PACE, and its citizens were deprived of the opportunity to apply to the 'only fair Russian court.'

You can read more about cases before the ECtHR here.

However, Russia is a violator of international law not only in terms of these conventions.

In general, whether due to a significant lack of intelligence or poor education, Putin has always perceived international law as a 'limitation of Russia's sovereignty.' In his understanding, he can do whatever he wants, and any indication of inadmissibility is a restriction of sovereignty and 'interference in internal affairs.' It is not surprising that with such an approach, it turns out that the violation of international rules is a 'strengthening of sovereignty,' and

following them is its 'weakening.'

Accordingly, the violation of international treaties has become the norm for Putin, and even, it turns out to a kind of goal.

Since 2014, he has violated 80 of 482 bilateral international treaties. Their spectrum is the most diverse, from the UN Charter to the Treaty on the Non-Proliferation of Intermediate-Range Missiles, which Putin violated by developing the Iskander-K missiles.

You can find more information about this here.

Naturally, paragraph 4 was very disturbing to Putin. He did not come up with anything better than to introduce, among the "amendments" to the Constitution of 2020, an "amendment" to Article 79, which stated that "decisions of international bodies adopted based on the provisions of international treaties of the Russian Federation in their interpretation, contrary to the Constitution of the Russian Federation, are not enforceable in the Russian Federation." Which, of course, made a literal, logical contradiction between paragraph 4 of Article 15 and Article 79 of the Constitution. Under these conditions, even formally, paragraph 4 ceased to operate.

So, Article 15, despite its importance for the legal field of Russia, is also wholly inoperative. And we come to the last article of the first chapter of the Constitution.

ARTICLE 16 OF THE CONSTITUTION

The full text reads as follows:

"1. The provisions of this Chapter of the Constitution shall constitute the fundamental principles of the constitutional order of the Russian Federation and may not be changed except in accordance with the procedure established by this Constitution.

2. No other provisions of this Constitution may conflict with the fundamental principles of the constitutional order of the Russian Federation."

We'll talk about changing the Constitution, particularly about Putin's "amendments" to it. Including the order of adoption and the contradictions between themselves and chapters 1 and 2 of the Constitution. I will note in advance that the order was violated, and as a result, the Constitution turned, at best, into a lump of total contradictions. Moreover, there were so many of them that the Constitution ceased to be a working document, even if someone would try to apply it.

It is due to the fact that the law must be logically consistent. This allows one to build a system of acts based on this logic and some general law principles. If one article in the law contradicts another, then the authorities, depending on the specific situation and their wishes, can apply either article and, when it is beneficial for them, another. This contradiction of rules gives rise to legal chaos - when it is not known how the legislation should be applied, or to the contrary — it is known — because it is beneficial to Putin.

The Constitutional Court could not remove such a contradiction (even if it wanted to): formally, both such contradictory articles are included in the Constitution. Therefore, none of them contradicts the Constitution itself.

That is why paragraph 2 was introduced into the Constitution, prohibiting the adoption of such laws and amendments in general; they kill the whole meaning of the Constitution. What, however, Putin needed.

So this article doesn't work either.

ARTICLE 17 OF THE CONSTITUTION

And we are moving on to the most important (in the past) chapter of the Constitution, Chapter 2, dedicated to the rights and freedoms of man and citizen. Such a clarification (of a person and a citizen) indicates that many of its provisions apply to Russian citizens and to any person in principle. Remember we talked about the theory of natural rights? That human rights belong to him from birth and arise simply by the fact of birth and are not bestowed by the state? Here is the same thought: the chapter is not aimed at regulating human rights but at restricting the state and its obligations concerning these rights. These are the state's restrictions, and, in theory, it can neither get rid of them nor deprive someone of these rights.

So, the full text of Article 17 reads as follows:

"1. In the Russian Federation human and civil rights and freedoms shall be recognized and guaranteed according to the universally recognized principles and norms of international law and this Constitution.

2. Basic human rights and freedoms shall be inalienable and shall be enjoyed by everyone from birth.

3. The exercise of human and civil rights and freedoms must not violate the rights and freedoms of other people."

As in the analysis of article 15, the provisions of paragraph 1 of article 17 once again emphasize the importance of human rights and freedoms and that nothing can violate them. Moreover, these rights are guaranteed by the Constitution and international treaties (in particular, the Universal Declaration of Human Rights and the Convention for the Protection of Human Rights and Fundamental Freedoms).

And just as when commenting on paragraphs 1 and 2 of Article 15, I have to say that the whole essence of this book is how the provisions of paragraph 1 of Article 17 of the Constitution correspond to reality. Unfortunately, I think you have already understood that this rule does not work. There is nothing more secondary for Putin than human rights and freedoms.

At the same time, it is difficult to disagree with the second paragraph of the commented article. It quotes verbatim the theory of natural rights, which we discussed earlier. However, the problem is that the Russian authorities do not believe in this. The most crucial evidence of this is the class structure of Russian society. And if, in theory, all people, being born, receive the same rights, then in Russian reality, their rights are different and can vary depending on the class, obedience, and appetites of those who are higher on the social ladder.

And if concerning Putin's fellow officials, or let's take it from the other end, oppositionists, one can assume some equality at the initial stage and further stratification later, then this paragraph does not work in principle concerning gays and lesbians. They initially do not have the same rights as heterosexuals (more on the situation can be found here).

I will discuss this in detail when analyzing Article 19 of the Constitution.

145

Naturally, this issue is closely intertwined with the issue of equality of all before the law and the courts (a topic repeatedly raised in the Constitution). Still, from the point of view of the existence of rights and their protection, this paragraph should also provide them.

Therefore, we have to conclude again that the article does not work.

Point 3 of the commented article is somewhat counterintuitive. It suggests that the solution to acute issues should be made on the basis of compromise, discussion, and agreement. However, given that state bodies do not work in Russia, the parliament does not discuss the laws passed down to it from the presidential administration, and the president does not care about the opinion of absolutely any person except himself, of course, not a single issue is resolved through negotiations, search compromise and discussion. All this was replaced by a class system (which we discussed above) and propaganda, imposing the authorities' point of view through direct deception and falsification of information through the state media.

Without at least some representatives who would defend the interests of society before the authorities, citizens naturally resort to protests, which, in turn, are trying to disperse the same government as much as possible. Therefore, among the demands put forward at the demonstrations, many very broad questions exist.

From political (the protests we have already mentioned on Bolotnaya Square and Sakharov Avenue in Moscow against the falsification of presidential elections); environmental (for example, against the cutting down of the Khimki forest by the authorities for the construction of a highway, or at the Shies station against the opening of a landfill); to rallies against arbitrariness of police (March against kidnappings and arbitrariness of people in Makhachkala (2011) or the case of Ivan Golunov); rallies against the construction of another temple of the Russian Orthodox Church (protest in the square of Yekaterinburg (2019)) or a truckers' strike (in connection with the establishment of the 'Platon' system—further on, we will talk about this when analyzing Article 57 of the Constitution).

The variety of issues on which protests arise indicates an extensive range of authorities that, solving specific problems raised from above, begin to implement them without even bothering to ask the opinion of citizens, which is a sign of the total degradation of the political system in Russia, and of course, a direct violation of the commented paragraph.

This is exacerbated by the fact that Putin does not like to act under pressure. He does not dismiss officials for whom massive violations of corrupt legislation have been revealed; he does not cancel unconstitutional laws signed by him, etc. For some reason, it seems to him that he does not look like a fool trying to break through the wall with his forehead, but like a cool macho who never makes a mistake—this inability to see and admit mistakes results in their number increasing to a large extent. Ironically, if Putin had turned his attention to the total theft in almost all spheres of power, revealed by the Navalny team, then his army would not have turned out to be a gang of hungry and demotivated hicks in the war with Ukraine but at least more combat-ready. True, though, in the event of a decrease in corruption, there would be no war at all. In addition, when the rallies are dispersed, the number of dissatisfied people is not decreased—on the contrary, there are more of them—but the discontent changes from open to hidden. Sooner or later, such discontent ends in a social explosion, which we have seen more than once in world history and even in Russia itself.

Separately, we will discuss rallies in more detail when analyzing Article 31 of the Constitution.

In any case, the class system of Russian society created by Putin is literally designed to ensure that the upper classes satisfy their interests at the expense of the lower classes. This applies from stealing from the budget to pumping out resources and polluting the environment, transferring shares in state-owned enterprises 'for feeding' to friends, relatives, and mistresses, hunting on Red Book animals until fines are imposed to replenish the very budget, which officials ruin.

One of the clearest examples of solving problems at the expense of a particular group of people is the 'Platon system.' This system charges trucker money for road repairs (in addition to the two taxes that all car owners pay: transport tax and excise tax on fuel). In Russia, there has always been a big problem with the quality of roads precisely because of total corruption: officials steal a lot of money to repair poorly built roads. The state decided: why fight systemic corruption when you can take money for repairs from citizens? In a nutshell, in 2017, the government introduced a system that tracks the movement of oversized vehicles and collects a fee for every kilometer of roads traveled. At the same time, Putin helped his friend, Arkady Rotenberg, who became the manager of this system. For this hard work, Arkady is annually allocated 10 billion (sic!) Rubles (about $165 mil), regardless of fees collected by the system. Isn't it great?

More about the problem here. As a result, we again have to state that this article of the Constitution also does not work completely.

ARTICLE 18 OF THE CONSTITUTION

The full text of the article reads as follows:

"Human and civil rights and freedoms shall have direct force. They shall determine the meaning, content and implementation of laws, the functioning of legislative and executive authority and of local self-government, and shall be guaranteed by law."

It is sad to say, but there is nothing further than this in Russia. Another legal joke says, "The rights and freedoms of a person and a citizen are directly applicable, and we all know who this person is."

But as I said when analyzing Article 15 of the Constitution, I cannot study this article and prove that this is not true. Its failure will be visible after all of my work is completed. At the current stage, I am only forced to leave a big spoiler; the article does not comply with the current Russian legislation or the authorities' actions. Instead, on the contrary, for Putin, there is nothing more insignificant than the rights and freedoms of his citizens. He refuses to admit they have rights and negates their subjectivity and free will!

So let's move on to the next article.

ARTICLE 19 OF THE CONSTITUTION

"1. All persons shall be equal before the law and the court.

2. The State guarantees the equality of human and civil rights and freedoms regardless of sex, race, nationality, language, origin, material and official status, place of residence, attitude to religion, convictions, membership of public associations, or of other circumstances. All forms of limitations of human rights on social, racial, national, language or religious grounds shall be prohibited.

3. Men and women shall enjoy equal rights and freedoms and equal opportunities to exercise them."

This article echoes Article 6 of the Constitution, where I showed that, in fact, society in Russia is a class society with a completely different set of rights and obligations. However, I have already promised twice to analyze the legal status of gays and lesbians in Russia, which I will now do. Formally, even the presence of one group of persons with discriminated rights already confirms the inconsistency of this article. Still, as we determined in the analysis of Article 6 of the Constitution, there are much more such groups. Here, I will add to what was said earlier, the report of the Moscow Helsinki Group on the situation of gays and lesbians for 2021 (full text can be found here):

"It cannot be said that LGBTQ+ people [an association of gays, lesbians, transgender people, etc. - A.M.] can feel safe anywhere in Russia. We can say that in the centers of large cities, the level of security is higher than in residential areas. At the same time, as research shows, LGBTQ+ people may be attacked in the center of Moscow, but they may not be touched in a village in the Sverdlovsk region. Those most at risk of violence or any other manifestation of xenophobia are those whose visual representation ("gender display") either does not unequivocally read as feminine or masculine or does not correspond to traditional ideas about the standards of masculinity and femininity.

"Assessing the situation of LGBTQ+ people in Russia as a whole and in certain regions, the experts we interviewed, as well as research and monitoring materials, speak of duality, being at the intersection of multidirectional trends. On the one hand, many note the growth of tolerance in society, especially among young people, confirmed by public opinion polls and expert observations. On the other hand, in 2020, an increase in violence was recorded at the national level (according to online survey data, 78.4% of respondents experienced violence and/or discrimination in 2020 and 64.4% in 2021) and in individual regions.

"At the same time, when faced with violence and discrimination, LGBTQ+ people cannot always count on help from law enforcement agencies. Moreover, the appeal to the police is often not only presented but also turns out to be almost more dangerous than the experienced offense itself. Police officers may begin to insult using homophobic or transphobic language, blame the victim, refuse to accept a statement, or not respond to a received report [this is a violation of Articles 20, 22 of the Constitution - A.M.]. Cases of discrimination, blackmail, and police violence against LGBTQ+ people have been recorded in all federal districts. Also, almost everywhere, law enforcement officers put pressure on LGBTQ+ activists, disrupting events, detaining, and starting criminal and administrative cases [violation of Article 31 of the Constitution - A.M.]. Experts call the actions of police officers one of the main factors that negatively affect the situation of LGBTQ+ people.

"In almost all districts, experts noted an increase in the activity of ultra-conservative, homophobic, and transphobic organizations. Followers of ultra-conservative movements staged harassment on social networks, published personal data of activists, called for violence and reprisals, and directly participated in attacks on LGBTQ+ people [violation of Articles 22 and 23 - A.M.]. In most cases, when the victims are contacted, the police do not take any action to find and punish the perpetrators. Some traditionalist associations are not only not persecuted by the state but are also endowed with official status and powers, such as the Cossacks. Both ultra-conservatives and other perpetrators know that most LGBTQ+ people, when faced with an offense, will not go to the police, fearing that they will face additional violence and discrimination there, and if they do, they are unlikely to receive appropriate assistance; therefore, they feel with impunity.

"The COVID-19 pandemic has affected the relationship between different forms and types of discrimination and violence. Due to overcrowded hospitals, many trans people have additional challenges in obtaining clearances and services related to the transition. Problems arose among LGBTQ+ people who needed psychotherapy (prescribing drugs). Many have lost their jobs, and sources of livelihood, and had to give up renting separate housing and move into housing with other tenants or start living with their relatives. Thus, this group found itself more vulnerable and often dependent on others (for example, relatives). This has led, as noted in several regional LGBTQ+ monitoring reports, to violence becoming more intimate and domestic and less public."

Accordingly, since the first paragraph of the commented article does not work, paragraph 2, which is designed to guarantee the equality of people regardless of gender, race, and other qualities, does not work either.

153

Paragraph 3 of the article specifically refers to the equality of men and women, duplicating the first two paragraphs. Well, let's also analyze the situation in modern Russia on this point.

The big problem of the oppression of women is the theme of their oppression in traditional communities. In particular, in Chechnya and Dagestan.

So, in Dagestan, in some settlements, female circumcision is still practiced, as in African countries! The practice continues to this day. So, in the fall of 2022, four girls had to flee Russia for fear of this circumcision or death. Moreover, the border guards tried in every possible way to detain them instead of assisting. You can read more about female circumcision here. In addition to equal rights for women, such a procedure violates women's constitutional rights to health, security, and personal integrity. The problem is widespread in the Caucasus; it is especially "acute in Dagestan, where about 1240 girls are subjected to this mutilation yearly. In Ingushetia, this is practiced by members of the brotherhood of Batalkhadzhins; in Chechnya, circumcised can be found among older women," says the material of the publication "This is the Caucasus."

You can read more about female circumcision in Ingushetia, here. I want to separately note that in this case, the circumcision procedure was carried out in an official clinic (sic!) and surfaced almost by accident, becoming the reason for a journalistic investigation.

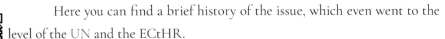
Here you can find a brief history of the issue, which even went to the level of the UN and the ECtHR.

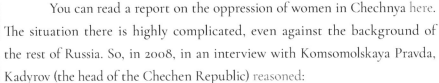

You can read a report on the oppression of women in Chechnya here. The situation there is highly complicated, even against the background of the rest of Russia. So, in 2008, in an interview with Komsomolskaya Pravda, Kadyrov (the head of the Chechen Republic) reasoned:

"I have the right to criticize my wife. The wife does not. Our wife is a housewife. A woman should know her place. A woman should give love to us. A woman should be the property. And the man is the owner. With us, if a woman walks naked if she behaves incorrectly, the husband, father, and brother are responsible. According to our custom, if she walks, her relatives kill her … It happens: a brother killed his sister, and a husband killed his wife … As a president, I cannot allow them to kill. So don't let them wear shorts."

So you understand the logic? Kadyrov cannot "allow the killing" of women, so it is women who should behave accordingly, not men. Such a wild Middle Ages calmly exists in Russia.

It cannot be said that the situation with the equality of men and women is also that badly neglected in other parts of Russia. However, they cannot be called entirely equal either. According to the World Bank report Women, Business and the Law 2019, Russia ranks slightly lower than the global average of 73.13 points out of 100 possible, with an average score of 74.71.

Among others, there is a list of professions issued by the Ministry of Labor, which expressly prohibits female labor in specific jobs (the official text is here).

The list was created in 1974 to preserve women's reproductive health. It allowed many types of hard labor but prohibited the professions of the boatswain, electric train driver, and bus driver on intercity and international routes was repeatedly recognized by the UN as infringing on the rights of women and became a vivid example of the so-called "glass ceiling."

According to even Rosstat data, women, on average, receive 30% fewer wages than men (More details here and here).

Women have similar problems in the political sphere. On the issue, you can read the report of Transparency International, which indicates that "in the ranking of gender equality in the political sphere, Russia ranks 122 out of 152 and is between Sierra Leone and Morocco."

The reproductive rights of women in Russia are similarly infringed. I admit that it is somewhat strange to talk about the inequality of men and women in this particular issue. Still, you can consider this an additional topic on which the Russian authorities do not want people to express their opinions. Let me elaborate for the foreign reader. There are two simultaneous tendencies of power that are perplexing: to take away the rights and ruin their citizens and to strive to ensure that there are as many citizens as possible. A sort of desire of the farmer to quickly cut the herd into meat and skins and breed it. This explains the state's eternal concern about the birth of children (including the promotion of "traditional values" and anti-abortion propaganda) and complete passivity during the recent COVID epidemic (when about one million (sic!) People died in Russia (the excess of births over deaths compared to the past year)) and the conduct of the war, during which tens of thousands of citizens have already died, hundreds of thousands were injured and about a million left the territory of Russia.

Be that as it may, one of the topics that irritate the Russian authorities is the topic of abortion and the "childfree" culture — the conscious abandonment of children.

This is what gender equality is in Russia.

I think the above is enough to firmly state that Article 19 of the Constitution also does not work entirely.

HOW RUSSIA BECAME A ZOMBIE STATE

ARTICLE 20 OF THE CONSTITUTION

The full text of Article 20:

"1. Everyone shall have the right to life.

2. Capital punishment until its complete abolition may be established by federal law as an exclusive form of punishment for particularly grave crimes against life, and the accused shall be granted the right to have his case examined by a court with the participation of a jury."

Violations under this article are the most significant crime of Putin and his gang.

I want to make a few comments right away.

Firstly, the right to life does not simply mean the obligation of the state not to kill anyone; it is entirely natural. In any law in any country in the world, murder is a criminal offense. The meaning of the article was supposed to be much broader. The state must investigate crimes, punish those responsible for their commission, and take all measures so that such cases do not occur ever again.

I mentioned some things before, but here I will supplement them, and I will try to set out those mentioned earlier in as much detail as the format of the book I have chosen allows. However, having said this, we will see that Putin not only failed to ensure citizens' right to life, but he also put the killing of citizens (and not only) on stream! This is not just an "uh-huh killer" but a real serial maniac.

So let's get down to the bottom.

In Chapter 3 of this book, I briefly explained that Yeltsin appointed Putin as his 'successor.' After the default of Russia announced in 1998, the old, alcohol-abusing Yeltsin was practically abandoned by all his former associates. He was terrified of prosecution for corruption of his family (in particular, his daughter, Dyachenko, at that time (her last name is now Yumasheva)). Only Putin remained next to him, who also helped Yeltsin to get the Prosecutor General of that time, Yuri Skuratov, out of the way by arranging a sex scandal for him (more about the scandal here). Under such conditions, Putin's choice seemed not a bad option to Yeltsin. Besides, he guaranteed immunity to Yeltsin and his family (we already discussed this earlier. Remember? Where Putin canceled the Criminal Code by presidential decree, namely the law).

Putin's rating was weak; a former KGB officer without much charisma aroused little sympathy among the population. And suddenly, quite by accident, in the fall of 1999, several residential buildings were blown up in Moscow, Buynaksk, and Volgodonsk, as a result of which 307 people died, and 1,700 were injured. Against this background, Putin, who promised during his election campaign to "drown terrorists in the toilet," and besides a former security official, significantly improved his rating; he sternly pledged to deal with the terrorists, and the people fell for this bait.

Roman Badanin (a well-known Russian journalist and editor-in-chief of the Proekt and Agency publications), in the light of recent "discoveries" on murders organized by the FSB, promised to raise the issue and re-conduct a full investigation into this case. Currently, the work is not finished yet, but I'm talking about it here so that you can find the materials when they come out. As we mentioned, there are still many blind spots in this whole story.

The strangest was the story of the so-called "Ryazan sugar." Against the background of those explosions of houses, the population mobilized throughout Russia. Citizens independently organized patrols and checks of all the basements of their residential buildings. And on September 22, 1999, residents found bags with a mixture in one of the houses in Ryazan, the primary express analysis of which showed the presence of an explosive, hexogen. The police (then still, the police) opened a criminal case under Art. 205 part 1 of the Criminal Code of the Russian Federation (attempted terrorism). All the explosives were, of course, seized and handed over to the FSB laboratory.

The FSB maintained deathly silence for three days. After which, the then director of the FSB, Patrushev, declared that the bags contained not RDX but sugar, and exercises were allegedly held in Ryazan.

This story smelt too bad. Many suspected that the FSB was behind all these explosions. The lieutenant colonel of the Soviet and Russian state security in 1988-1999—an employee of the KGB—FSB, where he specialized in the fight against terrorism and organized crime, Alexander Litvinenko spoke about this in detail. Notice this name; we'll talk more about it a little later. For now, I'll go in chronological order.

As a result, Putin starts the second Chechen war, his rating soars from 30% to 80%, and he wins the elections (more on this issue here and here).

At that time, no one could have imagined that senior officials, in principle, were capable of organizing the terror of their population (namely, terror, by definition, the use of violence to achieve political goals). Now, after the poisonings of Litvinenko, the murder of Nemtsov, the attempted assassination of Skripal, and the Bellingcat investigation into the poisoning of Navalny, everything that happened in September 1999 sparkled with entirely different colors. So, let's continue.

On August 12, 2000, one of the most significant disasters in the history of the Russian submarine fleet occurred; the nuclear submarine K-141 Kursk sank in the Barents Sea. According to the main version, a torpedo exploded on the sub, immediately flooding the control room. The submarine sank, and it was impossible to blow through the tanks to make the ascent. However, there were surviving sailors. They locked themselves in the ninth compartment and waited for help.

All nearby ships, including foreign ones, responded to the SOS signal. However, Putin rejected any help. He considered that he would rather risk the lives of the sailors than allow foreigners to visit the submarine. As a result, no assistance was provided, and the sailors remained forever in the ninth compartment of the flooded submarine.

Subsequently, to the question of a CNN journalist asked, "What happened to the Kursk submarine?" With a vile grin, Putin will answer about the death of 118 people: "It drowned." Putin has shown a complete lack of empathy or even understanding of the value of human life.

After Putin met with the sailors' widows, he simply called them "ten-dollar whores."

You can read more about the sinking of the Kursk submarine here.

Putin showed the same complete indifference to the lives of ordinary people in all its glory during the hostage-taking by terrorists in the theater in Dubrovka. The theater, together with the audience and the actors of the play "Nord-Ost," was seized by Chechen fighters led by Movsar Barayev. They demanded an end to the Chechen war and the withdrawal of Russian troops from Chechnya.

The negotiations ended in nothing. And the FSB special unit went on the assault, having released an unknown gas into the theater premises. The FSB refused to disclose the gas composition to the doctors, which significantly complicated the assistance to the hostages who suffered from its action. In addition, the FSB did not even begin to capture the unconscious militants; they were all killed, and, as a result, there was no trial.

The primary justification for the need to use gas during a special operation to free the hostages is the presence of weapons and explosive devices in the hands of the terrorists; if triggered, all the hostages could die. The gas blown into the building did not affect everyone: some of the hostages remained conscious, and some terrorists continued to shoot back for 20 minutes, but there was no explosion.

The main cause of death of many hostages is called the "exacerbation of chronic diseases." During a press conference in October 2002, Minister of Health Yuriy, Shevchenko said: "To neutralize the terrorists, a compound based on fentanyl derivatives was used." According to an official statement from the FSB, it was also said that "a special formulation based on fentanyl derivatives" was used at Dubrovka.

Specialists from the laboratory of scientific and technological safety foundations in Salisbury (UK) found that the aerosol included two anesthetics, carfentanil and remifentanil. Still, the text of the study was published only in 2012. The study, however, was unable to establish the proportions and original composition of the mixture. The exact composition of the gas used by the security forces during the assault remained unknown.

On December 20, 2011, the European Court of Human Rights ruled in Finogenov and Others v. Russia, unanimously finding that the inadequate planning of the rescue operation and the absence of an effective investigation by the Russian authorities of the rescue operation a violation of Article 2 (*on the right to life* [emphasis mine - A .M.]) ECHR [European Convention on Human Rights - A.M.] and awarding compensation to 64 victims in the total amount of 1.3 million euros; in the very decision of the Russian authorities to use gas, the court, also unanimously, did not see any violations.

You can read more about the events at Dubrovka here.

In general, crisis and borderline situations reveal everything hidden in a person. This attitude towards people revealed in Putin his inferiority complex: "Let people die, but I must not show that I can make concessions."

This complex manifests itself in him during the next terrorist attack.

On September 1, 2004, terrorists seized hostages at school No. 1 in the city of Beslan (North Ossetia) during a solemn assembly dedicated to the beginning of the school year. For three days, they kept 1,128 people, children, parents, and school staff in the mined building.

As always, the authorities failed to reach an agreement with the terrorists, and they did not find anything more ingenious than to start an assault on the school using a tank gun, flamethrowers, and machine guns.

More than 700 hostages were injured, and 334 people, including 186 children, were killed.

Between 2007 and 2011, more than 400 victims of the attack filed several group applications with the European Court of Human Rights (ECtHR). The applications were consolidated into one case under Tagayeva and Others v. Russia. The plaintiffs alleged violations by Russia of several articles of the European Convention on Human Rights, particularly Article 2 ("Right to life"). In June 2015, during the preliminary hearings, the ECtHR declared most of the applications admissible.

On April 13, 2017, the ECtHR delivered its decision in the case. The judges came to the following conclusions:

• The Court unanimously ruled that the violation of the right to life had taken place because the Russian authorities had sufficient information about a terrorist attack being prepared by Chechen separatists, timed to coincide with the beginning of the school year and related to the taking of hostages in educational institutions; however, the authorities **did not take all the necessary measures to prevent it** [highlighted by me - A.M.].

• The ECHR also noted a violation of the procedural obligations under Article 2, mainly because the investigation could not determine whether the authorities' use of force was justified in the circumstances.

• In a majority decision (5 to 2), the court found that the right to life had also been violated by the authorities' use of "tank guns, grenade launchers, and flamethrowers."

The decision can be found here. I recommend that everyone interested in the problem gets acquainted because the court also sets out all the facts and the chronology.

The European Court of Human Rights ordered Russia to pay the plaintiffs a total sum of EUR 2,955,000 in compensation for non-pecuniary damage; another 88,000 euros was intended for their representatives.

The next muddy story related to Putin and his political opponents was the poisoning of Ukrainian politician, Viktor Yushchenko.

Ukrainian presidential candidate Viktor Andreyevich Yushchenko had been attempted assassination during a dinner on September 5, 2004.

On September 17, 2004, Vice Speaker of the Verkhovna Rada A. Zinchenko made a statement from the rostrum of the Verkhovna Rada that on September 5, 2004, presidential candidate V. Yushchenko was poisoned by an unknown poison. The version of dioxin poisoning arose a week after Yushchenko (during treatment in an Austrian clinic) had "facial asymmetry"—the external signs of poisoning were quite typical for dioxin intoxication. However, Yushchenko's "political opponents" spoke mainly about food poisoning. Former director of the Kyiv Research Institute of Pharmacology and Toxicology, Professor Ivan Chekman, said: "During the Vietnam War, forests were treated with dioxin to rid the trees of foliage. Naturally, the Vietnamese hiding in the forests suffered from the action of this poison. And after that, their faces were the same as Viktor Yushchenko's now. But the Vietnamese as a nation did not die out. So there is no reason to talk about a bad prognosis for Viktor Andreevich."

However, the version of dioxin poisoning was confirmed by studies conducted in an Austrian clinic. Its dose was exceeded by 50,000 times, and its accidental ingestion into the body of a politician was practically impossible. The case was not thoroughly investigated. Therefore, it is impossible to say for sure whether the Russian special forces were behind the poisoning of Yushchenko or not; however, in the light of subsequent events, I believe that we will have yet many surprises in this story (you can read about all versions of the poisoning here).

During his second term, Putin had already 'settled' and grown bolder. He realized that his indifference to people's lives did not cause any solid negative either inside Russia or outside of it. Without thinking twice, he allowed operations to eliminate his enemies abroad.

On December 13, 2004, in the capital of Qatar, Doha, Zelimkhan Yandarbiyev, one of the commanders of the Chechens who fought against Russia in the second Chechen war, was killed. He was declared a terrorist (including by the UN Security Council Committee on Sanctions against the Taliban, Al-Qaeda, and related persons) and was hiding in Qatar. You can talk for a long time about his moral or legal portrait. Still, according to tradition, Russia rarely captures people it calls "terrorists"; therefore, there is usually no trial (more about him and his biography can be found here). That's what happened this time as well.

On December 13, 2004, Yandarbiev was blown up in his car along with his 13-year-old son and two guards. In connection with the murder, the Qatari authorities detained Anatoly Belashkov and Vasily Bogachev by a "strange" coincidence, who turned out to be employees of the Russian special services. They were sentenced to life imprisonment.

Then Russian intelligence officers detained three citizens of Qatar at the airport, accusing them of currency smuggling, and subsequently exchanged them for Belashkov and Bogachev.

The next high-profile death was the death of Sergei Magnitsky in prison.

He was a lawyer for the British investment fund Hermitage Capital. At some point, the special services searched the fund and seized documents and seals from the fund's office. With these documents, nominees went to court, recognizing the company's debts of more than 20 billion rubles. Hermitage Capital paid 5.4 billion rubles of its time to the budget as income tax. Since the debt was confirmed, there was no profit after the recalculation, and all tax paid was subject to return.

It was this embezzlement in the amount of almost $220 million at the exchange rate of that time that Sergei Magnitsky discovered.

However, instead of engaging in actual theft from the budget (sic!), the authorities opened a case against Sergei Magnitsky himself under the article on tax evasion.

He was tortured for a year in the Butyrka pre-trial detention center (a pre-trial detention center—a kind of prison for those accused or suspected of committing crimes).

As Sergei Magnitsky himself wrote in his letters:

"By evening, the entire floor of cell No. 35 was already flooded with sewage water several centimeters thick. Walking on the floor was no longer possible, so we moved around the cell, climbing on the beds like monkeys ...

"Cell No. 61 did not even have window frames. On September 11, 2009, I submitted an application asking for glass frames to be installed. Because of the cold in the cell, I had to sleep in clothes, covering myself with a blanket and jacket, but the frames were not inserted. On September 18, 2009, we filed a complaint that due to the lack of window frames and the resulting cold, we all caught a cold ... "

The investigation wanted Sergei to drop the investigation and slander the head of Hermitage Capital, William Browder, but he did not break down.

As a result, a year later, Sergei Magnitsky died.

More details can be found here.

The case caused an international outcry. USA (The Magnitsky Act, formal name: the Russia and Moldova Jackson–Vanik Repeal and Sergei Magnitsky Rule of Law Accountability Act of 2012), Great Britain, and then Canada (Justice for Victims of Corrupt Foreign Officials Act (Sergei Magnitsky Law)) adopted the 'Magnitsky Law,' which made Putin and his accomplices very angry. Neither Putin nor his gang initially intended to live in Russia. They used population and resources for personal enrichment and intended to leave at some point and live in the West, enjoying material benefits and legal guarantees (guarantees of property rights, personal security, and even a fair trial.) Even in 2022, during the Russo-Ukrainian war, most of the high-ranking officials' children and wives lived in Western countries, and the prospect of remaining in Russia was unbearable for them.

They adopted a number of laws 'in retaliation' for these laws that had been passed, including a law dubbed by the opposition as the 'law of scoundrels' — banning the adoption of Russian children by foreigners, which I mentioned earlier, violating once again the right to life not only in relation to Sergei Magnitsky (whose killers until Russia has not yet been punished, although they all are known, but also in concerning unfortunate orphans, many of whom by the time the law was passed had already found adoptive parents from America.

Putin's next victim was Alexander Litvinenko, the same one who investigated the bombings of houses in Moscow, Buynaksk, and Volgodonsk, which we discussed earlier. Based on the materials of his investigations, he wrote the book *"The FSB blows up Russia"* (ISBN 0-914481-63-0). In 2000, Litvinenko was forced to flee Russia to England, where in 2006, he was poisoned and killed by Russian FSB Officer Lugovoi (materials of the English investigation can be found here).

An unusually exotic method was used to kill him—radioactive polonium. The FSB had already realized that it was still somewhat problematic to kill people loudly and in plain view, and they were looking for ways to eliminate them inconspicuously. However, the uniqueness of the poisoning method allowed British investigators, on the contrary, to investigate the murder faster; the radioactive mark was well traced.

According to the investigation by the British police, Litvinenko was poisoned by FSB Officer Lugovoi. London demanded that Lugovoi be extradited to him and put him on the international wanted list. Putin did not even begin to conduct any investigation and placed Lugovoi in the State Duma, thus endowing him with immunity from any legal prosecution, de facto confirming all the conclusions of the British investigation, as well as his involvement in this murder.

Another very suspicious case of the 'completely accidental' death of Putin's political opponent is the death of Polish President Lech Kaczynski.

He died on April 10, 2010. His plane, along with 95 other high-ranking Polish officials, crashed near Smolensk; they flew to honor the memory of the captured Polish officers shot by the Chekists by their good tradition in 1940. One could attribute the death of the presidential plane to a tragic accident if the Kremlin respected the right to life in terms of a complete and impartial investigation. However, Moscow did everything to throw the investigation off course, which ultimately raises questions about Moscow's innocence in the assassination of the Polish president.

So, according to the examination of the remains of the dead, carried out by the Polish side, "the dead received injuries characteristic of explosions of TNT and similar substances. In particular, the bodies of most of the victims were torn to pieces, more than half of the dead were found without clothes, and approximately 47% of the passengers were severely burned. Moreover, many bodies were riddled with foreign objects, fragments of skin, glass, and even parts of a metal structure. This indicates an explosion that occurred inside the aircraft.

The remains of the aircraft itself have not been transferred to Poland even now. As a result, the investigation of such a critical case also reached a dead end. (You can read more about the situation, about how Russia interfered with the Polish investigation, here, including links to the investigations of the Polish Miller commission and the report IAC).

Among the reasons Putin would want to kill Lech Kaczynski was his assistance to Georgia during the 2008 Russian-Georgian War.

I also want to remind you that, in Russia, a criminal case should be opened simply on the fact of the death of people (Article 140 of the Code of Criminal Procedure of the Russian Federation). However, this case was not even prosecuted! And this is about the president of another country! The culprits have not been found and punished. The circumstances of the case have not been tried even in a Russian court.

Let me remind you that the 'right to life' is also the state's duty to investigate crimes and prevent their recurrence. Even if Moscow did not set up a disaster for the Polish plane (which I have some doubts about, given its behavior after the disaster), the interference in the investigation by the Polish side and the suspension of its investigation is an absolute violation of the right to life.

In 2014, as we discussed earlier, Putin launched aggression against Ukraine. He annexed Crimea and brought his militants into the Donbas, assuming that the local population there would also happily welcome them, like the pro-Russian local population of Crimea. However, he was wrong again. Fights began with the Ukrainian army.

At that moment, Ukraine was actively using aircraft. Since Russian mercenaries actively pretended to be local 'rebellious miners' who purchased tanks and military weapons from a nearby store, they did not have the means to combat aircraft.

Putin decided to rectify the situation and sent the militants an air defense system, BUK. However, the very first use of it was more than tragic: the militants thought that they would shoot down the Ukrainian IL-76 involved in the transportation of the Ukrainian military, but instead, they shot down a Dutch passenger plane Boeing 777 of Malaysia Airlines, which was performing a scheduled flight MH17 on the Amsterdam-Kuala Lumpur route. All 298 people on board were killed (283 passengers, including 80 minors, and 15 crew members).

The BUK was urgently returned to Russia, and propaganda poured out dozens of versions (one more idiotic than the other) of who exactly shot him down.

Needless to say, from the very beginning, even though the plane belonged to the Netherlands company, it flew from Malaysia to the Netherlands, was shot down, and crashed on the territory of Ukraine; however, propaganda, official bodies, and persons of Moscow ran around with a thousand versions based on "this not us," causing almost 100% impression that it was Moscow that was involved in this?

This has been confirmed. It was highly unlikely that the transfer of the BUK to combatants in Donbas took place without the consent or approval of Russia's top military officials. The trial of the defendants in the case ended in the Hague (all materials can be viewed here), where the participation of Russian militants in this crime was proven.

The question of whether Russia conducted its objective investigation and punishment of those responsible, I think, can be considered rhetorical. The only thing that Russia did was to try to interfere with the investigation of the Netherlands, again violating that same right to life.

I want to note that all these cases were accompanied by the murders of journalists who conducted specific investigations. I give a far from a complete list of them.

- Abashilov, Gadzhi Akhmedovich

- Akhmedilov, Malik

- Bogomolov, Lev Viktorovich

- Magomed Uspaev

- Evloev, Magomed Yahyaevich

- Ivanov, Valery Evgenievich

- Kalinovsky, Sergey Arturovich

- Kamalov Khadzhimurad Magomedovich

- Karimov, Farhad Asker

- Kuashev, Timur Khambievich

- Napiorkovskiy, Anton Yulianovich

- Popkov, Viktor Alekseevich

- Sidorov, Alexey Vladimirovich

- Skryl, Natalya Vladimirovna

- Tsilikin, Dmitry Vladimirovich

- Chaikova, Nadezhda Vladimirovna

- Shevchenko, Leonid Vitalievich

- Estemirova, Natalia Khusainovna

- Yudina, Larisa Alekseevna

You can read more here.

At some point, Putin ultimately suffered. Probably, the sanctions imposed by the vigilant West, after almost 15 years of terror by Putin of his population, greatly angered him; for the first time, he felt at least some punishment for his crimes.

However, instead of stopping criminal activity, Putin has sharply increased it.

In 2015, Nemtsov, a former deputy prime minister and opposition politician under Yeltsin, was assassinated. Most likely because of this phrase (in the interview, he said Putin was 'fucking mad'), or for his oppositional political activities in, let's say, aggregate.

He was killed on a bridge in the center of Moscow, directly opposite the Kremlin, with four shots in the back. Subsequently, the Bellingcat research team will discover that even a year before the murder, special services were monitoring Nemtsov.

By an utterly unsuspicious coincidence, the Kremlin cameras looking at the bridge at the time of the murder were not working.

And although five perpetrators were caught and convicted, neither the customer nor the organizer of the crime were ever found. The investigation requested an interrogation of the alleged organizer of the murder, Ruslan Gereemyev. Still, this requirement was not met: FSB operatives only once left for Geremeyev's place of residence and later wrote in a report that 'no one opened the door to the household.' Let me provide an example of how searches are carried out at the homes of oppositionists in Russia. Well, true; how can murder be compared with political activity?

And additional facts about his murder (non-working cameras, surveillance, 'special zeal' in interrogating the alleged organizer) raise many further questions.

In any case, an unsolved crime, as we said, is a violation of the right to life, even if suddenly, somehow, the FSB has nothing to do with it.

 In 2015, the FSB may have used the now widely known Novichok poison (more about Novichok here) for the first time on its political opponents. Human rights activist, Vladimir Kara-Murza, was poisoned. He was one of the people who helped investigate Magnitsky's death and also lobbied for the Magnitsky Acts issued by countries on the matter. Naturally, he was not forgiven for such a blow. Kara-Murza was hospitalized with symptoms of poisoning in May 2015. Years later, the Bellingcat investigative team revealed that he was being followed by the same group of FSB operatives that had poisoned Navalny.

The assassination attempt failed, and he was poisoned later in February 2017. There was no doubt that it was poisoning; it was even in official diagnoses, designated as 'poisoning by an unknown substance.' At that time, no one knew about the existence of the Novichok poison. It would be known later.

However, none of these events were prosecuted.

 You can read more about the poisoning of Kara-Murza here.

The next major poisoning was committed in 2018. On March 4, former Russian intelligence officer, Yuri Skripal, and his daughter were found unconscious in a park in Salisbury (UK).

Police said the Skripals had been exposed to a nerve toxin. The police sergeant in charge of the investigation, investigating the Skripals' home as part of the investigation, was also admitted to hospitals. The investigation continued until the summer, and the police collected about 2,300 different pieces of evidence and examined more than 4,000 hours of surveillance video.

The investigation also revealed that resident, Dawn Sturgess, and her friend, Charlie Rowley, were hospitalized with similar symptoms. After analyzing the substance with which they were poisoned, the investigation concluded that they were poisoned with a substance belonging to the Novichok group of nerve agents. Dawn Sturgess passed away a few days later. And the police, having searched her house, found a perfume bottle that contained traces of the specified substance.

As a result, the police found out that three FSB officers carried out surveillance of the Skripal family. They smeared the handle of their front door with Novichok (the poison is transmitted through the skin) and threw the bottle with the remnants of the poison into the trash, where Charlie Rowley found it, subsequently giving it to his girlfriend.

The identity of the employees became known, and the UK again demanded their extradition. But, as always, Russia was not going to extradite its killers, who could be used elsewhere.

Particular attention should be paid to the fact that this is already the second directly proven case where Russia acted not just as an indifferent actor, passively not investigating crimes, but precisely as the customer, organizer, and perpetrator of the crime. Secondly, Russia began to kill citizens of other countries (Litvinenko had already received British citizenship by the time of his death, like Skripal; moreover, Don Sturgess died from Novichok), directly or indirectly. Thirdly, the chosen method of murder, no matter how cynical it may sound, was dangerous for others and even in violation of the Chemical Weapons Convention (add it to the list of conventions violated by Putin).

More information on the poisoning of the Skripals and the identification of poisoners can be found here.

All the same, Putin answered the accusations only with counter questions and whataboutisms (from "What about you?" or such childish excuses in the style of "but you ..." or as in the old Soviet joke, "and you have Blacks lynched there!").

Minor sanctions were imposed on the poisoning of the Skripals, and Putin continued his mafia activities.

In 2019, Russian poet and writer, Dmitry Bykov, was hospitalized with poisoning. Again, the fact that Novichok was used and that the same group of murderers in the service of the state did this became known after the poisoning of Navalny. The motives are hard to explain. Dmitry Bykov opposed Putin, but he was not a politician. This is most likely because of this slogan (Bykov himself has a poster in the third photo from above). Putin often told his oppositionists, "Don't rock the boat," meaning that the protest could allegedly lead to the death of the whole country. Bykov wittily supplemented this phrase: "Do not rock the boat, our rat is seasick." Whether Putin is so pitiful and petty as to order the murder of a person for one sentence is not clear, but the more you look at him, the more you realize that this is quite likely.

You can read more about who Dmitry Bykov is and how Bellingcat found out about his poisoners here.

In 2019, there was another murder. On August 23, 2019, Zelimkhan Khangoshvili, a participant in the second Chechen war and one of the field commanders close to Shamil Basayev and Aslan Maskhadov, was shot dead in the very center of Berlin. The court found the Russian Vadim Krasikov guilty and sentenced him to life imprisonment. During the investigation, it turned out that he was assisted by employees of the Russian diplomatic mission, who were declared persona non grata. Should I say that Vadim Krasikov was an employee of the Russian special services (here and here)?

 A brief description of the court hearings, in this case, can be found here.

And finally, the most high-profile attempt on the life organized by the special services was the poisoning of the Russian politician and opposition leader Alexei Navalny in 2020.

At one time, he was a minority shareholder of Gazprom and, at some point, tried to find out a significant overpricing in the purchase of pipes for gas pipelines by Gazprom. He tried to appeal this, but everywhere, he ran into obstacles. This is how he understood that corruption was not a separate shortcoming of the system; it is the backbone of Putin's vertical.

Since then, he and his team have released hundreds of investigations into the luxurious lives of Russian officials, their children, wives, and mistresses. As a lawyer, he, unlike many other investigative journalists, provided documents that could be obtained from official open sources (you can watch them here).

And you can read more about Alexei and his biography here.

Naturally, such activities irritated Putin and his entire gang. The matter was complicated (for Putin) by the fact that Navalny had all the evidence of corrupt activities. Any criminal libel case would lead to the fact that even more details about corruption could emerge (by exploiting the rights of a defendant, it would be possible to demand additional documents and information from the accusing party). That is why the Russian authorities have taken a course to initiate any criminal cases against him, except for 'slander' (you can read more about them here).

Of course, Putin, seeing the growth of his popularity, decided to get rid of him.

Navalny's associates even made a separate website where they collected all the information and evidence on Navalny's poisoning.

I take a quote from there so as not to retell it.

"In August 2020, Alexei Navalny went on a business trip to Siberia to shoot videos about the corruption of local deputies and officials, members of the United Russia party on the eve of regional elections. He was accompanied on this trip by six employees of the Anti-Corruption Foundation — Maria Pevchikh and Georgy Alburov from the Investigation Department, lawyer Vladlen Los, operator Pavel Zelensky, FBK press secretary, Kira Yarmysh and assistant Ilya Pakhomov. The first group arrived in Novosibirsk on August 13; the next day they were joined by Alexei, as well as Kira and Ilya. In Novosibirsk, Navalny filmed an investigation with the team and held a meeting with his supporters at the headquarters.

"On August 17, Alexei and his team left Novosibirsk for Tomsk in one minibus. They arrived there at about 7 pm and stayed at the Xander Hotel, each in a separate room on the second floor. In Tomsk, Navalny, together with his team, also filmed an investigation and met with supporters at the headquarters.

"Alexei spent August 19 on the streets of the city and in an apartment rented specifically for filming. At about 8 pm, he had a meeting at the headquarters, and then went to the village of Kaftanchikovo to swim in the Tom River. At about 11 pm, he returned to the hotel and met with the team at the hotel restaurant Velvet. There he ordered a Negroni, but it turned out to be so unpalatable that Alexei only took a couple of sips and went to bed at midnight.

"Navalny, along with Kira Yarmysh and Ilya Pakhomov, flew to Moscow a day earlier than the others, on August 20. At 6 am, Alexei met Kira and Ilya in the hotel lobby, they got into a taxi and went to the airport. At that time, Navalny was feeling great. At the airport, he drank tea at the cafe called "Viennese Coffee House", bought some candy at a store to bring the family as souvenirs, and then went to boarding.

"The plane took off with a slight delay, at 8:01 am Tomsk time (4:01 am Moscow time). About 20 minutes after the start of the flight, Navalny felt sick.

"As Alexei later said, he broke into a cold sweat, he lost concentration, he could not focus. There was no pain, only the feeling of impending death, which is impossible to describe. Alexei refused the water, which was distributed by the flight attendants, and went to wash his face in the toilet. He spent about 20 minutes there. At 8:50 am Tomsk time (4:50 am Moscow time), the flight attendants found out that a person on the plane became ill, and began to provide him with first aid. After 10 minutes, they asked over the speakerphone if there was a doctor among the passengers and reported the situation to the pilot. At 8:20 am Omsk time (5:20 am Moscow time) the board requested permission to land from the dispatchers of the Omsk airport. Permission was granted. A few minutes after that, the airport received a call with a bomb threat, and the evacuation of passengers began, but like two previous reports of bomb threats this month, it turned out to be a false alarm. The board landed unhindered.

"The plane with Navalny landed in Omsk at 9:01 am local time (6:01 am Moscow time). A medical car from the Omsk airport was waiting for him on the runway. The medics got on the plane, examined Alexei and called the resuscitation team. When the ambulance arrived at the scene, Navalny was loaded onto a stretcher, placed in an ambulance and taken to the Ambulance Hospital No. 1 in Omsk. Kira Yarmysh went with him in the ambulance, Ilya Pakhomov arrived at the hospital later with Alexei's things. The ambulance left the airport at 9:37 am (6:37 am Moscow time).

"...Navalny spent 44 hours there. On August 21, the family decided to evacuate him to Germany, and on August 22, at 7:59 am local time (4:59 Moscow time), the medical plane carrying Alexei Navalny, who was in a coma, flew from Omsk to the Berlin clinic Charité.

"Alexei Navalny recovered from the coma on September 7. Since September 22, after being discharged from Charité, he continued his rehabilitation in Germany. At the end of October, Alexei and FBK employees were contacted by Christo Grozev, an investigative journalist for Bellingcat, who said that he had a hypothesis about who could have poisoned Navalny. FBK, Bellingcat and The Insider launched a joint investigation.

"By that time, it was already known that chemical weapons from the Novichok group had been used against Navalny. On August 24, Charité stated that numerous laboratory tests had proved that Alexei had been poisoned with a substance from the group of cholinesterase inhibitors, which includes chemical warfare agents. Bundeswehr experts conducted an examination and found out that Navalny was poisoned by Novichok. Later, at the request of Germany, the Organization for the Prohibition of Chemical Weapons (OPCW) conducted its independent research in laboratories in Germany, France and Sweden and confirmed the conclusions of scientists from the Bundeswehr (more on this in the "International Position" section).

"Novichok has been the subject of interest for Bellingcat investigators for several years now. In 2018, while investigating the attempt on the life of Sergei and Yulia Skripal in Salisbury, they established that the current GRU officers Anatoly Chepiga (Petrov) and Alexander Mishkin (Boshirov) participated in a special operation to poison the Skripals by Novichok in Great Britain. In the fall of 2020, Bellingcat and The Insider released an investigation about the continued production of chemical warfare agents in Russia in violation of the Chemical Weapons Convention, and the Moscow-based Signal Scientific Center, which is affiliated with the special services and plays an important role in their development. According to investigators, on the eve of all operations with the use of Novichok, including the one in Salisbury, GRU officers would call and meet with scientists from Signal. Bellingcat's hypothesis was that Navalny's poisoning could have been coordinated along the same lines.

"Bellingcat's main method of operation is to analyze open source data and data that can be bought on the black market. In Russia, there is a developed market for "running people down": for a small cost, you can get data from mobile network operators, airlines, police, border services, and so on. This is how Bellingcat investigators gained access to the details of calls made by **Artur**

Zhirov, the director of Signal, and his subordinates. An analysis of the phone calls on the eve of Navalny's poisoning and directly after it showed an unusual surge in conversations between Signal employees and several subscribers whose identities were yet to be established. Investigators found out that these numbers are used by FSB officers.

"This was established primarily through the use of special applications that allow you to determine how a particular number is recorded in the contact lists of other people. Some of the subscribers with whom the employees of Signal called up were saved in their contact lists as "Stanislav FSB" or "Vladimir FSB". With the help of similar applications, you can find out which social network pages are tied to this number, whether the number is used to pay parking fees or fines and find out other information that allows you to identify, with a high degree of accuracy, the identity and places of residence and work of the subscriber.

"Most of the FSB officers with whom Zhirov communicated are associated with the Institute of Criminalistics of the Center for Special Technology of the FSB. Zhirov's main contacts in those days were Colonel General **Kirill Vasiliev**, the director of this institute, and his chief, the director of the entire Center for Special Technology, Major General of the FSB **Vladimir Bogdanov**. They, in turn, often called **Stanislav Makshakov**, deputy head for science at the Institute of Criminalistics. Previously, Makshakov worked as a military medical scientist in the city of Shikhany, Saratov Oblast. Subsequently, it turned out that he had been studying the effect on the body of poisons similar to Novichok for many years. In Soviet times, Shikhany was home to the institute where this poisonous substance was created.

"Officially, the Institute of Criminalistics (aka NII-2 FSB) is the main place for conducting examinations for the needs of the FSB. However, Belligcat and The Insider managed to find out that in the structure of this institute there is also a secret subdivision responsible for poisonings with chemical weapons. You can read more about this in the "Chemical Weapons of the FSB" section.

"One of the divisions of the laboratory is located in Moscow, at the intersection of Akademika Vargi Street with Teplostansky Proezd, the other is in the Moscow Oblast, near the Podlipki sanatorium. Billing data indicated that it was from these two locations that FSB officers most often called Signal employees.

"The detailing of Makshakov's calls showed that before and after the poisoning, he communicated with a group of about ten other FSB officers. Bellingcat then bought data on the movements of these people — and it turned out that some of them, starting in 2017, have followed Alexei Navalny on almost all his trips, both work and family.

"The principle of surveillance was as follows. FSB officers usually traveled in twos or threes, in different combinations. To buy tickets, both fake passports (with slightly changed dates of birth and surnames) and original documents were used. As a rule, they did not take the same flight as Navalny, they came to where Alexei was supposed to be on the eve of his arrival, and left one day before him or one day later.

"In total, since 2017, FSB officers associated with the laboratory that deals with chemical weapons have accompanied Navalny on more than 30 trips.

"Later, after examining the database of air tickets and data from telephone conversations, Bellingcat found another permanent companion of Alexei — Valery Sukharev. He traveled with Navalny in Russia at least 15 times, and before and after the poisoning he constantly called up with the already well-known team of poisoners. Valery Sukharev works in the Service for Defense of Constitutional Order and Fight against Terrorism of the FSB. For more information about this organization, which has a secret department responsible for political assassinations, see the "Chemical Weapons of the FSB" section"

 (the quote is taken from here, you can find the whole investigation and proofs, Navalny's team had to gather on their own).

This investigation revealed not just individual killers but a whole state department of the FSB, in Orwellian, called "for the protection of the constitutional order," but directly involved in political assassinations of citizens objectionable to the regime.

In addition, Navalny and his team are a group of highly educated investigative lawyers. Having poisoned him, the FSB officers gave them threads that revealed that the special services were behind the murders and attempted murders of other persons (in particular, Kara-Murza and Bykov) (more on the identified persons can be found here) that we talked about earlier.

On the fact of poisoning, the investigative committee even refused to open a criminal case. Navalny's team even applied several times to the "court" demanding to start a formal investigation, but they were denied this.

Summing up, I hope it is evident that Putin violates Article 20 of the Constitution not only by not investigating cases of violence against journalists, oppositionists, and other persons but even by having a unit of special services directly involved in liquidating opposition activists! Moreover, their activities are not limited to the territory of Russia and are often dangerous for their targets but for random people as well.

Article 20, paragraph 2, is of lesser importance. Although the death penalty has not been abolished in Russia, its use is subject to a ban by the Constitutional Court (Decree of the Constitutional Court of the Russian Federation of February 2, 1999, No. 3-P). Indeed, it is not applied, although formally, it is present in regulatory legal acts. It is not known how the situation will unfold further. Still, more and more Russian politicians are calling for the abolition of this decree (they refer to the moratorium imposed by President Yeltsin, but that moratorium is void because the presidential decree cannot repeal the norms of the law).

However, point 2 can be recognized as working at the time of writing this book.

As a result, it can be said with certainty that the right to life is not respected in Russia. It does not fulfill the duties of investigating cases but is directly involved in murders.

Therefore, when facts arise about the atrocities of Russian troops in Ukraine, I readily believe this: if murders are not investigated within the country itself, why would a Russian soldier, with weapons in his hands, suddenly begin to respect the right to life of others? I don't need to look at the evidence presented by the Ukrainians on Bucha. I am more than sure that this is the work of Putin's soldiers, for this is the very nature of Putin's power—no one will be punished for either murder or theft.

Therefore, unfortunately, the shelling of Mariupol, which razed the city to the ground, is not surprising, nor the indiscriminate bombardment of civilian targets by rockets; Putin has no empathy for people at all. Not only did he not start an investigation into the atrocities in Bucha, but this worthy successor to Stalin's KGB executioners even awarded the direct perpetrators of the tragedy that occurred there! This "lawyer" and "legalist" do not understand law basics, even at the most primitive level. The concept of "killing is bad, stealing is bad" is inconceivable to him. He does not understand this so much that he is packing his luggage to heaven. Undoubtedly, he even prepared a golden harp to boast luxury in front of the angels (here and here).

ARTICLE 21 OF THE CONSTITUTION

The text of the article states:

"1. Human dignity shall be protected by the State. Nothing may serve as a basis for its derogation.

2. Nobody should be subjected to torture, violence, or other severe or humiliating treatment or punishment. Nobody may be subjected to medical, scientific or other experiments without voluntary consent."

In general, 'dignity' is a rather vague term. It means respect for the person, recognition of equality and human rights, and respect for his opinion and desires.

We had already said more than once, when we discussed gays and lesbians, that the state not only does not respect their honor and dignity but is directly engaged in their discrimination and humiliation.

However, they are not the only ones whom the government openly despises.

And again, to talk about respect (especially for rights), the rights must first be respected, which, as you probably already noticed, is entirely wrong.

However, not only the violation of rights is degrading to human dignity. To the lack of rights, poverty is added. That does not allow people to solve their problems on their own. More, officials neglect the lower classes and groups.

A prime example of the former is asking the authorities on their knees (sic!) for help (here, here and here). Typically, such requests end in initiating criminal cases, not against officials or law perpetrators but against people who thus turned to Putin or high officials with their pitiful pleas.

In general, Putin's central thesis that Russia has some kind of "greatness" pales somewhat against the background of a video about pensioners who are forced to climb garbage dumps in search of expired food (a quick search on YouTube). Does the homeless have greatness or dignity? In my opinion, this is a rhetorical question.

Most officials in Russia are not elected by the population but are appointed from above. Even if an official has gone through formal election procedures, in most cases, he is still appointed by upper levels of authorities, and the elections are falsified. With such an approach to hiring, the people cease to be a source of power, and the officials begin to feel that they are not managers appointed to solve the people's problems but petty kings or barons who were put in charge to supervise slaves.

Very often, such an internal feeling of officials breaks out, causing some scandals.

So, the head of the department of youth policy of the Sverdlovsk region, Olga Glatskikh, said at a meeting with young people in 2018, "The state did not ask you to give birth."

The governor of the Arkhangelsk region, Igor Orlov, called the protesters against the construction of a landfill at Shiyes "scums."

And the head of Chuvashia, Mikhail Ignatiev, made a fire department officer jump for the keys to a new fire engine.

Labor Minister of the Saratov Region Natalya Sokolova said that one can survive on minimum wage because pasta always costs the same. In response to such a bold statement, she was offered to live a month on a minimum salary herself. But Natalya Sokolova refused, saying that her status did not allow her to do that.

Nikolai Smirnov, Minister of Energy and Housing and Public Utilities of the Sverdlovsk Region, expressed such an elegant and respectful phrase: "I will answer plainly. Girls, cover your ears. How the fuck do we collect money? Your task as the owner is to pay for the service that is provided to you. Everything else is none of your business."

Mikhail Balakin, deputy head of the State Labor Inspectorate for the Sverdlovsk region, also noted. He said the following maxim: "People in bankrupt enterprises continue to go to work for months. Hundreds and thousands of them go, and then they shift their duties to the supervisory authorities. They say they don't pay us a salary, and you don't help us to get it. But I shouldn't. It wasn't me who led you there by the hand. You can get into your Zhiguli [cheap car - A.M.] and temporarily work as a taxi driver."

You can find many other exciting and respectful phrases here.

If it seems to you that this is an exception and officials are very respectful of ordinary people, then this is very unlikely. Most likely, the rest are smart enough not to talk about it so openly on cameras or in front of journalists.

Even the very presence of "flashing lights" and blocking traffic for the sake of the passage of a cortege of officials indicates how much an official puts his convenience above the interests and even the life and health of other citizens, as we talked about earlier.

Officials, however, not only openly humiliate citizens but also openly threaten them. In particular, Peskov (President's spokesman) suggested "smearing the liver [of the protesters] on the asphalt."

The propagandists do the same. Thus, one of the most famous propagandists, Solovyov, directly called the protesters "2% of shit."

I can go on for a long time to show the sheer contempt of the Russian government for its citizens. After analyzing Article 20 of the Constitution (the right to life), no one should have any doubts about how the Russian government treats a person and his dignity.

The second paragraph of the commented article explicitly stipulates the prohibition of torture. I have already mentioned the direct torture of prisoners in the analysis of the class character of Russian society. With their help, FSB officers knock out the testimony they need from people or extort money, threatening otherwise to make the torture video public. Here

is the evidence. This link contains videos with tortures (CAUTION, VERY VIOLENT CONTENT 18+).

Vladimir Osechkin obtained 40 GB of video data. As he said, his colleagues managed to take out of Russia, a man who had been serving a sentence in one of the institutions of the Federal Penitentiary Service for five years. Osechkin did not name him but specified that he was a programmer who "was beaten and tortured, and then [FSIN - Federal Penitentiary Service] decided to use him as a professional." Hence, from 2018 to 2020, he had access to computers and video recorders of the department employees. The video archive, according to Osechkin, concerns employees of three regional departments of the Federal Penitentiary Service, Vladimir, Saratov, and Irkutsk.

According to the founder of Gulagu.net, more than 200 people went through torture and rape, but only 40 were tortured on video.

If you think that after the publication of the torture video, the authorities in Russia opened criminal cases against the FSB and FSIN officers, then you most likely have not read about the class nature of Russian society carefully enough. Of course, a criminal case was initiated against Osechkin for disclosing the "classified materials"!

However, torture is not necessarily an active activity. The content in prisons and pre-trial detention centers (PDC) and the transportation of people takes place literally "under torture conditions" (here and here).

And like the Russian matryoshka, the prison has its internal prison, ShIZO (penalty cell). Prisoners who have violated one or another rule of internal order are placed there. Depending on the prisoner and the administration's mood, they can be placed there for practically anything. So, Navalny was placed in a punishment cell for an unbuttoned button on his collar.

You can read more about ShIZO here, and in general, you can read about all the placings of Navalny in ShIZO here. In a nutshell, he ended up in a ShIZO for the fact that:

1. A button on his collar was unbuttoned.

2. He did not immediately remove his hands behind his back.

3. For citing the decision of the ECHR three times.

4. For refusing to wash the fence.

5. "Badly cleaned the yard" and called the employee "lieutenant"...

Here is an excerpt from the above article regarding the conditions of detention in the ShIZO:

•   "There was no exhaust ventilation in the cell, no daylight came through the window, there was no drain tank above the sanitary unit, it was cold, damp and damp," one of the prisoners describes the punishment cell in his complaint against PDC-1 in the Orenburg region.

- In the same PDC-1, according to another prisoner, "there was an open toilet in the cell, from which an unpleasant smell emanated, which made it impossible to eat. It was also impossible to go to the toilet because the video camera was aimed at the bathroom."

- While being placed in a ShIZO, offenders cannot buy even the most necessary things on their own; therefore, they are entirely dependent on the colony employees. Thus, a convict from IK-4 in the Arkhangelsk region complains that he "was not given toilet paper, soap, washing powder, toothpaste, a brush, shaving accessories, bed linen."

- Deprived of a bed, a prisoner from IK-16 in the Murmansk region was forced to sleep on the floor, on which rats ran, and had a cold in his back. In court, the plaintiff admitted that "due to the existing conditions of detention, he was forced to open his veins" and "showed a rodent in a plastic bottle that he fed." The judge exacted ten thousand rubles (about $150) from the Federal Penitentiary Service.

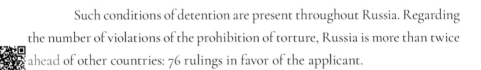

Such conditions of detention are present throughout Russia. Regarding the number of violations of the prohibition of torture, Russia is more than twice ahead of other countries: 76 rulings in favor of the applicant.

One of the goals of torture, in addition to previously stated coercion to testify or extortion, is the state policy aimed at intimidation. Real state terrorism. It is not enough for the authorities to deprive a person of freedom; it needs to humiliate and morally destroy him, depriving him of the ability to resist. And although the purpose of detention under the Code of Criminal Procedure is the "correction" of the prisoner, it is clear that such conditions have entirely different goals: to intimidate those who remain free. Frightened people are easier to manage and manipulate and are easier targets for robbing and extortion.

For a complete picture, I give a link to the Human Rights Watch report on torture in the Ukrainian city of Izyum.

Based on the above, I think, dear reader, it is clear that Article 21 of the Constitution does not fully work.

ARTICLE 22 OF THE CONSTITUTION

The full text of Article 22 reads:

"1. Everyone shall have the right to freedom and personal inviolability.

2. Arrest, detention and keeping in custody shall be permissible only under a court order. A person may not be detained for more than 48 hours without a court order."

"Freedom" in this article is used narrowly as the absence of physical restrictions on movement and not the lack of legal barriers.

The article says that authorities cannot arbitrarily restrict the movement of a person or seize and beat him.

These restrictions are closely linked to two other rights: the right to peaceful procession and assembly (Article 31 of the Constitution) and the right to a fair trial (Article 46 of the Constitution).

As we have already discussed more than once, protests cause a very painful reaction from the authorities. Putin even created a special body of security forces whose only task is to suppress any events unauthorized by the authorities—the National Guard (Rosgvardia). In total, there are about 350,000 people in the Russian Guard. At the head of the National Guards, Putin put his former bodyguard, a man with unusually low intelligence, Zolotov, who was personally devoted to Putin.

Naturally, such "useful" people belong to the upper class, according to our classification. Being classic guardsmen, they are not affected by the law and do not hesitate to use force to disperse any rallies or even single pickets. Many examples can be seen here.

One of the high-profile moments was a kick in a woman's stomach by a security officer. Naturally, this worthy husband did not receive any responsibility: according to official information, they simply could not find him among their employees. This is what the right to personal integrity looks like in Russia.

Also, OVD-Info made an additional report about detentions at protest actions by (a Russian human rights organization).

In general, I think it is not particularly appropriate talking about some kind of personal integrity of citizens in Russia after the story of actual murders and torture (as we analyzed when analyzing articles 20 and 21 of the Constitution).

Regarding the right to freedom of assembly and peaceful marches, I will quote a few figures that Human Rights Watch notes in its report on detentions at anti-war protests in March 2022. "According to the human rights project OVD-Info, since February 24, when Russian troops entered Ukraine, 13,500 people have been arbitrarily detained.

"Social media posts documenting the March 6 protests contain footage of peaceful demonstrators being detained for holding placards, marching in groups, chanting "No to war!" wearing blue and yellow clothes, ribbons, videorecording of detentions or just passing by.

"There were repeated instances of the use of force by the police against demonstrators. OVD-Info reports at least 34 situations where law enforcement officers beat protesters on March 6.

"Numerous videos from different cities contain footage of police using excessive force during arrests. In a video from Moscow, five police officers take away one man, and one of them kicks the detainee. In a video from St. Petersburg, law enforcement officers knock a man down and beat him with fists. In Moscow, a policeman beats a protester with a baton while carried to a police van.

"In St. Petersburg, a video was filmed showing four to six policemen beating a man on the ground with batons, after which they allegedly used a stun gun. He shouts that he "did not rally." Using a stun gun on an already detained person violates the prohibition of torture and other cruel, inhuman, or degrading treatment.

"The detainees complained of cuts, abrasions, and burns from a stun gun. One person allegedly suffered a concussion, and another had an open head wound, which he claims was sustained during his arrest. Several detainees were hospitalized.

"Police officers did not, in all cases, have a badge on them; sometimes, as far as one can judge, it was sealed with black tape. Officers carried out some arrests in civilian clothes.

"In Moscow, 22-year-old Marina Morozova was taken to the Brateevo police department on suspicion of participating in an anti-war protest. There she managed to record what was happening on the phone. In the audio recording she subsequently provided to Novaya Gazeta, three police officers ask her questions. One unidentified employee is behaving aggressively: insulting Morozova, hitting her on the head, threatening her with a gun, and brandishing a chair.

"26-year-old Aleksandra Kaluzhskikh also managed to covertly record on a dictaphone what happened to her in the Brateevo police department. Later, she handed over the recording to the OVD-Info project. Allegedly, the same officer who interrogated Morozova hits the Kaluzhskys in the face with a water bottle, grabs her hair, threatens her with electric shocks, and smashes her mobile phone.

""What do you think, that will we be punished for this? Putin told us to [kill] ... That's it! Putin is on our side! You are the enemies of Russia; you are the enemies of the people,... They will even give us a bonus for this," the employee says on the recording.""

More details can be found here.

I believe I have provided enough evidence that Article 22 of the Russian Constitution also does not work and is not respected.

ARTICLE 23 OF THE CONSTITUTION

The full text of the article states:

"1. Everyone shall have the right to the inviolability of his (her) private life, personal and family privacy, and protection of his (her) honour and good name.

2. Everyone shall have the right to privacy of correspondence, of telephone conversations and of postal, telegraph and other communications. This right may be limited only on the basis of a court order."

We again need to break the first paragraph into separate parts. The first concerns the secrets of private life, and the second concerns the protection of honor and good name. You can read more about the right to privacy here.

The secret of private life is one of the favorite ones for violation by the KGB officer Putin. For example, we can recall the sex scandal with prosecutor Dmitry Skuratov, where a video of "a person who looks like the prosecutor general" having fun with two prostitutes became the basis for its removal.

As you understand, the public publication of such a recording was a direct violation of Article 23 of the Constitution.

Of course, such techniques were subsequently used by the security forces more than once. So, they leaked a scandalous video to the network with a famous writer, playwright, and satirist, Viktor Shenderovich. He became famous for his criticism of the authorities and solid moral rhetoric. As planned by FSB, this incident was supposed to destroy the honest image of the writer. If you want to know the details of this scandal, google "Shenderovich and the Mattress" with all due respect, I will not provide a link to this abomination in my book.

The FSB even had a special lady who met and slept with opposition politicians. They planned to use such materials for blackmail or discredit.

Is it necessary to say that such methods violate several articles of the Constitution at once?

Also, as we mentioned above, gays and lesbians have big problems with the right to privacy.

Human Rights Watch report "License to Harm: Violence and Harassment against LGBT People and Activists in Russia" dated December 15, 2014.

Gays are especially persecuted in Chechnya. Moreover, this is precisely what the very bodies should monitor.

With the help of torture, which we spoke about earlier, they are forced to give up all the gays they know and then openly shown on stage in front of their relatives.

Here is a quote from the BBC investigation:

"Zaur spent 14 days under arrest. Then he, along with other detainees, was brought to a room that looked like an assembly hall, where their relatives had previously been taken - "they were sitting there as if they had come to a concert." From Zaur's family, there were his father, brother, and uncles.

On the stage where the arrested were taken, a man was sitting, in whom Zaur recognized the speaker of the Chechen parliament, Magomed Daudov: "He said in plain text that these people are sleeping with men, we caught them. Then figure out what you will do with them; we give them to you."

After that, Zaur was released and went home with his relatives. He describes their reaction to what happened in the assembly hall as follows: "I can't say that they reacted normally, but not bad either."

"Chechnya, traditions, adats. They are brought to a hall where there are a lot of people, and they publicly declare that their son, nephew, and brother sleep with men. Of course, this is a shock for Chechnya," Zaur explains. The topic of his orientation in the family was no longer raised, and it remained taboo: "They did not want to discuss this with me, and I did not want to tell them."

You can read more about the problem here.

In principle, it is difficult to imagine the right to privacy in a state where methods of state terror and torture are used. However, I want to note that the desire to "get into bed" is one of the main signs of a totalitarian state. That is why gays and lesbians have always been persecuted in dictatorships; they were too different from some "true Aryan" or "ideal communist," or from some of their "perfect human." As you understand, this sign is also in the "Signs of Fascism by Umberto Eco" cited by us earlier.

Let's move on to the second part of Article 23. It is devoted to the secrecy of personal correspondence.

In the case of Russia, the secrecy of correspondence is directly violated right at the legislative level. As in any totalitarian state, the state fears independence, horizontal communication, and people's connections. Therefore, the destruction of communication between people (public speeches, rallies, pickets, correspondence, and so on. Even conversations) is one of the goals of any dictatorship. Another Roman principle, divide et impera—divide and conquer—helps the unpopular, not based on the people, to last longer.

The Federal Security Service (FSB) provides for itself the ability to control communications with the help of systems of technical means for ensuring operational-search activities in communication networks (the so-called "SORM"). SORM requirements are approved by order of the Ministry of Communications of the Russian Federation of 01.21.93 and the Ministry of Defense of the Russian Federation of 01.25.93 No. 513, the order of Gostelecom of Russia No. 15 of July 9, 1999, for mobile radiotelephone communications, the order of the Ministry of Communications of Russia No. 5 of January 19, 2001, for the Russian segment of the global personal mobile satellite communications Globalstar. SORM makes it possible to intercept Internet traffic, including e-mail messages, entirely, and directly redirect data to the local FSB office. At the same time, the Russian feature (but not an exception) is that judicial control in many cases does not work because if law enforcement agencies get access to information about users by a court decision, then the FSB can track, intercept, and interrupt the communication of any Internet user remotely, without contacting the telecom operator. In addition, when imposing sanctions on wiretapping, the judge does not have the opportunity to get acquainted with the case materials to the extent necessary to make an objective decision. Judge of the Constitutional Court of the Russian Federation A.L. Kononova pointed out this in his dissenting opinion in connection with the consideration of the case on the complaint of citizens M.B. Nikolskaya and M.I." (Website "Privacy"). In addition, in Russia, in principle, there is no control over the activities of the FSB, so there is simply no one to grab their hand.

In accordance with the rules of interaction approved by Government Decree No. 538 of August 27, 2005, "an operator who has received a license from Roskomnadzor is obliged to contact the FSB of Russia within 45 days."

The department will appoint an authorized person with whom the operator will further interact on implementing SORM.

If there is no plan, the authorized division of the FSB, within three months from the application's submission date, together with the operator, develops it. The final document should be drawn up in three copies: for the FSB, the territorial department of Roskomnadzor, and the operator.

According to the plan, the FSB issues technical conditions, and the operator installs SORM TS **at his own expense**. Then they are tested, and the act of commissioning is signed.

In addition, in 2018, the so-called "Yarovaya Law" was adopted.

"According to the Yarovaya law, from July 1, 2018, operators must store telephone conversations, text messages, images, sounds, video recordings, and other electronic messages of users. Operators must store conversations and messages for 6 months and messages via the Internet for 30 days. Operators were required to increase storage capacity by 15% annually over five years. But the government has postponed this requirement until September 2021 in accordance with the economic recovery plan, which was adopted on September 25."

The desire of the state to get into communication between citizens is costly for telecom operators. So, according to Kommersant:

"To fulfill the requirements of the Yarovaya Law, Rostelecom in July 2019 has already purchased 3 billion rubles (about $45 mil). Data storage systems (SHD) "Kupol" manufactured by National Technologies LLC (in April 2019, Rostelecom bought 49% of this company from the structures of ICS Holding).

"Other operators have also already started investing in the enforcement of the law. For example, back in May 2018, MegaFon purchased the Kupol storage system for 923.5 million rubles. MTS, in March 2019, signed a contract to supply SORM equipment to Norsi-Trans, and storage systems for 14 billion rubles (about $218 mil) purchased from the Yakhont company (owned by the structures of AFK Sistema, Rostec, and Norsi-Trans). Tele2, owned by Rostelecom, intends to buy services for implementing the Yarovaya Law from the parent company; the companies have already entered into an appropriate agreement for 4.3 billion rubles (about $67 mil), Kommersant reported on November 21.

"MTS, MegaFon, Vimpelcom, and Tele2 do not comment on the details of the implementation of the law. Previously, the most prominent operators estimated their potential costs for it at 40-50 billion rubles (about $625 mil - $781 mil) within five years for each."

Of course, telecom operators shifted the costs of spying on citizens to the citizens themselves, raising communication tariffs.

Moreover, at one time, the Russian court fined Google for violating the secrecy of correspondence since its algorithms checked letters by keywords and issued contextual advertising in accordance with this (case materials can be viewed here).

As you understand, Article 23 of the Constitution also does not work in full.

ARTICLE 24 OF THE CONSTITUTION

As usual, let's start from citing the full text of the article:

"1. Collecting, keeping, using and disseminating information about the private life of a person shall not be permitted without his (her) consent.

2. State government bodies and local self-government bodies and their officials shall be obliged to provide everyone with access to documents and materials directly affecting his (her) rights and freedoms, unless otherwise envisaged by law."

In principle, the first paragraph is closely intertwined with the content of paragraph 1 of Article 23 of the Constitution, which we analyzed earlier. But if paragraph 1 of article 23 spoke about the right to privacy in principle, then the paragraph of this article says that it is impossible not only to interfere in private life but even to collect information about it.

The concept of "collection of information" also intersects with the meaning of Article 23. For example, violation of the secrecy of correspondence also occurs, mainly for "collecting, storing, using" information.

Accordingly, the SORM systems and the "Yarovaya Laws" (which we discussed when analyzing the previous article) violate this article; they are created to collect, store and use information about citizens' activities.

Naturally, correspondence surveillance is not the only source of such informational espionage. So, special services use the installation of hidden cameras and direct surveillance. If you remember that when we talked about the poisoning of Navalny and other oppositionists and journalists, they were all being monitored. Of course, in the context of an attempted murder, this does not seem to be such a malicious offense. However, such information was also collected illegally in order to prepare for the murder more thoroughly.

I would like to draw attention to the fact that criminal cases have not yet been initiated against those oppositionists, and accordingly, there was not and could not be any court sanction.

This is such a legal tangle: when the special services begin to ignore some norms of the law, sooner or later, they will sink to the point that they will violate them all.

But back to surveillance.

In terms of spying on Navalny, it was admitted by Putin himself. He, due to his stupidity or total legal illiteracy, apparently did not realize that illegal surveillance was a criminal offense (Article 137 of the Criminal Code of the Russian Federation).

However, Navalny is far from the only one directly monitored. The Agora human rights organization made a whole report on the surveillance of politicians and journalists in Russia (the full report can be viewed here, and here you can find a summary table on surveillance).

Please note that this report was published in 2016. And the situation with surveillance, at least, has not changed.

Agora noted: "At the same time, and obviously in connection with this, a series of provocations, revelations, and campaigns to discredit political opposition and civil activists began. Publications of wiretapping of telephone conversations, CCTV recordings, and printouts of documents from e-mail traditionally become part of it."

The Meduza publication, commenting on the Agora report, points out:

"The authors of the report identified 28 cases of politically motivated surveillance in 2007, two cases in 2008, and 17 to 33 cases in 2011, 2012, 2013, and 2015. In 2009 and 2010, not a single case was recorded, in 2014, there were 177 of them, and in January-May 2016, there were already 53...

"The paper describes specific areas of surveillance in detail: movement control, complex simultaneous surveillance of activists in different regions, wiretapping, covert video and audio surveillance and GPS tracking, account hacking, and collection of biometric information (DNA samples and fingerprints).

"The paragraph on movement control talks about the Surveillance Control database of the Ministry of Internal Affairs, into which the data of potential extremists are entered (the agency denies the existence of such a database, but its existence was established in 2011 by the European Court of Human Rights). This database includes not only representatives of ultra-right and nationalist organizations but also political and civil activists. According to various estimates, the database contains up to 6,500 surnames.

"At the beginning of 2007, the data of the Nizhny Novgorod human rights activist Sergei Shimovolos were entered into the Surveillance Control (the authors of the report claim that he was included in the database under the category "Human Rights Defenders"). Interior Ministry officials tried to stop him as he was on a train to Samara to investigate the detentions of activists protesting during the Russia-EU summit. On the same days, the "March of Dissent" authorized by the authorities was supposed to take place in Samara, and many opposition activists from other cities could not come there. The arrests followed the same pattern. In particular, Sergei Udaltsov, coordinator of the Left Front, and Denis Bilunov, then a member of the Solidarity movement, were detained on the platform of the Kazansky railway station. Several dozen politicians and journalists were prevented from boarding the plane at Sheremetyevo airport. All of them were told that they were in a specific base and checked the documents exactly until their transport left Moscow.

"The ECHR acknowledged that surveillance does not meet the standards of legality and legal certainty. The inclusion of Shimovolos in the base and his detention at the Samara railway station were recognized as violating human rights.

"A similar case is described in the paragraph of the report, which tells about the complex Surveillance of activists in different regions. In September 2014, several delegates to the UN World Conference on Indigenous Issues could not fly to New York due to strange circumstances.

"The border guards returned one of the delegates, a passport with a page cut out, saying that his document was invalid. The other car was stopped three times by traffic police officers, and during one of the stops, an unknown person attacked the delegate; he knocked her to the ground and tried to take away the bag with the passport. The police officers did not intervene in what was happening and prevented the attacker from being caught. On the eve of departure, the third delegate had his passport taken away on the street by people in balaclavas. The fourth had their front door filled with glue, causing the delegate to miss her plane.

"The authors of the report conclude that by the middle of the 2000s, a complex control system had been formed in Russia, the purpose of which was human rights and political and civil activists. At the same time, government officials involved in account hacking, covert filming, and other surveillance methods remain unpunished. This speaks to the "complete insecurity of the privacy of civil and political activists in modern Russia, and therefore of all ordinary residents of the country," Agora concludes."

The principles of surveillance methods are: movement control, eavesdropping, covert video and audio surveillance, GPS tracking, mobile phone tracking, billing data collection, biometric information collection, account hacking, and e-mail interception.

You can read about each surveillance method here.

The Agora concludes:

It is safe to say that by the middle of the 2000s, a comprehensive control system had been formed in Russia, which was purposefully applied to political, civil activists and human rights defenders, which was only improved in the future. This system included:

a) control over movements within the Russian Federation and border crossings;

b) wiretapping and interception of communications;

c) covert audio and video recording;

d) interception of e-mail and hacking of accounts in Internet services; and

e) collection and analysis of biometric information.

The complex of these measures is aimed at collecting information, and the results of operational activities can also be used to discredit in the eyes of the public those whom the state calls the "fifth column" and "national traitors."

The described cases show how a system formally created to prevent and investigate crimes, in the absence of public and judicial control, turns into an instrument of political investigation when people who are not involved in any criminal activity become objects of surveillance.

In addition, the authorities have at their disposal such methods of surveillance as the analysis of the activity on social networks, the control of financial transactions, the collection and analysis of biometric data, as well as provocations and falsifications involving state media, primarily television.

At the same time, not a single case of hacking mail and social networks, interception of correspondence, telephone conversations, covert audio and video recording, and outdoor surveillance without legal grounds has led to the trial and punishment of the perpetrators. This looks exceptionally bright against the background of the criminal prosecution by the German authorities of Sergei Maksimov, better known as Hacker Hell.

This testifies to the complete impunity of government officials and the same complete insecurity of the private life of civil and political activists in modern Russia, and consequently of all ordinary residents of the country."

The developed surveillance system through cameras stands apart. In particular, it is installed in the Moscow metro. Cameras are used to search and identify criminals and oppositionists. The system is connected to street and access cameras, and it works in both directions: by uploading a photo, you can follow the entire path of a person. Thus, according to OVD-info (a human rights organization in Russia), "On June 12, 2022, police detained at least 43 people in the Moscow metro, clearly fearing protests. Among them were journalists and activists, whose photos were clearly marked in the system in a special way. In this case, as soon as the right person enters the station, the system informs law enforcement agencies."

You can read more about the camera system and face recognition here.

Consequently, paragraph 1 of Article 24 of the Constitution does not work.

What about point 2? Let me remind you that it sounds like this: "State authorities and local self-government bodies, their officials are obliged to provide everyone with the opportunity to familiarize themselves with documents and materials that directly affect their rights and freedoms unless otherwise provided by law."

This self-explanatory and yet essential rule exists in all legal systems; it is impossible to protect your rights if you do not even have a copy of the document that affects them.

However, to complicate the defense, the investigating authorities often use various tricks to make it difficult for the defendant or his representative to familiarize himself with the case.

They limit the familiarization time and the ability to make copies and take photographs. For example, in the rather sensational case of Ivan Safronov, in which lawyers, until the last moment, did not understand what exactly their client was accused of. He is a journalist who did not have access to state secrets and made investigations into significant thefts in the Ministry of Defense. Safronov's defenders were given two weeks to familiarize themselves with the materials of the case, which consists of 22 volumes. At the same time, they were forbidden to make recordings and make copies of the materials.

Safronov's lawyer commented on the indictment as follows:

"We still do not understand what we are protecting ourselves from, what specific information, how, from whom, to what extent our client received, from what sources, under what table he sat, overheard, with whom he interacted: when he found out what, we don't know what. The accusation is absurd," Talantov said.

He noted that "he saw many miracles in his 30 years of activity," but he had never seen anything like it.

"We still do not understand what material bonuses Safronov received from transferring secret information abroad," Talantov said. Separately, he stressed that the figures of "material rewards," which the investigation stated, "do not beat," contradict each other and was obtained strangely: "Neither the nature of the calculation, nor where the money came from, and, moreover, in different parts of the accusation have different amounts. Sometimes they are called "illegal income," sometimes "criminal income." Sit down, choose what you like."

Talantov once again noted that Safronov did not have access to state secrets and could not judge whether his actions violated the law, which the defense also mentioned in the petition. "The investigation response to this contains an original wording—they say, take our word for it, that this [what Safronov did] cannot be done," the lawyer said. (quote from BBC).

None of the above prevented the court from sentencing Ivan Safronov to 22 years.

More details about the miracles in the case of Ivan Safronov can be found here. In general, you can read about the violation of the right to defense here.

We also mentioned the order of the Ministry of Internal Affairs of September 12, 2013, No. 705-dsp "On certain issues of departures of police officers, federal state civil servants and employees of the Russian Ministry of Internal Affairs system for private affairs outside the territory of the Russian Federation," which prohibit ordinary police officers from traveling abroad. So his text is completely classified. The police tried to somehow appeal against it, but the Supreme Court rejected the complaint about the illegality of this order.

We also talked about citizen tracking systems, in particular, the Surveillance Control system. The human rights organization, Agora, points out: "[In] the "Wanted-Mainway" system, which includes (1) persons wanted by Interpol; (2) foreigners suspected of committing crimes in Russia; (3)

foreigners who are restricted from entering Russia; (4) persons suspected of certain serious or severe offenses: illegal transportation of weapons, ammunition or explosives, illegal transportation of antiques or their smuggling out of the Russian Federation, premeditated murder, acts of terrorism, drug trafficking, financial crimes; (5) leaders of ethnic communities, leaders and active members of organized criminal groups. The order on the creation and operation of the base "Rozysk-magistral" has never been published.

"In 2005, this database was supplemented with a section that included information about potential extremists. The section was given the code name Surveillance. The Government of the Russian Federation provided the European Court with an affidavit from a police officer, from which it followed that **the decision to enter the name of an individual in the database is made by the Ministry of Internal Affairs or its regional division based on confidential** **information**" (from here, page 7).

The absence of an officially published order significantly hinders the understanding of its content and appeal, which of course, leads to the arbitrariness of the security forces.

These examples are enough to say that Article 24 is fully non-operational.

ARTICLE 25 OF THE CONSTITUTION

The Articles sounds like this: "The dwelling shall be inviolable. Nobody shall have the right to enter a dwelling place against the will of those residing therein, except in those cases provided for by federal laws or on the basis of a court order."

Dwelling here is understood in a broad sense: any place where a person lives, regardless of the characteristics of the premises (say, a tent is also a 'dwelling' within the meaning of this article).

In theory, the security forces have the right to enter the dwelling without the permission of the owner only if they have a court sanction (an analog of the Western "warrant") or there is reason to suspect that a crime is taking place there, or the pursued criminal has run into the dwelling.

In practice, breaking into homes and searches have become extremely common and are often carried out without a court warrant, and are carried out for pressure, intimidation, and banal robbery.

The report of the Institute of Law and Public Policy entitled "Search, examination, examination: human rights and the interests of the investigation" notes:

"Russian courts satisfy about 96% of the requests of the investigating authorities for searches, inspections, and examinations (the courts copy the requests of law enforcement agencies without requesting additional material and without specifying the subjects of the search). At the same time, both at the preliminary stage and during the subsequent control of the legality of searches, the courts do not emphasize that by doing so, they sanction the most restrictive and psychologically oppressive investigative action. They do not assess the grounds and proportionality of the interference with the rights of citizens and very rarely recognize searches as illegal, thereby neglecting constitutional rights ...

"Since a search requires a criminal case, the Russian investigation increasingly uses two other procedures for operational-search activity. Inspection and examination of the premises are only minimally regulated, but they allow the investigating authorities to do almost everything they do during a search. The boundaries between these procedures in law, science, and legal practice are not clearly drawn. Police officers are almost never charged with abuse of power when, instead of, for example, conducting an inspection, they search, declaring the place of the search as an "accident scene."

""Examination" is becoming even more popular with the investigating authorities. This procedure can be carried out on anonymous requests and unverified operational information. Only 18% of examinations end with the initiation of cases, while the number of illegal seizures of property and documents is increasing. There are almost no restrictions on the conduct of examinations and inspections by the investigating authorities, and in fact, these procedures cannot be distinguished from a search (for example, in all these cases, the investigating authorities prohibit movement, communication, and use of communications).

"The procedures of operational-search activity (examination and inspection) gave law enforcement agencies the opportunity to actually conduct searches without initiating a criminal case, according to an unclear procedure, and without the ability to appeal against them quickly and according to clear rules. This substitution is against the law and violates the rights of citizens and organizations."

The most terrible incident that shocked the public was a search at the home of journalist, Irina Slavina.

"On October 1 [2020], searches were carried out at Slavina's house. "Today at 6:00 am, 12 people entered my apartment with a petrol cutter and a crowbar: employees of the TFR, police, SOBR, witnesses," she wrote on Facebook. According to Slavina, the security forces were looking for materials related to Open Russia [another media outlet persecuted in Russia - A.M.]. According to her, she was not allowed to call a lawyer.

"They took what they found—all flash drives, my laptop, my daughter's laptop, computer, phones—not only mine, but also my husband's—a bunch of my notebooks, on which I scribbled during press conferences," the journalist wrote.

"Thank you for allowing my husband to take medicine because he survived a severe stroke and takes drugs for life. Fortunately, no force was used on us; otherwise, it is not known what it would have resulted in for her husband's health," she said on the eve of her suicide in conversation with "Nn.ru." (BBC quote)

At the same time, Slavina was not even accused in the case! She was in the status of a "witness." This is, in principle, Russian "legal" know-how—to conduct searches of witnesses.

As a result of this "search," everything on which she earned money was confiscated from Slavina: she was a journalist, and in the modern world, it is impossible for a journalist to work without the appropriate equipment. And without work, she could not earn money for new equipment.

As a result, on October 2, 2020, she committed self-immolation. Before her suicide, Irina wrote a post on Facebook with the words, "I ask you to blame the Russian Federation for my death."

As you can guess, there was no investigation into the persons who conducted the search at Irina's place. The Nizhny Novgorod Department of the Investigative Committee stated, "There was no connection between the search and the suicide."

According to Novaya Gazeta, if in 2007 the courts granted 155.8 thousand requests for a search or inspection in a residential building, then in 2020, 212.7 thousand. Searches may not occur immediately after the issuance of a permit, but assuming that law enforcement searches an equal number of apartments each day, Russia experiences an average of about 600 searches daily.

As you might guess, there are no prerequisites for reducing the number of searches.

Accordingly, Article 25 of the Russian Constitution is also invalid.

ARTICLE 26 OF THE CONSTITUTION

The full text of the article looks like this:

"1. Everyone shall have the right to determine and declare his (her) nationality. Nobody shall be forced to determine and declare his (her) nationality.

2. Everyone shall have the right to use his (her) native language and to a free choice of the language of communication, upbringing, education and creative work."

We have already passed an article prohibiting discrimination based on many grounds, including nationality (Article 19 of the Constitution). Why was a separate article needed, which in its meaning is not of particular importance if the rights of different nationalities were equally respected? Here, we must remember the history. In the days of the USSR, nationality was directly indicated in the passport. This greatly complicated the lives of representatives of some races, Jews, Gypsies, etc.

In the logic of the founders of the Constitution, if a person does not indicate his nationality, then he will not be persecuted for this reason. However, it seems to me that this logic is somewhat crooked. It resembles the situation with gays and lesbians: it seems like everything is fine before "coming out" and the "don't ask, don't tell" system.

The critical problem is that although the person may not indicate his nationality, the authorities can do this for him.

That there is discrimination, we said earlier. At that time, I deliberately left out discrimination based on nationality. And now, we are going to address this issue in more detail.

In principle, xenophobia is one of the main features of fascism (the fifth point in Umberto Eco's "signs of fascism" we cited earlier), and Russia, under the system created by Putin, could not help but bypass it.

To some extent, it is surprising how many derogatory nicknames of other nationalities were created in Russia! Rodents (Georgians), Khokhols (Ukrainians), Khachi (some unifying "term" for all representatives of the Caucasus), Dzhamshuts (for guest workers from Central Asia (from the character of the 2000s comedy show 'Nasha Russia'—Dzhamshut)), Chukchi (although there is such a nationality, its name is often used as a negative label, denoting naive, gullible and narrow-minded people), Azeris (for Azerbaijanis), and of course Pindos (Americans), Gayropeans (for all representatives of European countries), frog-eaters (especially for the French), pasta lovers (and this is for the Italians), psheks and lakhs (for the Poles), kitaezy (narrow-eyed) (for the Chinese and, in principle, people from East Asia), jids (of course, for the Jews, where without hatred for them?), etc. (You can read about the history of the issue here, and here you can find a complete list).

Again, this could be considered some feature of the language and communication if the state had not deliberately cultivated natural xenophobia.

Certain peaks of hatred coincided depending on who Russia declared its enemy. So, in the 90s through to the early 2000s, all hatred was concentrated on the Chechens, whose houses at that time Russia leveled to the ground; in the late 2000s, on the Georgians; in 2010, the peak fell on Ukrainians and Americans, a little later, propaganda also coined a special term Anglo-Saxons, having made a mistake with the relevance of about 1500 years. It is strange that the Visigoths and Vandals do not arouse so much hatred in propaganda. On the other hand, blaming propaganda for inaccuracies in terms is entirely useless.

Hatred frankly pours from the TV screens:

Here, propagandist Kiselev proposes to turn the United States into radioactive ashes.

Here is the well-known propagandist, Solovyov, talking about the Chechens.

Here, another propagandist, Krasovsky, calls for drowning or burning Ukrainian children.

And these videos are more than enough. None of the propagandists responsible for their hateful speeches was even fired.

Against the backdrop of the war in Georgia, the authorities organized real persecution of Georgians, up to checks on students in schools.

It should be noted that anti-Georgian propaganda began long before the war with Georgia in 2008 and most likely prepared public opinion for an inevitable armed conflict and Human Rights Watch report on the subject.

The interesting point is that the authorities persecute Russian nationalists in the same way as oppositionists—that is, with all the might of the repressive apparatus. You can read more about this here. It is unclear whether these are the remnants of the understanding that any hatred leads only to destructive results or the Russian authorities' harsh rejection of everything it does not control. But in the end, it turns out a paradox that in Russia, there is hatred for everything foreign, but radical nationalist "Russian" organizations are persecuted in the same way. This probably happened due to Putin's actual lack of any principles and ideas. He uses hatred to divide groups of people and divert their attention from the real issues. In this vein, the built-in estates of Russian society do not allow the lower classes to take a more advantageous position without Putin's desire. But the conditional group of "Russian nationalists" has nothing to offer him in the form of services or money as this is a relatively marginal and little influential group of scumbags. As a result, their speech is suppressed equally with speeches against the authorities.

Against all this, propaganda endows Russians with a unique "spirituality" inherent only to Russians. In the best traditions of any fascist state, "spirituality" is that property that makes Russians better than any other people and allows them to accuse, give advice, and dictate their will. Dissertations are even being written on this topic (see, for example, here, here, here and here). In her view, Russia is the only island of some exceptional purity, which is opposed to the "spiritless West," in which, for some reason, gays have some rights! What this "spirituality" is expressed in, apart from homophobia, is not entirely clear. Of those values inherent in all people (family, love, and others), Russians historically had only one thing that Europeans did not have, 'snokhachestvo'—the cohabitation of a father with his son's wife, his daughter-in-law. But for some reason, it seems to me that it is not because of this that Russian thought declared Russians unique and sublime. Therefore, in order to somehow separate their "spirituality" from European "spiritless," the central thesis was the rejection of "European values implanted by the hostile West": freedom of speech, freedom of rallies, democracy, and so on. According to the theorists of "Russian spirituality," these are all immoral things, and any adherent of them is an immoral person and is a priori an enemy of Russia.

The right to determine one's nationality was violated even by Putin himself (who would have thought, right?). In his pseudo-historical article — worthy of a loser who barely learned to write and is not versed in history —

"On the historical unity of Russians and Ukrainians," he generally denies the nationality of Ukrainians. He directly says that there are no such people, and all Ukrainians are Russians; therefore, they are destined to "reunite" with Russia, gaining "historical justice." This pseudo-historical nonsense is not only a direct violation of the commented article, and led Putin to unleash an aggressive war in Ukraine.

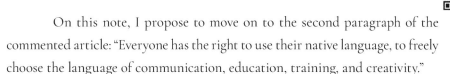

You can read more about nationalism in Russia here.

On this note, I propose to move on to the second paragraph of the commented article: "Everyone has the right to use their native language, to freely choose the language of communication, education, training, and creativity."

The language serves as a continuation of the leading national idea in Russia. Indeed, there are a lot of nationalities in Russia. Still, they all speak Russian in one way or another (considering that, in accordance with the law on the "Official language in the Russian Federation" dated June 1, 2005 No. 53-FZ, this is the only state language in which all official office work is carried out, this is not surprising).

The law establishes Russian as the state language and indicates that the republics in the country have the right to develop their state languages, which are used along with the state language of the Russian Federation. At the same time, the right of the republics to establish their state languages does not mean the right of national minorities to the state status of their languages, which in many cases leads to a violation of their linguistic rights. In particular, in the Republic of Karelia, the state status of the Karelian language is not recognized, despite the insistence of the Karelian population itself.

Despite the lack of direct consolidation in the Constitution of the right of autonomous okrugs and autonomous regions to establish their state languages, these subjects of the Russian Federation establish the official status of these languages by their charters and laws. However, as a rule, in the subjects of the Russian Federation, only Russian is the only official language.

As we can see, the language issue is strongly distorted towards the "republics" that are part of Russia (Tatarstan, Adygea, Kalmykia, etc.).

However, it is not without incidents. Thus, the Supreme Court of the Republic of Adygea, considering the statement of the Deputy Prosecutor of the Republic of Adygea that "the mandatory consolidation of the obligation to study the Adyghe language by schoolchildren contradicts parts 1 and 2 of Article 9 of the Law on the Languages of the Peoples of Russia, which establishes the right of citizens of Russia to freely choose the language of education and training, noted following.

The requirement to study the Adyghe language for students of Adyghe and the introduction of the Adyghe language as a compulsory subject cannot be given an imperative character since this leads to a violation of the principles of equality of rights and freedoms of a person and a citizen guaranteed by the Constitution of the Russian Federation and the fulfillment by citizens of Russia of equal duties throughout its territory, including in relation to the realization of the right to education, and linguistic rights and freedoms.

The introduction by the law of the subject of the Russian Federation of the requirement for the critical study of the national language of the republic, even if it is also the state language, is not provided for by federal legislation and violates its legislation on education, the obligation to study the Adyghe language by Adyghe students, which infringes and limits the rights of citizens in their language and nationality.

Taking into account the analysis of the current legislation, the court considered that the requirements of the prosecutor in the above part were justified. And admitted paragraph 5 of Article 6 of the Law of the Republic of Adygea No. 156 "On education" as invalid (Decision of the Supreme Court of the Republic of Adygea dated December 19, 2006 No. 3-32/2006 "On invalidating part 5 of article 6 of the Law of the Republic of Adygea dated 06.01.2000 No. 156 "On education." Soviet Adygea, No. 11, 23.01.2007).

Often, the Russian authorities use language as the basis for their crimes. Thus, the Ukrainian Crimea and Donbas were seized precisely under the pretext of protecting the "Russian speakers" from phantom oppression, in this case, Ukrainians (there were similar cases in the Baltic countries, but so far, there has been no military intervention). Why did Russian authorities and propaganda use such a strange term? Because these same "Russian speakers" were neither citizens of Russia, nor even Russians, they just spoke Russian. Agreeing to "protect" the citizens of another country does not sound like "protection" of "ours" who speak the same language.

Ironically, it is precisely the spread of the Russian language and culture that is harmed by such a policy since all countries with a large spread of the Russian language among their populations have been hit by such a sudden "liberation."

Also, in 2018, the Russian authorities took several actions regarding books in the Ukrainian language. It even reached the point that the director of the Library of Ukrainian Literature was arrested and tried for extremism and "inciting hatred using official position," and the library itself was closed (here and here). Even if we now admit for a second that the director was engaged in giving access to "extremist literature," the question still arises of why the library itself had to be closed.

Based on the above, we can conclude that Article 26 is also consistently violated.

ARTICLE 27 OF THE CONSTITUTION

"1. Everyone who is legally present on the territory of the Russian Federation shall have the right to travel freely and freely to choose the place of temporary or permanent residence.

2. Everyone may freely leave the Russian Federation. Citizens of the Russian Federation shall have the right freely to return to the Russian Federation."

The article, as you understand, concerns freedom of movement. Historically, in the USSR, there was an institution of 'propiska': a person was obliged to live in a specific place, which was "signed" in his passport. Remember that in the USSR, there was no right of private ownership of real estate; it all belonged to the state. So the absence of a person outside the place of registration for more than six months could serve as a basis for his eviction.

In Russia, the situation has changed slightly since the emergence of ownership of real estate. Still, the 'propiska' institution became very convenient for the authorities, and the institution of "registration" replaced it.

There are still a lot of rights attached to the registration. These relations are regulated by the law with the ironic title "On the right of citizens of the Russian Federation to freedom of movement, choice of place of stay and residence within the Russian Federation" (Law of the Russian Federation of June 25, 1993, N 5242-1). Its essence is quite simple: "We guarantee you freedom of movement by establishing an institution of control over your movement and place of residence."

Although the original version of this law contained the phrase "registration does not affect rights and obligations," it soon became clear that the phrase itself destroyed the built system and was removed.

Among the rights that depend on registration are: the right to receive medical care (many require registration to go to the local clinic; the situation has improved somewhat recently when it has become sufficient to present a health insurance policy), the right to education (especially for preschool and school education), etc.

There is even a fine for not having a residence permit (Article 19.15.1 of the Code of Administrative Offenses).

Why does the state need it? For control, of course. This free man can move and live wherever he wants, while the slave has a collar with a bell so that he does not get lost. On the registration, among other things, tax accounting and military registration are tied (which, in connection with the unleashed war, has become very important).

A separate issue was with the owners of the apartments. I'll explain a little. "Residential premises" in Russia are recognized as premises directly intended for living. The list of properties that such a room should have can be found here. In terms of cost, such premises are, of course, much more expensive than non-residential ones. In a situation where the population is quite poor, to increase demand, some developers do not transfer some premises to the category of "residential," selling the so-called "apartments" — premises, although formally not residential, intended for living. The owners of the apartments have been breaking spears in the courts for many years to obtain the very "registration at the place of residence" to remove restrictions on some of their rights (which we discussed above) but to no avail.

However, in connection with the mobilization by Putin, I think this unwillingness of the state to register residence in apartments ironically helped their owners a lot.

You can read more about registration here.

Let us now turn to the second paragraph of Article 27 of the Constitution. And again, I want to tell you where this norm came from. Of course, it arose as a reaction to the policy of the USSR in the field of travel abroad. For a person to leave the USSR, he had to get a reference from his place of work and apply for an exit (sic!) visa. For many reasons, few citizens could even go to the countries of the "Eastern Block," not to mention the Western countries. And in most cases, the family members couldn't leave; they remained hostages in case of non-return.

Of course, this practice was the first to be abandoned during the collapse of the USSR. However, the desire to control the movement of their citizens and not let them see how the "decaying West" actually lives remained.

We spoke about one case (and more than once)—restrictions on the exit of ordinary police officers who do not even have access to state secrets. We said that they were prohibited from leaving by order of the Ministry of Internal Affairs of September 12, 2013 No. 705-dsp "On Certain Issues of Departure of Police Officers, Federal State Civil Servants and Employees of the Ministry of Internal Affairs of Russia on Private Matters Outside the Territory of the Russian Federation." The text of the order itself is classified. Given its unconstitutionality under several articles of the Constitution (as we said, the very existence of such a secret decree contradicts Article 24 of the Constitution of the Russian Federation), its secrecy is logically justified. As we remember, however, the Supreme Court rejected the complaint about the illegality of this order.

This article's second block of violation is the prohibition on the departure of debtors. As an incentive to fulfill obligations, among the restrictions that the court may impose on the debtor is a ban on such a debtor leaving the border of the Russian Federation. I want to note that within the meaning of Articles 16 and 18 of the Constitution, no legal action can serve either to violate the Constitution or to diminish the rights granted by this Constitution. The right to leave is unconditional and unlimited. To make it dependent on obligations (according to the type of transaction)—you are for me, I am for you—is legal nonsense. With the same success, it is possible to condition other constitutional rights, such as the right to life or freedom (not far from debtors' prisons).

But in a sense, this is true; the Russian authorities, in principle, have conditioned all human rights and freedoms by loyalty to themselves. If you don't oppose the authorities, you have more rights; if you don't like something, the authorities take these rights away.

That is why the existence of Article 67 of the Law "On Enforcement Proceedings" is so dangerous. Yes, it was adopted to facilitate the work of bailiffs, but at the expense of the constitutional rights of citizens, which also violates the provisions and paragraph 3 of Article 17 of the Constitution.

The third group of violations of paragraph 2 of Article 27 is the unlawful obstruction to the movement of the opposition. We also touched on this earlier when we talked about shadowing the opponent.

For example, in September 2014, Pussy Riot members Nadezhda Tolokonnikova and Maria Alyokhina reported problems with passport control at Sheremetyevo.

The human rights organization Agora in the same report on surveillance of oppositionists and journalists, states: "In September 2014, some delegates to the UN World Conference on Indigenous Issues were unable to fly to New York. For example, the director of the Center for Assistance to the Indigenous Peoples of the North, Rodion Sulyandziga, was not allowed out of the country, citing the invalidity of his passport—handing over the document to the border guard, Sulyandziga received it back with a page cut out.

"The car of the chairman of the Saami Parliament of the Kola Peninsula, Valentina Sovkina, who was heading from Lovozero (Murmansk region) to Kirkenes airport (Norway), was stopped three times for inspection by traffic police without drawing up any protocols. During one of the stops, a young man attacked Sovkina, knocking her to the ground and trying to snatch the bag from her hands. Everything happened in front of the police officers, who failed to protect the woman and prevented her driver from detaining the attacker. On the attack on Sovkina, a criminal case was even initiated under the article of attempted robbery; however, for a year and a half, the culprit was never identified. Given the circumstances, Sovkina has no doubts that the purpose of the attack was to take away her bag with her passport, thereby eliminating the possibility of crossing the border, and the attacker was a law enforcement officer.

"Another Russian delegate to the conference had her front door sealed with glue, so she couldn't get into her apartment and missed her plane. The director of the International Fund for Research and Support of the Indigenous Peoples of Crimea, Nadir Bekirov, was confiscated by unidentified people in balaclavas on the street on the eve of the flight" (from here).

Based on the above, I believe that I was able to show that Article 27 of the Constitution also does not work.

ARTICLE 28 OF THE CONSTITUTION

The full text of the article reads:

"Everyone shall be guaranteed freedom of conscience and religion, including the right to profess individually or collectively any religion or not to profess any religion, and freely to choose, possess and disseminate religious and other convictions and act in accordance with them."

Freedom of conscience means that a person has the right to profess some religion and not to profess any.

We had already touched on the religious question earlier when we discussed the equality of organizations. Let's freshen it up a bit.

There are two points here: the attitude towards atheists and believers of other religions than historical Orthodoxy.

Despite the presumption that any opinion and belief about God (gods) is equal, within the meaning of this article of the Constitution, the Russian authorities believe, almost according to Ludwig Feuerbach (see his

"Essence of Christianity"), that a people have some special "religious feeling" that distinguishes it from animals. Accordingly, whoever is not religious is a priori less developed than the same "spiritual person." Stating this, the Russian authorities defended these "religious feelings" by amending the criminal code (remember, they were introduced immediately after the Pussy Riot punk prayer on the pulpit of the Cathedral of Christ the Savior "Mother of God, drive Putin away" in 2012). However, by highlighting such feelings and endowing them with special protection, the authorities violate the principle of equality and the principle of a secular state.

This was manifested in the same trial of Maria Alekhina (one of the participants in this very punk prayer), at which the "court" quoted the canons of the Trullo Cathedral (sic!) (691-692 AD, Constantinopol), turning this political case into some kind of crazy inquisitorial performance.

According to the authorities' plan, the rule on insulting the feelings of believers was supposed to stop any criticism of the Russian Orthodox Church (ROC). However, it turned out exactly the opposite and showed the hypocrisy of the ROC itself. In theory, the main strength of Christianity was in forgiveness. Some not very famous to Russian Orthodox Church citizen, Jesus Christ, in his Sermon on the Mount (unauthorized, we note, by the local authorities), called in response to a slap in the face to turn the other cheek. But, as I understand

it, this mister is not a great authority for the Russian Orthodox Church, which initiated the transfer of "insulting the feelings of believers" from the Code of Administrative Violations to the Criminal Code.

In this regard, the Russians have created many memes. For example, see fig. 1.

In itself, the trial of Pussy Riot was completely legal and even logical nonsense. If a person is a genuine Christian, he cannot write a statement on a person for insulting his religious feelings precisely because of the canons of Christianity about forgiveness—"forgive them, as they do not know what they are doing." Suppose such a "believer" wrote a statement. In that case, he is not a real Christian, and this fact should already serve as a basis for dismissing the accusation since non-believers do not have these very "special religious feelings." But when did such obscure things like logic stop the Russian authorities?

The very recognition of "religious feelings," which the state is eager to protect, puts believers and non-believers in an unequal position, which contradicts the meaning of this article. However, the problem does not end there.

Гр. И. Христос в момент совершения преступления предусмотренного ст. 148 ч.2 УК РФ. Художественная реконструкция гр. Джованни Франческо Барбьери.

Fig. 1. Mr. J.Crist in the moment of committing a Criminal offense under point 2 Article 148 of Russian Criminal Code. Artistic reconstruction by Mr. Giovanni Francesco Barbieri.

We have also already discussed that authorities treat beliefs and cults differently. It openly helps the ROC, including direct funding and patronage.

But it also directly prohibits other religions, as in the case of Jehovah's Witnesses (you can remember this in more detail by referring to our analysis of Article 14 of the Constitution).

In total, the activities of 26 religious groups and organizations are prohibited in Russia. This alone puts an end to whether this article is observed or not.

The head of the US State Department, Anthony Blinken, named Russia among 10 countries where systematic and "egregious" violations of religious freedom are allowed.

"In Russia, out of 89 organizations recognized as extremist, 26 are churches, religious groups, and associations.

Only against the followers of the Church of Jehovah's Witnesses, 262 criminal cases were initiated, 570 believers were charged, 31 people were under house arrest, and 73 were in custody. Several Jehovah's Witnesses have been imprisoned for eight years.

 Svetlana Solodovnik, head of the religious section of the Daily Journal, believes that Russia's place on the "black list" is well deserved. In her opinion, the State Department, in this case, cannot be accused of bias. "In recent years, we have seen large-scale persecution of Jehovah's Witnesses and Muslim movements that do not deserve such treatment," added the source of the Voice of America Russian Service. "And the fact that all Protestant nominations today are under quite strong pressure is also an obvious fact."

"In turn, **Alexander Soldatov**, a religious observer and editor-in-chief of the Credo.Press information and analytical Internet portal noted that Russia took place in the anti-rating, which "largely corresponds to." According to him, entire religious denominations are banned in the country, which has long been a big question for the international human rights community.

"Statistics show that the number of criminal cases and sentences related to a confession of faith is only growing over time," he stressed. "Another thing is that, due to the specifics of Russian legislation, it is difficult for me to give assessments or call for measures that seem to follow the promulgated decision (of the State Department - V.V.)."

Meanwhile, the Plenum of the Supreme Court (SC) of Russia recently ruled that religious meetings of believers are not a criminal offense, despite the liquidation of legal entities of confessions. The Supreme Court clarified that the ban on religious organizations does not mean a ban on freedom of conscience and religion, including the joint practice of religion or worship. Supreme Court rulings are binding on lower courts.

However, Alexander Soldatov thinks that the decision of the Supreme Court will have little effect in practice. The religious scholar recalled that this is not the first ruling regulating the enforcement of Russian extremist legislation: "There was also a corresponding ruling of the Supreme Court in 2010, and it was poorly implemented, which I experienced from my own experience. I was the defendant in the case of recognizing materials as extremist, and in my case, this decision did not work."

Here, you can read in detail about the state of affairs in connection with freedom of religion in Russia.

And finally, the cherry on the cake. Explaining the reason for the aggression against Ukraine, Aleksey Pavlov, Assistant Secretary of the Russian Security Council, said that the next stage of the war against Ukraine should be "de-Satanization."

"I believe that with the continuation of the "special military operation" [the war in Ukraine - A.M.], it becomes more and more urgent to carry out the de-Satanization of Ukraine, or, as the head of the Chechen Republic Ramzan Kadyrov aptly put it, its "complete de-Shaitanization."

He claims that in Ukraine, "hundreds of sects are operating, sharpened for a specific goal and flock." Pavlov is especially concerned about the "Church of Satan," which allegedly "spread across Ukraine" and "is one of the religions officially registered in the USA."

Yes, yes, that's exactly what this fool thinks a secular state that respects all beliefs and religions looks like (not to mention the apparent archaism in the form of a crusade in the 21st century). You can feel from such speeches the level of education and intellectual development (better yet, degradation) of Putin's advisers.

On this, I should conclude that Article 28 of the Constitution is also not observed by the Russian authorities. Moreover, the authorities deliberately use religious motives to justify their crimes, singling out "correct" and "incorrect" religions. You can delve deeper into the issue from the links above. In the meantime, we will begin to study the most (spoiler) violated article in the Constitution.

ARTICLE 29 OF THE CONSTITUTION

The full text of the article looks like this:

"1. Everyone shall be guaranteed freedom of thought and speech.

2. Propaganda or agitation, which arouses social, racial, national or religious hatred and hostility shall be prohibited. Propaganda of social, racial, national, religious or linguistic supremacy shall also be prohibited.

3. Nobody shall be forced to express his thoughts and convictions or to deny them.

4. Everyone shall have the right freely to seek, receive, transmit, produce and disseminate information by any legal means. The list of types of information, which constitute State secrets, shall be determined by federal law.

5. The freedom of the mass media shall be guaranteed. Censorship shall be prohibited."

This article can be divided into three substantial parts: 1) freedom to freely express any thoughts and speak in any form (freedom of speech); 2) a ban on hate speech—words that excite hatred and enmity; 3) freedom of the media and lack of censorship. Points 3 and 4 are practically a paraphrase of points 1 and 5.

In my opinion, this is the most violated article of the Constitution by the authorities. The Russian government is long and stubbornly fought any independent view, regardless of how it is expressed.

If you remember the story about the formation of the legal system under Putin, you may remember that the first thing he started with when he became president was the liquidation of independent media, the establishment of total censorship, and the direct persecution of any dissenters or even journalists who show the inside out deceitful and thieving power.

In Russia, there are many laws that, in one way or another, restrict the expression of one's thoughts, up to and including criminal prosecution for individual words.

This is where we will start.

On February 24, 2022, Putin launched an aggressive war against Ukraine. He, as a cowardly person and, besides, a KGB officer, called it a "special military operation." The word "war" has become taboo. I want to note that Russian legislation has no concept of "special military operation" at all. But there is a word "war." In particular, Article 353 of the Russian Criminal Code provides responsibility for starting and waging an aggressive war. And Article 354 of the Criminal Code provides criminal liability for its incitement. The concept of "aggression" is defined by international documents; in particular, it is defined in General Assembly resolution 3314 (XXIX) of December 14, 1974.

In particular, in Article 1:

"Aggression is the use of armed force by a State against the sovereignty, territorial integrity or political independence of another State, or in any other manner inconsistent with the Charter of the United Nations, as set out in this Definition."

And in Article 3:

"Any of the following acts, regardless of a declaration of war, shall, subject to and in accordance with the provisions of article 2, qualify as an act of aggression:

(a) The invasion or attack by the armed forces of a State of the territory of another State, or any military occupation, however temporary, resulting from such invasion or attack, or any annexation by the use of force of the territory of another State or part thereof;

(b) Bombardment by the armed forces of a State against the territory of another State or the use of any weapons by a State against the territory of another State;

(c) The blockade of the ports or coasts of a State by the armed forces of another State;

(d) An attack by the armed forces of a State on the land, sea or air forces, or marine and air fleets of another State;

(e) The use of armed forces of one State which are within the territory of another State with the agreement of the receiving State, in contravention of the conditions provided for in the agreement or any extension of their presence in such territory beyond the termination of the agreement;

(f) The action of a State in allowing its temtory, which it has placed at the disposal of another State, to be used by that other State for perpetrating an act of aggression against a third State;

(g) The sending by or on behalf of a State of armed bands, groups, irregulars or mercenaries, which carry out acts of armed force against another State of such gravity as to amount to the acts listed above, or its substantial involvement therein."

I remind you that Putin held shameful "referendums" on the annexation of some parts of Ukraine: Crimea, Zaporizhzhia, Lugansk, Donetsk, and Kherson regions and officially put them into the Constitution of Russia as its subjects.

It is not surprising that Putin and his accomplices are so concerned that the war is not called by its name.

 As a result, the very word "war" became a criminal offense. It is somewhat amusing that even the well-known slogan "peace to the world," which is the opposite meaning of the word "war," is also punished since it involves protests against military actions.

The authorities, in principle, considerably tightened repressions with the outbreak of war with Ukraine. They conduct searches and arrests and give real terms to people who oppose it.

The most egregious case was the conviction of municipal deputy Alexei Gorinov to seven years in prison for (evaluate Orwellianism) "spreading fakes about the Russian army." On March 15, 2022, during an open meeting of the council of deputies of the district, Gorinov made several statements "containing untrue data about the Armed Forces of the Russian Federation."

At the trial, a meeting recording was provided, including a five-minute excerpt in which Gorinov argues with another deputy about holding a competition for children's drawings. Gorinov suggested that during the war, such a competition would look like a "feast during the plague." He was supported by the Municipal deputy, Elena Kotenochkina; she also became a defendant in a criminal case but managed to leave Russia.

You can read more on the issue of prosecution of people for anti-war statements here.

It should be noted that persecution for expressing opinions began well before 2022. At that moment, the system generally ceased to reckon with the law, logic, and people's rights.

We have already mentioned a number of issues for which the authorities are persecuting people: LGBT "propaganda" (Remember? "Statements that imply the equality of traditional and non-traditional relationships"), insulting the "feelings of believers," criticism of the authorities and journalistic investigations about corruption. For this, the authorities long and stubbornly prosecuted Navalny and his associates, depriving him of almost all the rights provided for by the Constitution. But, of course, he is not the only one who is persecuted by the authorities for these reasons. For example, Ivan Safronov was sentenced to 22 years for his open-source investigation of the Defense Ministry embezzlement (which we mentioned earlier).

It is not only investigators and the opposition who are being persecuted; even the people who like and reposts their posts on social networks are persecuted!

Human rights groups "Agora" and "Roskomsvoboda" published a report on persecution for opinions on the Internet. You can see it here (and here is the full text of the report).

They point out: "In 2019, international human rights organizations again noted the tightening of Internet censorship and the worsening situation for journalists.

"In the Press Freedom Index published by Reporters Without Borders (RSF), Russia fell from 148th to 149th place out of 180 countries, and the country's rating deteriorated by 0.34 points. According to RSF, the situation in

Russia is worse than in Venezuela, Cambodia, and Palestine but better than in Belarus, Turkey, and Azerbaijan.

"According to the Freedom on the Net 2019: The Crisis of Social Media annual report prepared by the non-governmental organization Freedom House, with a score of 31 out of 100, Russia remains in the group of 21 countries with non-free Internet for the fifth year in a row along with China, Saudi Arabia, Cuba, and Sudan. At the same time, the organization's experts consider the presence in the country of blocked social networks, Internet services, and individual sites, the activity of pro-government Internet commentators, and the arrests of users.

"We state that the general course toward establishing total state control over information, users, and communication networks remain unchanged. Laws on "internet isolation," "fake news," and "disrespect for authority" came into force. Once again, officials threatened to block VPN services, Twitter and Facebook, and to "finally" resolve the issue with Telegram.

"Several new trends that have developed in 2019 clearly demonstrate the isolationist intentions of the Russian authorities. First of all, this is the further spread of the practice of regional and local politically motivated shutdowns (Internet Government Shutdown is a deliberate disconnection from the Network or other electronic means of communication, which makes them inaccessible or actually unsuitable for use by a specific group of the population or is usually used to gain control over the flow of information) and increase pressure on IT businesses and software developers, expressed, in particular, in several criminal cases against Internet entrepreneurs, as well as the first censorship of a computer game in the history of Runet.

"One of the mechanisms of isolation is the coercion of the owners of global Internet platforms to cooperate. In the previous report, we assumed the beginning of a real turn of state policy in the field of the Internet towards control over large entities that have access to information about users and a real opportunity to limit the dissemination of information.

"In general, we can say that the repressions in Runet have become less massive but more severe and targeted. The most active critics and opponents of the authorities, public figures, civil activists, and, as it turned out, successful IT entrepreneurs are under threat.

"Moreover, the persecution is not necessarily directly related to Internet activity but can only be used as a formal reason for intimidation or the collection of operational information. An example is the searches at the homes of relatives of the leading Telegram channel Stalingulag and the Twitter and Instagram accounts of the same name Alexander Gorbunov" (from here, p. 5). We note once again how searches are used as a means of intimidation and blackmail.

OVD-Info, Memorial, Network Freedoms, and the Media Rights Defense Center sent an analysis of the situation in Russia to the UN Special Rapporteur on freedom of opinion and expression Irene Khan. Based on this material, the expert will be able to include in his report, paragraphs on the restriction of human rights in Russia to record violations at the international level.

In their document, Russian NGOs recorded the following:

Since February 24, the Russian authorities have blocked more than 5,300 websites (Roskomsvoboda wrote about this here).

The law on "fake news" about the Russian army allows blocking any information that contradicts official information and prosecuting the authors of messages and those who disseminated them. Any information that is not confirmed by official sources is considered "false."

New amendments to several laws relating to the dissemination of information and the media provide additional grounds for blocking or discrediting the RF Armed Forces. In particular, they authorize the Prosecutor General's Office to extrajudicially suspend the activities of the media for up to

6 months, prohibit the activities of foreign media, and block websites without the possibility of unblocking them.

The authorities have begun to actively enforce laws on "foreign agents" (66 new "foreign agents" since the beginning of the "special operation") and "undesirable organizations" against the media; many media outlets have closed or emigrated;

There is a purge of independent sources of information in the country through the adoption of new repressive laws and the arbitrary use of old ones, as a result of which Russians may remain in informational isolation;

New articles in the Criminal Code provide a penalty of up to 4 years in prison in case of repeated public display of prohibited symbols (e.g., related to Smart Voting).

The role of social media has changed since February 24. Prior to this, IT giants (Google, Meta, Twitter, etc.) complied with Russian law; for example, in September 2021, Apple and Google LLC removed Navalny's application from their stores), but they reacted negatively to the "special operation." In March, a Russian court found Meta's activities "extremist" and banned Facebook and Instagram in Russia." (Quote from here). The full text of the appeal can be read here.

In June 2017, the human rights organization, Human Rights Watch (HRW), published a report on the problem of freedom of speech in Russia. A study entitled "Online and on all fronts. Assault on Freedom of Expression in Russia" is available here.

Further quote from RBC:

"The Russian government launched a 'massive campaign' against civil society following the mass protests of 2011-2012 and the return of Vladimir Putin to the presidency in May 2012, and restrictions on freedom of speech are part of it, the report says.

"Human rights activists believe that after the mass protests of 2011-2012, the government began to "tighten the screws"—fighting its critics under the guise of fighting extremism and passing laws that restrict freedom of speech and information ...

"Since 2012, human rights activists have recorded a significant increase in the number of allegations of speaking extremism on social networks—under the guise of "fighting extremism," the government persecutes those who criticize it, they say.

"Amendments to the legislation, already adopted or just being considered by the Russian parliament, regulate the content of materials posted on the Web and allow the collection of personal data of users, HRW experts say.

""These laws provide the Russian government with a wide range of tools to restrict access to information and censorship under the guise of fighting extremism," the document says.

"According to the organization, between 2014 and 2016, approximately 85% of convictions for "extremist speech" were for writing online, with penalties ranging from fines or community service to actual jail time. Over the past year and a half alone, from September 2015 to February 2017, the number of people imprisoned for extremist statements has almost doubled, from 54 to 94 people, human rights activists note.

"Among the examples of criminal cases cited by the human rights organization are the case of blogger Ruslan Sokolovsky, the case of blogger from Tyumen Alexei Kungurov, sentenced to two years in prison for criticizing Russia's actions in Syria, the case of Daria Polyudova, who in 2015 received two years in prison on charges of inciting separatism for posting a satirical post on the Vkontakte social network calling for the separation of the Kuban from Russia, and many others.

"Among the laws mentioned by HRW as infringing upon freedom are all the resonant legislative initiatives of recent years.

"These are the bill on the deanonymization of messenger users, the bill on banning VPNs and anonymizer programs, the Yarovaya package, which obliges information dissemination operators to store user data for several months, federal law No. 242-FZ, which obliges companies to store and process personal data of Russian citizens on servers located in Russia, a law prohibiting "gay propaganda" among children (No. 135-FZ).

"The 2014 law "On bloggers," which obliges blog owners with an audience of more than 3 thousand people to register with Roskomnadzor, and the "Lugovoy law" (No. 398-FZ), adopted in 2013, which allows the authorities to 24 hours and without a court order to block online resources that disseminate calls for riots, extremist actions or participation in unauthorized mass events, as well as several other legislative initiatives of recent years.

"A separate report on press freedom was made in 2022 by the public organization Reporters Without Borders (RFS). She published the 2022 World Press Freedom Index report. Russia took 155th place out of 180, worsening its position even in comparison with 2021 by five points.

"The report states that "in Russia itself, the government has taken full control of news and information, imposing extensive censorship for the duration of the war, blocking the media and persecuting unruly journalists, forcing many of them to leave the country." Especially strong pressure on journalists began in 2021 after media workers began to be massively recognized as "foreign agents" and prosecuted for covering the fate of opposition politician Alexei Navalny."

The RFS believes that Russia controls the press beyond its borders.

The Kremlin is imposing its vision of war on some of its neighbors, especially Belarus (153rd), where independent journalists continue to be harassed for their work, and more than 20 media workers languish in prison."

The RSF report recorded Russian pressure on the Central Asian governments on the media to cover the conflict in Ukraine in a more "neutral" way. In Turkmenistan (177th), the press—all controlled by the government—ignores the war in Ukraine."

However, the propagandists themselves acknowledge state control over the press. Thus, the Director General of Russia Today (RT), Margarita Simonyan, openly stated on the official channel "Russia 1" that "no great country can exist without control over information" and subsequently called for the abolition of the ban on censorship in the Constitution.

Human Rights Watch additionally cites evidence of pressure on the media and journalists: "Since December 2020, the number of individuals and legal entities has rapidly increased, recognized as "media-foreign agents". By the beginning of November, there were 94 positions in the corresponding register. As a rule, well-known investigative journalists and independent information resources were included in the register.

In April, the FSB searched the home of Roman Anin, editor-in-chief of Important Stories, who had recently published an investigation into one of the leaders of this special service. That same month, a criminal case was filed against the editors of the independent student magazine DOXA, who were groundlessly accused of involving minors in unsanctioned protests.

In July, the Prosecutor General's Office declared Project Media Inc., the legal entity of the Russian publication Proekt, known for high-profile anti-corruption investigations, to be an "undesirable organization." The editor-in-chief of the Project, Roman Badanin, and four of his journalists were included on the same day in the register of foreign media agents. Shortly before that, a search was conducted at Badanin's apartment, and he himself was brought in as a suspect in a criminal libel case. Employees of the "Project" were evacuated from Russia.

In May, the Ministry of Justice included the legal entity, the administrator of the independent information resource VTimes, into the register of "media-foreign agents." In June, the editorial office announced its closure, citing risks for journalists.

In August, the websites of the media project Open Russia, MBKh Media, and Open Media, as well as the website of the project Human Rights Postcards, were blocked.

In July, police raided the apartments of The Insider editor-in-chief Roman Dobrokhotov and his parents. The searches appear to have been linked to a criminal libel case. In August, Dobrokhotov left Russia. In September, a criminal case was opened against him for illegally crossing the border, as part of which new searches were carried out at his home and at his parents'.

Despite journalists complying with the requirement to wear a vest and press badge, police detained and sometimes used force against journalists covering the protests.

In February, a court in Moscow sentenced Mediazona editor-in-chief Sergei Smirnov to 25 days of administrative arrest for retweeting a comic post that contained information about a rally in support of Navalny.

In January, the amendments came into force, imposing additional restrictions on freedom of expression. One of the amendments allows the authorities to initiate cases of an administrative offense on charges of insult in the absence of the applicant **and the victim** [highlighted by me - A.M.]. Other amendments expanded the criminal offense of "slander." In addition, imprisonment was introduced into the list of sanctions under this article.

Authorities continued to persecute expressions of artistic freedom with critical or high-profile overtones.

In November 2020, Pavel Krisevich received 15 days of administrative arrest for a performance dedicated to political prisoners near the FSB building on Lubyanka. After that, he was expelled from the university. In June, he was detained on Red Square during another political performance dedicated to political prisoners. A criminal case of hooliganism was initiated against him, and at the time of writing this review, Krisevich remained in the pre-trial detention center.

In December 2020, police in Moscow detained Maria Alyokhina and Rita Flores from the punk band Pussy Riot and two other participants in a performance against the police state. Alyokhina also spent several months under house arrest in connection with a social media post supporting the January protest and was sentenced to a year of confinement in September. In June-July, several Pussy Riot activists were repeatedly arrested for up to 15 days on extremely dubious protocols of disobedience to police. Three of the activists left Russia.

In March, civic activist, Karim Yamadayev, was sentenced to a fine for "insulting a government official" and "public calls for terrorist activities" for a video with a mock trial of "Vladimir Putin," "Dmitry Peskov," and "Igor Sechin." Before that, Yamadayev spent more than a year in a pre-trial detention center.

In August, police detained more than two dozen visitors to a street photo exhibition in St. Petersburg. Law enforcement officers were interested in some photographs, including those with words about the police and with the silhouette of church domes. Protocols were drawn up against the organizers for violation of the procedure for organizing and holding public events.

In September, an investigator of the Investigative Committee interviewed the famous actress Liya Akhedzhakova in connection with her character's monologue in the play, perceived by some as an insult to the memory of veterans and propaganda of same-sex relationships. In October, famous rapper, Morgenstern, questioned the need for significant spending on the annual Victory Day celebration in an interview. Shortly after that, the chairman of the Investigative Committee was instructed to conduct a check to see if there were violations of the law in the statements of the perpetrator, as a result of which a criminal case could be initiated. In the same month, the Investigative Committee launched a check in connection with the demonstration of a painting by a St. Petersburg artist, which depicted a crowd of people with portraits of the dead. Those who complained about the work saw an allusion to the action in memory of the Immortal Regiment.

In October, the blogger and his girlfriend were sentenced to 10 months in prison for insulting the feelings of believers for a photograph of simulated oral sex in front of St. Basil's Cathedral. The next day in St. Petersburg, a woman was detained under a similar case, posing in a thong against the backdrop of St. Isaac's Cathedral. The court refused to choose a measure of restraint for her. In 2021, several women received from 2 to 14 days of arrest for obscene performances at police stations and in the Kremlin area.

During the year, authorities expelled or deported foreign nationals whose reporting, criticism, or activism displeased the authorities, including BBC correspondent, Sarah Rainsford, Tajik activist, Saidanvar Sulaymonov (with a 40-year travel ban) ,and Belarusian stand-up comedian, Idrak Mirzalizade. In the latter case, the stand-up comedian was banned for life for a joke that the authorities considered "inciting hatred and enmity towards persons of Russian nationality."

I believe that the given examples and legislative acts are enough to make a confident choice that Article 29 of the Constitution is also de facto not valid.

 Additionally, you can read the Human rights watch report on freedom of speech in Russia.

ARTICLE 30 OF THE CONSTITUTION

"1. Everyone shall have the right of association, including the right to establish trade unions for the protection of his (her) interests. The freedom of activity of public associations shall be guaranteed.

2. Nobody may be compelled to join any association or to stay there."

Again, we touched on this a bit when we talked about equality. Of course, the primary key to the problem lies in the class and the desire of the authorities to suppress civil society.

The authorities directly ban some organizations (like Memorial (which became a Nobel laureate in 2022), or they don't allow the creation of others (like some LGBT organizations or the political party of Alexei Navalny) or recognize them as a "foreign agent" which significantly complicates their activities.

The rationale for this is as varied as it is idiotic. The Human Rights Center "Memorial" was engaged, providing legal assistance, compiling lists, and researching the fate of citizens who were repressed back in Soviet times. Also, the "Memorial" compiles lists of political prisoners in Russia, citizens convicted for their political beliefs.

On December 28, the Supreme Court of Russia satisfied the claim of the General Prosecutor's Office and liquidated the international historical and educational society Memorial, which was included in the register of "foreign agents." The prosecutor's office demanded that Russia's oldest human rights organization be banned because it allegedly violates the law on "foreign agents" and discredits the government. At the final meeting, prosecutor Zhafyarov said that Memorial was creating a "deceitful image of the USSR as a terrorist organization"... Lawyer Henry Reznik, representing International Memorial at the trial, noted that here "everything is turned upside down" and "such political cases are not based on legal considerations and result in unjust decisions."

The next day, the Moscow City Court also liquidated the Memorial Human Rights Center. During the debate, a representative of the prosecutor's office said that the human rights center participated in all protest movements and supported actions aimed at destabilizing the country. Memorial's lists of political prisoners are "aimed at creating a negative perception of the Russian judicial system and misinforming citizens." Before this, the prosecutor's office accused the human rights center of justifying extremism and terrorism and argued that the absence of a "foreign agent" label in Memorial's materials "may cause depression among citizens."

Representatives of gays and lesbians have big problems with self-organization in Russia, as we talked about earlier.

So, on April 21, 2022, a court in St. Petersburg, at the request of the Ministry of Justice, liquidated the Sphere charity foundation, which supports Russian LGBT initiatives. The representative of the Ministry of Justice at the trial stated that the foundation's activities "are aimed at changing the legislation, including the Constitution," and do not correspond to charitable purposes. According to the department, the fund only assists the LGBT community, while the Constitution enshrined "basic traditional family values."

You can read the report on the freedom of non-profit organizations here.

The authorities are not limited to liquidating organizations "according to the results of their activities"; they also prevent their creation.

So, back in 2005, gays and lesbians were denied registration of organizations. And in particular, the organization "Rainbow House" in Tyumen. The reason was that its "members undermine the state security, sovereignty and territorial integrity (sic!) of the Russian Federation **due to the reduction of its population** [emphasis mine - A.M.]". Only in 2019 did the ECtHR finish examining this case and, on July 16, 2019, issued a decision on this issue.

"The court found that the verdicts of the Russian courts to refuse registration contradict the freedom to participate in associations—this applies both to organizations that have submitted relevant applications, and to their founders and chairmen, individual applicants," the ruling says.

The document also clarifies that due to the lack of registration, the Movement for Marriage Equality could not be officially registered as a non-profit organization, and the Rainbow House in Tyumen and the Pride House in Sochi did not receive the status of legal entities.

Well, of course, I remind you of Navalny's attempts to register his political party registration. His associates even reached the Constitutional Court, but without success. This is due to Putin's cowardice: he already participated in regular elections once (remember when he worked in the mayor's office of St. Petersburg for Sobchak?) and lost them. Since then, he has never participated in fair elections and despised them. A favorite question, but a rather silly, of Russian propaganda, was: "If not Putin, then who?" Since, paraphrasing Lenin, any cook would do instead of Putin, his policy is to exclude any opposition from the "elections" completely.

At the moment, the issue of registering Navalny's party is being considered by the ECtHR. However, along with the shameful expulsion of Russia from the Council of Europe, the ECHR is no longer considering cases involving Russia.

Also, in the Russian "legal" field, there is such a thing as "undesirable organizations." If you remember, we mentioned this term in the context of the "Law of scoundrels" — a ban on foreigners from adopting Russian children. In the same "law," the term "undesirable organization" was also introduced. According to the "law," foreign or international non-governmental organizations that "pose a threat to the foundations of the constitutional order" and "the defense capability of the country or the security of the state" fall under the category of "undesirable."

According to the law, "Undesirable" organizations are prohibited from opening structural subdivisions in Russia, distributing their information materials, including on the Internet, and conducting their projects in the country.

Their activities are terminated on the territory of Russia, and, again, out of court (paragraph 4 of Article 3.1 of the Federal Law of December 28, 2012, N 272-FZ (as amended on July 14, 2022) "On measures to influence persons involved in violations of fundamental rights and human freedoms, rights and freedoms of citizens of the Russian Federation." And individuals are immediately under the fear of criminal liability in case of continuation of activities or even for "cooperation" with such an organization (Article 284.1 of the Criminal Code of the Russian Federation).

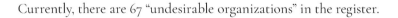

Currently, there are 67 "undesirable organizations" in the register.

In most other cases, the state violates paragraph 1 of article 30 in terms of "non-intervention." Especially now, the authorities stick the label "foreign agent" on any organization and people they simply don't like left and right (more details can be found here). They don't even need a judgment for this.

248

Such a label is not only discrediting and humiliating but greatly complicates the operational activities of the organization: from providing additional reports to paying enormous fines for each sneeze, forcing organizations to liquidate themselves or leave Russia.

In a nutshell, the duties of a person recongized by the Ministry of Justice as a "foreign agent" are:

1. Register a legal entity within one month after being included in the register (note that paragraph 2 of Article 30 of the Constitution is also violated here, which states that "No one can be forced to join or stay in any association").

2. Immediately after the legal entity registration, notify the Ministry of Justice about this. This new legal entity is immediately declared a "legal entity that performs the functions of a foreign agent."

3. Put a note about your status on each message and material, not only on media sites but also on social networks.

4. Once a quarter, submit a detailed report on all your income and expenses to the Ministry of Justice.

5. Once a year, it is necessary to undergo a mandatory audit and submit its results to the Ministry of Justice.

You can read about all the expenses (with amounts) that organizations and individuals incur after receiving such status here. The total mandatory spending is about 234,000 rubles (about $3,200).

There are LGBT activists, journalists (it's very funny that even foreign journalists, for example, Ukrainian ones, are included in the register, in particular, Taras Berezovets was included in this way and Roman Tsymbalyuk; as usual, logic is too hard for degenerate Putin's government), and, of course, oppositionists (since the status of a "foreign agent" a priori prohibits a ban on participation in any elections) and human rights activists. The human rights organization "OVD-info" even made a website with graphics to see all the people recognized as "foreign agents" and sort them according to one feature.

Regarding the effect of paragraph 2 of Article 30 of the Constitution, we have already mentioned it. The "law" obliges individuals, "foreign agents," to forcibly organize legal entities. This is done, of course, in order to simplify control and, possibly, to create additional inconveniences and difficulties. And failure to fulfill the obligation entails criminal liability under Article 330.1 of the Criminal Code of the Russian Federation.

In July 2021, Russia adopted the Federal Law "On the Activities of Foreign Persons in the Internet Information and Telecommunication Network." According to it, foreign IT companies with a daily audience of more than 500,000 users are required to open their branch in Russia, authorized legal entity, or representative office. Of course, this was done for the sole purpose of trying to control supranational IT companies. Opening a branch or legal entity means the Russian authorities can arrest these companies' employees and impose huge fines. In essence, this is a demand by terrorists to provide them with hostages.

I want to note that even though the law is directed at foreign companies, it is a pure violation of clause 2 of article 30 of the Russian Constitution since it was published on the territory of Russia and must not contradict the Constitution. The Constitution applies (in theory) to people who made the law and those who applied it.

Considering the above, we can conclude that Article 30 of the Russian Constitution also does not work.

ARTICLE 31 OF THE CONSTITUTION

The full text of the article:

"1. Citizens of the Russian Federation shall have the right to assemble peacefully, without weapons, hold rallies, mass meetings and demonstrations, marches and pickets."

It is also one of the most violated articles. During the massive rallies in 2012 and 2013 (Report of the International Expert Commission for Evaluating the Events on Bolotnaya Square in Moscow on May 6, 2012), Putin was very frightened. He brutally dispersed them and staged a show trial of random participants. Since then, he has done everything possible to deprive, as much as possible, a hypothetical opportunity for citizens to express any disagreement with the authorities.

Firstly, rallies since then must be coordinated with the authorities. Any spontaneous action, according to Russian law, is illegal.

According to the literal interpretation of Article 7 of the Federal Law of June 19, 2004, N 54-FZ (as amended on December 30, 2020), "On meetings, rallies, demonstrations, marches and pickets," the agreement is of a notification nature. That is, supposedly, the authorities have no right to refuse to hold a rally. The order turned out to be conciliatory; the authorities are doing everything possible not to authorize them.

 You can read more about the coordination of rallies in the OVD-Info report here.

 In 2014, according to the official report of the Commissioner for Human Rights in the Russian Federation, the number of refusals to approve events this year ranged from 8.5% in Yekaterinburg to almost a quarter (23%) in Samara. In March 2016, First Deputy Interior Minister Alexander Gorovoy openly stated: "We have noticed an increase in the number of refusals to hold rallies and demonstrations, and the number of disagreements is increasing."

 Of the reasons for the refusal (sic! - such a fantastic "notification" procedure), OVD-Info cites the following:

- Date of notification (although it was affixed);
- "Wrong" goal of the event;
- Absence of a "picketed" object;
- "Wrong" venue for the event (for bans in certain places (with maps and graphics), see this report);
- "Incorrect" date of the event;
- "Wrong" time of the event;
- Incorrect number (sic!) of expected participants;
- "Inappropriate" organizer. I would especially like to note that among the prohibitions for persons who acted as organizers of a rally, there is a prohibition for such "people whom the court in the recent past found guilty twice of violating the procedure for holding a public event or under some

other administrative articles." This is a direct violation of the unconditional wording of Article 31 of the Constitution.

- "Lack of information about the forms and provision of medical care."

Yekaterinburg journalists carried out an interesting experiment in coordinating various rallies and pickets. They filed notices of 18 pickets in various parts of the city, and none of them was approved on the first try. At the same time, they chose different topics and different places. You can find more details here.

The funny thing is that part 5 of Article 20.2 of the Code of Administrative Violations, which established responsibility for violating the procedure for holding rallies and picketing, was found in 2013 to be inconsistent with the Constitution by the Constitutional Court. However, this paragraph was not only not canceled but is still applied! (you can watch the practice here).

The authorities have even established criminal liability for "violating the rules for holding rallies" (Article 212.1 of the Criminal Code of the Russian Federation).

Any unauthorized rallies are severely suppressed. We have already mentioned this, but I want you to refresh your memory. On January 23, 2021, law enforcement agencies performed arbitrary mass detentions at a peaceful protest in St. Petersburg. A widely circulated video shows a young man being taken away by three officers in special equipment. A woman stands in front of them and asks: "Why did you guys grab him?" In response, one of the police officers kicks her in the stomach, and she falls to the ground. The woman, Margarita Yudina, needed treatment in intensive care. Although the police initially tried to apologize to her, authorities later refused to investigate the incident and said there was no wrongdoing in the policeman's actions. Moreover, in response to her demand for an investigation, the authorities threatened that they could demand custody of her 15-year-old daughter and threatened to conscript her eldest sons into the army.

Also, OVD-Info (a Russian human rights organization) made an additional report on detentions at protest actions. We have already quoted it before when analyzing Article 22 of the Constitution, but I consider it necessary to repeat it here in case someone reads this work, not in a row.

Human Rights Watch reports the following on arrests at anti-war protests in March 2022. "According to the human rights project OVD-Info, since February 24, when Russian troops entered Ukraine, 13,500 people have been arbitrarily detained.

"Social media posts documenting the March 6 protests contain footage of peaceful demonstrators being detained for holding placards, marching in a group, chanting "No to war!" wearing yellow and blue clothing or tapes, filming detentions, as well as detentions of people who appear to be just passing by.

"There were repeated instances of the use of force by the police against demonstrators. OVD-Info reports at least 34 situations where law enforcement officers beat protesters on March 6.

"Numerous videos from different cities contain footage of police using excessive force during arrests. In a video from Moscow, five police officers take away one man, and one of them kicks the detainee. In a video from St. Petersburg, law enforcement officers knock a man down and beat him with fists. In Moscow, a policeman beats a protester who is being carried to a police van with a baton.

"A video was filmed in St. Petersburg showing four to six police officers beating a man on the ground with batons, after which they allegedly used a stun gun on him. He shouts that he "did not rally." Using a stun gun on an already detained person violates the prohibition of torture and other cruel, inhuman, or degrading treatment.

"The detainees complained of cuts, abrasions, and burns from a stun gun. One person allegedly suffered a concussion, and another had an open head wound, which he claims was received during his arrest. Several detainees were hospitalized.

"Police officers sometimes have no badge on them, and as far as one can judge, it was sealed with black tape. Officers carried out some arrests in civilian clothes.

"In Moscow, 22-year-old Marina Morozova was taken to the Brateevo 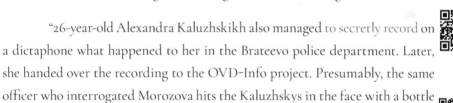 police department on suspicion of participating in an anti-war protest. There, she managed to record what was happening on the phone. On an audio recording she subsequently provided to Novaya Gazeta, three policemen ask her questions. One unidentified employee is behaving aggressively: insulting Morozova, hitting her on the head, threatening her with a gun, and brandishing a chair.

"26-year-old Alexandra Kaluzhskikh also managed to secretly record on a dictaphone what happened to her in the Brateevo police department. Later, she handed over the recording to the OVD-Info project. Presumably, the same officer who interrogated Morozova hits the Kaluzhskys in the face with a bottle 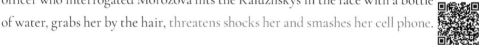 of water, grabs her by the hair, threatens shocks her and smashes her cell phone.

""What do you think? Will we be punished for this? Putin told us to [kill] ... That's it! Putin is on our side! You are the enemies of Russia; you are the enemies of the people, ... They will also give us a bonus for this," the employee says on the recording.""

And so on... I remind you that more details about this holiday of rights and freedoms can be found here:

The international human rights organization Amnesty International generally claims that the right to freedom of assembly and peaceful marches in Russia has been completely destroyed (here and here).

They point out in their report "Russia: No Place for Protest" that the legislation on gatherings, pickets, and marches has been destroyed in 13 stages over the past 16 years.

"Nine of these 13 amendments that have been used to restrict the right to freedom of peaceful assembly in Russia have been introduced since 2014 as part of a coordinated policy to restrict rights guaranteed by international human rights law and directly by the Russian Constitution.

"Moreover, local authorities were sensitive to the course taken at the federal level and introduced additional restrictions on peaceful gatherings. In addition to these changes, the police and the judiciary have also received an incentive to move towards more repressive practices: the police are using increasingly harsh methods to suppress and disperse peaceful protests, and the courts are imposing increasingly harsh punishments on protesters ...

"Since 2011, the number of specific, statutory violations of the law on mass actions has increased from three to 17. Maximum fines have increased from 2,000 rubles ($60 at the time) to 300,000 rubles ($4,000 in 2021), and the commission of 12 of these 17 offenses was established as a possible punishment in the form of administrative arrest for up to 30 days.

"The most repressive measure was the introduction in 2014 of criminal liability for repeated violations of the law on rallies and demonstrations with a maximum established penalty of imprisonment for up to five years.

""In addition to criminal liability for exercising their right to peaceful protest, detained protesters in Russia are also subjected to unfair, almost parodic trials, sometimes taking only a few minutes, without calling key witnesses and in which police reports are unconditionally accepted on faith," Oleg Kozlovsky said."

 You can read more about the rights to peaceful assembly of processions here and legal analysis here.

As we can see, the rights to peaceful meetings and marches in Russia are also ignored and even brutally suppressed by the authorities. Article 31 of the Constitution is also not valid.

ARTICLE 32 OF THE CONSTITUTION

The full text of the Article sounds like this:

"1. Citizens of the Russian Federation shall have the right to participate in managing State affairs both directly and through their representatives.

2. Citizens of the Russian Federation shall have the right to elect and be elected to State government bodies and local self-government bodies, as well as to participate in referendums.

3. Citizens who are recognized as incapable by a court, and citizens who are kept in places of imprisonment under a court sentence, shall not have the right to elect and be elected.

4. Citizens of the Russian Federation shall enjoy equal access to State service.

5. Citizens of the Russian Federation shall have the right to participate in administering justice."

To summarize, this article is the very article that, in theory, should make Russia a democratic state, that is, guarantee the participation of the people in the formation of state bodies and the administration of justice.

However, this article is also one of the most frequently violated by the Russian authorities.

Let's start at the beginning with points 1 and 2. At its core, point 2 only specifies the first point: how citizens can participate in managing state affairs: to elect and be elected.

Accordingly, we need to discuss voting rights.

We have already touched on this topic several times. In particular, when analyzing Article 3 of the Constitution, I cited a few pages of simple listings of changes to the electoral legislation made during Putin's rule.

But it is not even about the constantly changing, like cards in a cheater's hands, rules. The electoral system is absolutely controlled by Putin at every, and even the most insignificant, stage.

So let's start over.

First, quite officially, Putin forms the Central Election Commission (for accuracy: five members are approved by the lower house of parliament (State Duma), five members by the upper house (Federation Council), and five by the president, but given that the president controls the parliament, this is only formal clarifications).

Secondly, Putin is engaged in a real selection of suitable candidates, not allowing those who are not pleasing to the authorities.

For those who need help understanding the picture: imagine there is a beauty contest; there is an ordinary girl who is not particularly beautiful but is the daughter of the contest organizer. The competition begins, and all her rivals look like they should go to Halloween without a costume. The organizer's daughter will win such a competition, and I assure you it will be honest voting. Therefore, the selection of sparring partners is essential for falsification (in the sense of distorting the people's will) in Putin's "elections." Sometimes, hand-picked candidates are used for discrediting entire groups of individuals. So, in 2018, in the "elections" of the president, Putin appointed as his rival, the daughter of his former boss, for whom he was carrying a suitcase — Ksenia Sobchak — a scandalous presenter, with a somewhat ambiguous reputation. Of course, she did everything to discredit Russia's free-thinking people with her behavior. Against her, even Putin could seem more attractive (no matter how incredible it may sound). For this reason, Putin excluded the line "against everyone" from the voting bulletin in 2006.

As a result, the authorities are doing everything possible to deprive all dissenters of passive suffrage. According to the estimates of the Golos association, more than 9 million (sic!) people are disenfranchised in Russia, that is, more than 8.1% of the total number of voters (110 million as of 2021). For more information about persons who cannot be elected in Russia, you can read the report of the Golos association here and here. In addition, there is a bill in the State Duma to deprive citizens of voting rights recognized as "foreign agents" (I remind you that this label is not even attached by the court, but by the prosecutor's office).

For those who still have the right to be elected, the authorities have come up with a special "municipal filter"; a candidate must collect the signatures of municipal deputies in favor of his nomination. Here, for instance, is an example of an unsuccessful filter passage in the Perm Territory. The same report describes the entire mechanism for collecting signatures.

As a result, political parties cannot overcome this "municipal filter," and they have to ask for the votes of municipal deputies from United Russia (ER) (the ruling party). Accordingly, no political party can somehow criticize or put forward strong candidates against the EP, which leads to a lack of real competition.

Thirdly, of course, control over the financial flows of political parties. We also discussed earlier that political parties are funded from the federal budget.

The Golos association points out: "At the same time, state support for parties is not limited to budget financing; their corporate donors also receive government contracts. However, more than 90% of state contractors are donors to one party - United Russia.

"The system of support for parties through affiliated foundations and non-profit organizations is becoming more widespread, which makes these revenues opaque. The parties have practically ceased to attract private donations; their share is minimal...

"One of the main problems remains the gigantic income gap between United Russia and other parliamentary parties. The budget of United Russia in 2017 was 1.8 times higher than the total budget of the other three parties. This gap has been maintained since 2012 when it was 1.5 times. The current situation practically nullifies the chances for the emergence of competition in the electoral field - the resources at the disposal of the parties turn out to be incomparable. Especially when you consider that in addition to official funding, the "party of power" receives significant bonuses through the use of "administrative resources" by officials, which further widens the gap between it and other players" (quote

from here).

Fourth, Putin uses the media to promote pro-government candidates. The distribution of time for speeches and debates also has a significant bias towards the same pro-government candidates. I want to note that Putin has never participated in pre-election debates at all. Probably not without reason, fearing that his ignorance will be easily seen when he tries to answer unprepared in advance questions. Dmitry Peskov (presidential press secretary) did not

hesitate to say that Putin never participates in pre-election debates because "in his case, his candidacy, of course, proceeds according to other laws."

Administrative resources are also used for propaganda. For details, you can read the reports of the Golos association. For the 2021 elections; for the 2022 elections; and on the topic in general.

Additionally, the election process itself is held with huge violations. Among such violations of the voting process are:

- Pressure on state employees;

- Voting of "dead souls" - the local commission itself signs for a person who did not come to the polls;

- "Carousels" - voting by the same people several times;

- Stuffing - a one-time stuffing into the ballot box of a large number of ballots into ballot boxes with already affixed "ticks." Moreover, stuffing can even be carried out by the members of the election commission themselves (the mathematician, Sergey Shpilkin, whom I mentioned earlier and mathematician, Alexander Shen);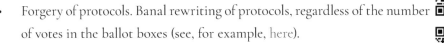

- Forgery of protocols. Banal rewriting of protocols, regardless of the number of votes in the ballot boxes (see, for example, here).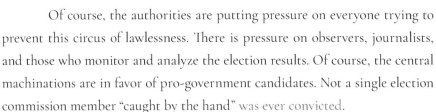

Of course, the authorities are putting pressure on everyone trying to prevent this circus of lawlessness. There is pressure on observers, journalists, and those who monitor and analyze the election results. Of course, the central machinations are in favor of pro-government candidates. Not a single election commission member "caught by the hand" was ever convicted.

Sixth, it is, of course, control over the courts. Not a single claim for the cancellation of obviously rigged elections was satisfied.

The last was invented solely to simplify the falsification of "electronic voting." It seems like a voter can leave his vote in electronic form, and a special CEC system will process it and give a specific result. I will immediately note that its very existence violates the electoral law. Thus, in accordance with Article 68 of the Federal Law of June 12, 2002, N 67-FZ "On Basic Guarantees of Electoral

Rights and the Right to Participate in a Referendum of Citizens of the Russian Federation," the final count of votes is carried out by the election commission, and not some "computer system."

In addition, the same Sergey Shpilkin was also involved in the analysis of electronic voting and revealed several significant violations (more details can be found here).

The very system of "electronic voting" is completely closed and classified.

In its report, the human rights organization "Golos" points out: "The Constitutional Court of Russia, in its Resolution of 04.22.2013 No. 8-P, indicated that the right of citizens to participate in government is not limited to ensuring only free participation in voting itself. Citizens are associated participants in popular sovereignty. Therefore, it is necessary to recognize their right to control the procedures related to counting votes and establishing voting results, as well as the possibility of a legitimate response to identified violations. Thus, the Constitutional Court of Russia points to the inalienability of the right of citizens to exercise control over compliance with the procedures for expressing will. Such representation is designed to guarantee the legitimacy of the decisions taken during the voting in the eyes of both their supporters and opponents.

"However, in the case of remote electronic voting, the legislator has not provided effective mechanisms that allow citizens to exercise this constitutional right: the voting and vote counting system is not transparent even for persons with special knowledge in the field of information technology, not to mention other voters. Thus, the current system of electronic voting does not meet the high requirements of electoral procedures being controlled by the society."

I want to separately emphasize the importance of control over electoral procedures in the context of Article 32 of the Constitution being commented on. The very control over electoral procedures literally is participation in "state affairs."

The "miracle" of e-voting happened in the 2021 Moscow municipal elections, where in one night, more than ten candidates supported Navalny's "Smart Vote" (consolidation of votes for one candidate in order for the pro-government candidate to lose), who confidently won the result of the usual (face-to-face) vote, lost to pro-government candidates after the release of "electronic voting." As a result, not a single candidate supported by "Smart Voting" made it to the Moscow Duma. At the same time, United Russia's ratings in Moscow have historically been minimal and, at that moment, did not exceed 20%.

In general, you can read the report of Golos about violations in the "elections" of 2021 here.

But foreign companies are also helping Putin in his uneasy struggle with the remnants of dissent. Thus, Google and Apple, at the request of the Russian authorities, removed the Navalny applications from their stores (Google Play and Apple Store), where it was possible to find a candidate from the "Smart Vote" at their address of residence, for whom Navalny and his team advised to vote. Telegram also removed a Smart Voting bot that performs the same functions. Durov, the founder of Telegram, said that Apple and Google demanded that Telegram remove "publicly available information in accordance with the laws of individual countries" under the threat of deleting the application from app stores.

"The basis for the removal of the application is the recognition of the Anti-Corruption Foundation as an extremist organization, follows from Apple's response ... Apple's message also says that, according to the Prosecutor General's Office, the application "violates Russian law by allowing it to interfere in elections."

"There is no and cannot exist a legal reality in which the publication of a list of supported candidates in elections is "extremism" or simply something illegal. These are registered candidates in official elections; anyone has the right to express their opinion regarding their support," Volkov [head of Navalny's campaign headquarters - A.M.] wrote on Facebook (quoted from BBC)."

Now, let's look at part 5 of this ill-fated article of the Constitution: "Citizens of the Russian Federation have the right to participate in the administration of justice."

 This means jury trials. I want to clarify right away that jury trials in Russia only try criminal cases (and even then, not all of them—initially, only in cases where the maximum punishment would be the death penalty or a term of imprisonment of more than 10 years) and only in some regions.

The range of cases that juries can hear is shrinking more and more. At the end of 2008, cases of treason, sabotage, **riots**, terror, business cases, and then cases of crimes against justice and **corruption** were withdrawn from the jurisdiction of the jury. The Supreme Court of Russia forbade the presence of jurors to talk about torture, which forced a confession from the accused.

 Since 2016, the volume of categories of cases considered by the jury has increased. Then, further changes were made to the Code of Criminal Procedure, which gave the right to trial by jury to persons accused of genocide, infringement on the life of a statesman or public figure, a person administering justice or a preliminary investigation, a law enforcement officer.

 But even with such restrictions, the use of jury trials is catastrophically minimal. So, in 2021, Russian courts considered about 770,000 (sic!) criminal cases. Of these, only 1,019, about 0.13% of the total number of criminal cases were tried by jury.

 Sergey Nasonov, in his article "Jury Trial in Russia: Trends of the Outgoing Year," points out:

"As in 2020, the share of jury acquittals remains stable and is growing slightly. Thus, in all jury trials in the first half of 2021, 31% (196) of defendants were acquitted (i.e., one in three). For comparison: in cases considered in the first half of 2021 by a single professional judge, only 0.3% of the defendants were acquitted.

"At the same time, a high percentage of acquittals overturned remained a stable trend in the practice of trial by jury in the outgoing year. As the statistics for the first half of 2021 show, 110 acquittals and 52 convictions were overturned on appeal, i.e., acquittals were canceled twice as often. In my opinion, these indicators testify to the existence of so-called "double" standards. After all, violations of the Code of Criminal Procedure of the Russian Federation cannot be detected mainly in cases that ended in an acquittal."

Using a jury also interferes with the consequences of a trial with the accused's participation. Retired judge Sergei Pashin says:

"If the accused chose a jury trial and was acquitted, it is easy to appeal the verdict in the Supreme Court and appoint a new trial, and if convicted, the judge tries to apply the most severe punishment. Secondly, there are a lot of prohibitions for lawyers—for example, you can't talk about torture (which we mentioned earlier). The Supreme Court ruled that the question of using unlawful methods of investigation is not within the jury's competence. They should not assess the credibility of the evidence. And the jury thinks: he confessed during the investigation, but now he's lying, you scoundrel.

"Another problem is the damage to the mechanism for selecting jurors to participate in trials, which was debugged in the 90s of the last century. If in 1994 92% of candidates were invited to the courts, today it is a catastrophe with ensuring the attendance of jurors: at best, every 20th of those summoned comes to court; trials are repeatedly postponed due to the failure of the required number of jurors to appear. At an unfortunate hour, they abolished liability for the loss of candidates for jurors to appear when summoned by the court. In countries where a "court of equals" has been introduced (and this is 52 states), such disrespect is considered as a serious offense, entailing a large fine and even imprisonment."

In addition, it is also more difficult for defense lawyers to participate in jury trials.

According to the expert, they have more than 30 bans, and most directly affect how the jury will perceive the case.

"The motive for the crime cannot be established. Whether or not a selfish reason guided the defendant is not within the jury's competence. But it's one thing when a person takes away his property—this is arbitrariness with a penalty in the form of a fine, and quite another—robbery, for which they give a term. Why does the judge decide this question? Pashin continues.

"Objectivity is also affected by the right of the presiding judge, before admitting a witness or a specialist from the defense, to interrogate them independently and decide whether they should participate in the process..."

There are significant problems with the formation of the jury. The procedure takes a lot of time: preparing the actions of the court to form a collegium, compiling a reserve and main list, selecting jurors, checking them, and the very formation of a collegium in a particular case.

Until all the formalities are met, it may take several months. Complicating the situation even more is the fact that few people in Russia want to administer justice. By law, participation in such a process is the duty of every citizen, but there is no real responsibility for avoiding it. It turns out that the chances of the defendants for a timely and objective consideration of the case are often reduced by the citizens themselves.

"'In some regions, they cannot start the trial for six months. From the point of view of criminal proceedings, the guilt of the defendant has not yet been proven, but the articles are grave, so that a person, as a rule, is in custody at that time,' Alexander Spiridonov, a lawyer at the European Legal Service, tells Izvestia."

You can read more about the statistics of cases involving juries here.

As a result, we can conclude the following: paragraphs 1-4 of Article 32 of the Constitution do not work almost completely. Putin has eliminated the institution of elections as a class, leaving only imitation procedures that are becoming increasingly indifferent to the people.

Paragraph 5 of the commented article is very limited. And categories of cases, the formation of a jury, restrictions in the process, and the rules of appeal. As a result, even those 0.13% of cases that are considered by jury can hardly be considered adequate for granting citizens the right to justice and trial by jury.

ARTICLE 33 OF THE CONSTITUTION

Again, let me start with the full text:

"Citizens of the Russian Federation shall have the right to appeal in person and make individual and collective appeals to State bodies and local self-government bodies."

Although it would seem that this is a completely obvious right: to ask officials to solve their problems, that is, simply to do their job; the Russian authorities manage to break even this simplest rule.

We also touched on this issue a little when analyzing Article 21 of the Constitution, where citizens had to turn to Putin on their knees (here, here and here). I also mentioned that such appeals often become the subject of criminal proceedings, not against officials, but against the citizens themselves (for example, here). Citizens of Russia even sometimes turn to foreign officials, in particular to German Chancellor Merkel.

But why do people even have to kneel before officials? This is forced by an extremely inefficient bureaucracy, an almost non-existent judicial system, a harsh suppression by the authorities of any rallies and pickets, control over the media (and their agenda), and the absence of any political party that could deal (even for the sake of PR) with the problems of certain citizens. This is a consequence of the authorities' actions in their attempts to not depend on civil society as much as possible. Since the authorities managed de facto not to depend on society (neither financially nor politically), they do not need to take care of this society. In the absence of feedback, people are left with only humiliating ways to let the authority know about their problems. (Similar ideas can be read here).

There are also cases of conscious resistance by the authorities to accept the plea. Of course, I again have to give the example of Navalny (a person whose rights the Russian Constitution does not cover at all). If you remember, we have already discussed his poisoning with Novichok. So, he (and his team) turned to the authorities with demands to initiate a criminal case of poisoning.

They even filed a lawsuit, demanding to initiate a case (you can review all their misadventures here). The following is a quote from that site:

"After the release of the investigation, which shed light on the detachment of poisoners from the FSB, and after the publication of the conversation with Kudryavtsev, the FBK lawyers filed applications to the Chief Military Investigation Department of the Investigative Committee, but they refused to conduct a check.

"The pre-investigation check on the poisoning, which was carried out by the transport police of Tomsk, lasted until February 10, 2021. Over the course of it, more than 210 persons were questioned and more than 60 different forensic examinations were assigned on 542 seized objects. As a result of the check, the investigators came to the conclusion that the poisoning of Navalny was a staging aimed at preparation of a provocation for political purposes. The key role in this staging was played by FBK employees, who took away bottles of water from

269

the hotel, as well as Navalny himself and his wife Yulia, who concealed Alexei's alleged illnesses from the investigation.

"The initiation of a criminal case was refused 'due to the absence of a crime event under Part 1 of Art. 111 of the Criminal Code of Russia.'

"'Taking this into account, the position of the Prosecutor General's Office of Russia looks absolutely untenable: over and over again, it demands from Germany some evidence of poisoning, referring to the European Convention on Mutual Legal Assistance in **Criminal Matters** [highlighted by me - A.M.] (for more details, see the section "Russia's Position")... Indeed, in order to count on assistance under this convention, Russia needs to start its own investigation and open a criminal case on the fact of poisoning.'"

 At the link, you can see a table with all complaints and attempts to appeal them in court.

They continue: "["Paradox" is that] In accordance with **Subparagraph "c" of Paragraph 1 of Part 2 of Article 151 of the Criminal Procedure Code of Russia**, a preliminary investigation in criminal cases of crimes committed by FSB officers is carried out by the Investigative Committee. It must also conduct a preliminary investigation in cases of crimes provided for in Article 105 of the Criminal Code, in accordance with **Subparagraph "a" of Paragraph 1 of Part 2 of Article 151 of the Code of Criminal Procedure of Russia**. The check on the assassination attempt was supposed to be carried out by an authorized body — the Investigative Committee, and not by the transport police, whose responsibilities mainly consist of ensuring public order at train stations and investigating thefts on electric trains.

"According to **Part 1 of Article 144 of the Code of Criminal Procedure of Russia**, the investigator is obliged to accept and check the report of any committed or impending crime and take a decision on it within no more than three days (with the possibility of a maximum extension of up to 30). Nevertheless, neither the Investigative Committee nor the FSB carried out checks within the framework of the Criminal Procedure Code. They did not take any procedural decisions, unlawfully excluding themselves from the execution of the duties assigned to them by law at the very initial stage of the criminal process.

"The fact of poisoning has been repeatedly confirmed by international authorities. The Organization for the Prohibition of Chemical Weapons released a report on October 6, 2020, according to which the tests carried out confirmed the content of a chemical warfare agent from the Novichok family in Navalny's biomaterials. The letter that UN special rapporteurs sent to the Russian government on December 30, 2020 following a four-month investigation says: "The use of chemical weapons is a 'sinister threat' and a 'gross violation' of customary international law." The reporters emphasized that the Russian authorities "have an obligation to investigate the crime committed against Alexei Navalny and to identify and punish everyone responsible, including those at the highest level of leadership"."

My personal experience cannot serve as a criterion for the truth of an argument. Still, I have more than once encountered the total incompetence of Russian officials or their unwillingness to solve someone's problems. So, I have already talked about removing the arrest on my car, having received a small fine (500 rubles or about $8). I paid the fine, and the enforcement proceedings (which I was not even informed about) were terminated, but the arrest was not lifted. I contacted the bailiffs several times, once directly to the traffic police, twice to the prosecutor's office, and even for the sake of laughter to the presidential administration (after all, even a tuft of wool from a black sheep). The solution to the problem took almost a year, a completely minor issue with a penny sum. At the same time, the solution to the issue took time for me, for at least six officials of various ranks, and delayed the sale of my car for almost a year. Now, imagine if the case had at least some grounds for ambiguity and controversy! It is not surprising that people have to invent ways to get through to that fool who removed all independence from officials and took all the levers of solving problems into his feeble hands — Putin.

Courts in Russia last long enough. On average, there are 3-4 sessions, with a 1.5-2 month break. Therefore, after the case is accepted, it will take about 6-8 months before it is resolved, depending on the workload of the court and the judge. Plus, a period is given for making a decision and a period for appealing it (30 days). The appeal of the decision may take another 2-4 months. A few more meetings, and the consideration of the case easily takes a year and a half.

Based on the above, this article also practically does not work. People have almost no opportunity to quickly solve their problems. They have to invent unique methods so that their issue is at least somehow resolved. This is not normal in a modern or even healthy society.

At the same time, it is impossible to trace this article's systematic nature of non-compliance (no judicial or regulatory action would somehow contradict it). Punishment for "improper" treatment or non-acceptance is an exception, and lengthy proceedings can hardly be formally considered a significant violation of it. So, this time, it would be fair to conclude that Article 33 of the Constitution still works, albeit badly and with egregious individual cases of its violation.

ARTICLE 34 OF THE
CONSTITUTION

The full text reads:

"1. Everyone shall have the right to use freely his (her) abilities and property for entrepreneurial and other economic activity not prohibited by law.

2. Economic activity aimed at monopolization and unfair competition shall not be permitted."

Note that the speech in paragraph 1 of Article 34 concerns not only entrepreneurial activity but also the personal abilities of a person for his self-realization and income generation.

And here, a huge problem has dramatically escalated since Russia's aggression in Ukraine.

As you have probably already seen, Putin is annoyed by any opinion that differs from his (considering his mental abilities, there is not even much effort needed here; the bar is literally on the floor). And, of course, it annoys him even more when famous and influential people express their opinion. This applies not only to journalists but even artists, musicians, stand-up artists, and bloggers. To force them to side with the Kremlin, or at least to keep quiet, the Russian authorities extensively use numerous obstacles in implementing their activities. Putin keeps complaining about some phantom "ban on Russian culture in the West," but no one has done more to ban Russian culture than he.

Some of the creative people were declared, of course, "foreign agents." These are, for example, rapper Face, cartoonist Sergey Elkin, comedian Sergey Schatz, writer Dmitry Glukhovsky, musician Nadezhda Tolokonnikova, rapper Morgenstern, humorist Tatyana Lazareva, musician Andrey Makarevich, humorist Maxim Galkin, rapper Oxxxymiron, and film-director Alexander Rodnyansky. We have already spoken about the restrictions imposed on "foreign agents."

There is an unspoken ban on concert activities for such musicians. In addition to official restrictions, there are unofficial restrictions. In particular, the Fontanka publication provides the following list of tacitly banned musicians. Meduza publishes a similar list, citing an anonymous source.

However, the effect of lists is fully verified by practice.

- So, on April 21, 2022, the concert of the DDT group was canceled in Tyumen. The official reason for the cancellation of the concert is unknown. Group leader, Yuri Shevchuk, suggested that this may be due to the group's refusal to perform in the hall with the letter Z.

- On April 28, the Bi-2 group canceled their performance in Omsk because of the banner "For the President," which hung at the Red Star concert venue. It was forbidden to remove the poster, so the organizers decided to cover it with a black canvas, but the club administration disagreed. As a result, the team just left.

- In September 2021, the Russian rapper, Face announced the cancellation of part of the autumn tour due to threats from the authorities to regional organizers. The musician associated the pressure with his civil position and support for the politician Alexei Navalny. The first two performances were to be held in Krasnoyarsk and Novosibirsk.

- Two concerts of the Kis-Kis group in Astrakhan and Volgograd were canceled "for moral reasons."

- The Moscow concert venue, "GlavClub," announced the cancellation of several performances on June 26, 2022. So, within the framework of the PunkRupor festival, Anacondaz participants will not take the stage, and the concerts of "Neschastny sluchai" and the singer Manizha have also been canceled. "We decided under pressure from state authorities. After several weeks of calls to us from various authorities, on Friday, June 24, within a couple of hours after our next refusal, we received notifications of two unscheduled inspections from Rospotrebnadzor and the Ministry of Emergencies," the site's official public page says.

- "Splin's" concerts have been canceled in five Russian cities. Organizers of performances write about it on social networks. Shows scheduled for the end of September to the beginning of October have been postponed to the next year. This happened with performances in Cherepovets, Yaroslavl, Vladimir, Nizhny Novgorod, and Tula. In almost all cases, the reason for the transfer was "technical reasons."

- The concerts of the "Nogu Svelo" group were also canceled. First, the group was banned from going on tour in Siberia, and then their concert on May 9 and in Yekaterinburg was suddenly canceled.

The concerts of the satirist writer Shenderovich, stand-up comedian Bely, and stand-up comedian Indrak Merzalidze was expelled from Russia (he did not have Russian citizenship, only a residence permit). A criminal case was opened against Director Kirill Serebrennikov. He spoke publicly on a wide range of issues. He criticized the persecution of LGBT people and, in this context, the influence of the Russian Orthodox Church on the life of Russian society. He talked about the increase in censorship, including in connection with the Pussy

275

Riot case, and about the strengthening of authoritarianism in Russia. He was also critical of Russia's role in the August 2008 war with Georgia.

 Authorities are persecuting comedian Danila Poperechny.

 The number of journalists persecuted for their activities and forced to leave Russia is in the hundreds.

The teachers are not left out. So, the history teacher, Tamara Eidelman, was declared a "foreign agent," which hurts me personally. She was a history teacher at the school where I studied, and I know her personally. And now she was forced to leave Russia.

 Of course, representatives of the LGBT community suffer simply because of their orientation. So, a student from St. Petersburg, Maxim Drozhzhin, was expelled from the folklore ensemble for being openly gay: the choir leader found out about this from his Facebook and asked him not to come to rehearsals anymore.

 They are persecuted, and not only those who actively oppose it. But even those whose work the authorities, in principle, do not like, such as rapper Morgenstern or hip-hop artist Instasamka.

 The ban on freedom of creativity and self-expression is also a ban on books by specific authors. Of course, books with LGBT relationships are in the first place, even though they are labeled 18+. Even a particular bill has been prepared to ban such literature. Similar threats are made against the work of Akunin, Bykov, Shenderovich, Glukhovsky, and Parfenov. Again, there is only an implicit ban on their promotion and sale (here and here), but censorship will probably become quite official soon.

 There are many such examples. The Russian authorities use the ban on creativity and self-realization to deprive a person of receiving income from their activities and thus force them to cooperate. Some people in creative professions are eventually forced to remain silent, and a more significant number simply leave Russia. Therefore, no one in the world has done as much as Putin did to abolish modern Russian culture.

The second part of the commented paragraph is related to entrepreneurial activity.

It should be noted that Putin, in principle, considers all entrepreneurs to be "crooks by definition" and "hucksters." Of course, this does not apply to his friends, mistresses, illegitimate children, and personal acquaintances, who, by completely random circumstances, occupy high positions in state bodies and state enterprises, and all of them without exception are dollar billionaires (here, here and here). Accordingly, there are two simultaneous trends: a huge monopolization and a literal milking of medium and small enterprises by law enforcement agencies.

As a result, according to official data (sic!), in 2019, the state's share in the economy was more than 50%. Government-owned companies also account for 50% of jobs. At the same time, the FAS (Federal Antimonopoly Service) indicates that the state's contribution to the economy is more than 70%.

Let's take a look at why this is the situation.

The following is a quote from Vedomosti:

"Business distrust in law enforcement and the judiciary has reached record levels [as of May 25, 2020 - A.M.]. This is evidenced by the data of a study by the Federal Security Service (FSO) [The service is engaged in the protection of the carcasses of senior officials and is forced to engage in surveys as independent sociology in Russia was destroyed by the Russian authorities; which gives an additional touch to the portrait, - A.M.]. Attached is the annual report prepared by the presidential commissioner for the protection of entrepreneurs' rights of entrepreneurs Boris Titov (Vedomosti managed to get acquainted with the text of the survey).

"The FSO Special Communications and Information Service asked for the opinion of experts (lawyers, prosecutors, human rights activists, and legal scholars) and businessmen who were subjected to criminal prosecution. In total, 279 experts and 189 entrepreneurs in 36 regions were interviewed.

"Three-quarters of respondents (74.3%) believe that doing business in Russia is unsafe — in 2017, 57.1% shared this opinion. The proportion of respondents who say that Russian legislation does not provide sufficient guarantees to protect businesses from unreasonable prosecution remains virtually unchanged and has remained at 70-71% over the past three years. On the other hand, the proportion of respondents who do not consider justice in Russia to be independent and objective has noticeably increased: from 50% in 2017 to 73.8% in 2020. Notably, 57.7% of the surveyed experts also do not trust the judiciary.

"Distrust of law enforcement agencies continues to grow: from 45% of respondents in 2017 to 70.3% in 2020. At the same time, almost three-quarters of respondents consider the qualifications of investigators insufficient for investigating crimes of an economic nature. And the vast majority of respondents (76.7%, including nearly half of the representatives of the prosecutor's office) believe that crimes in the field of entrepreneurial activity should be investigated by one specialized investigative body.

"Entrepreneurs most often (41.3%) cite the **personal interest of law enforcement officers as the reason for initiating criminal cases against them** [highlighted by me - A.M.]. In second place is a conflict with another businessman (37.6%). At the same time, 74.1% of respondents consider the activities of law enforcement agencies to combat corruption to be ineffective (in 2017, there were 61.1% of them)...

"**84.2% of the interviewed entrepreneurs reported that their business was completely or partially destroyed due to criminal prosecution. Half complain that the persecution resulted in the loss of their health and**

reputation, 33.9% lost most of their assets [highlighted by me - A.M.]". (Another source about this, the original report can be read here).

I want to emphasize here: 84.5% of the time, after a criminal case is initiated against entrepreneurs, their business ceases to exist. At the same time, in Russia, there is no liability for a legal entity. This is connected with the so-called theory of the "reality of a legal entity" in Russian law—it is (in view) an utterly independent subject of law—it should not be affected by any criminal prosecution of any of its founders or employees. But as we can see, security forces can easily rob or seize private enterprises.

Titov [Ombudsman for the Rights of Entrepreneurs - A.M.] said in 2022 further quoted from the Expert.ru website: "In terms of criminal prosecution, the conclusion is this: in recent years, many good and useful innovations have been introduced into laws, but practice lags behind them." As a result, under economic articles (Articles 159-159.6, 160, 165, as well as Chapter 22 of the Criminal Code of the Russian Federation), more cases are initiated every year."

This is not surprising since it is not the criminal law that requires reform, but the law enforcement agencies, which need to reduce their powers drastically, and the courts, which need independence. Not surprisingly, even such attempts to increase the number of dairy herds fail.

"So, according to the business ombudsman, in 2021, the number of criminal cases under economic charges increased by another 7.7% and amounted to 496,048 units. In 2020, the growth rate was 24.38%; in 2019, it was 15.78%" (ibid.).

More information about the problem can be read here.

Separately, I want to note that corruption and terrible legislation have a powerful effect on business: it is not impossible to conduct business honestly. In any case, a company that performs business honestly will always be in a deliberately disadvantageous position compared to a business that ignores rules or gives bribes to numerous inspectors so that they turn a blind eye to these violations.

At the same time, the authorities see only the initiation of criminal cases as the only way to combat economic violations. Often, civil law disputes quickly develop into criminal ones.

"...traditional popularity among "entrepreneurial" structures is maintained by criminal cases of fraud. The investigating authorities often "superficially" assess the facts of entrepreneurial activity and qualify the acts, not understanding their economic essence clearly enough. Lawyers consider this trend dangerous. "Corporate approvals of transactions, a complex business ownership structure, the amount of damage—these are some of the many issues that come up sharply in these cases but are lost from the field of view of the investigating authorities and the court," says Magomed Hasanov. In addition, businesses are often charged with fraud and embezzlement to remove the actions committed by entrepreneurs from special legal personality and thereby ensure their detention, Yakov Gadzhiev adds.

"Stories where entrepreneurs are prosecuted for actions that the business community does not consider illegal have traditionally caused a great public outcry. These include: criminal cases against borrowers of large banks who, for various reasons, did not repay the loan; cases of economically expedient disposal of funds of a legal entity, qualified as embezzlement; cases of transactions on market conditions, the price of which law enforcement officers later recognized as unreasonable and qualified actions of the participants in the transaction as theft and many others.

"In general, those circumstances that are established in the framework of arbitration and civil proceedings are increasingly not taken into account in the framework of criminal proceedings, despite the direct indication of Art. 90 of the Code of Criminal Procedure of the Russian Federation on prejudice. In the context of a criminal case, this sometimes entails issuing a decision directly opposite to what was previously taken in arbitration. Experts consider the

Vostochny Bank case a striking example, in which the investigation has long been considering an obvious corporate conflict through the prism of criminal law. Although the founder of the investment fund Baring Vostok, American businessman Michael Calvey, won the arbitration proceedings and all decisions up to the Supreme Court of the Russian Federation were made in his favor, his criminal prosecution continues" (quote from here).

This problem was recognized by Putin himself, who almost every year, calls on the security forces to "stop making business a nightmare." He cites statistics that 45% of cases initiated against business owners do not even reach court, and, as we remember earlier, the initiation ruins 83% of such enterprises. He, of course, does nothing to correct the situation and will not do anything. Such a scheme was built by him to create a "food base" for the security forces; this is much more profitable than maintaining this army of inspectors at the expense of the budget.

All this leads to a violation of paragraph 2 of the commented article: "Economic activity aimed at monopolization and unfair competition is not allowed." It's funny that the state becomes the main monopolist.

I also briefly described the monopolization of the Russian economy when analyzing Article 8 of the Constitution. I spoke about monopolization figures a little earlier when studying the current article.

With a vast level of monopolization, there is a tendency to increase it (charts can be viewed here).

Already in 2022, in connection with Russia's aggression against Ukraine, more than 500 foreign enterprises left Russia, which, as you understand, did not improve the situation with the competition.

Given the above, Article 34 of the Constitution also does not work.

ARTICLE 35 OF THE CONSTITUTION

As usual, here is the full text:

"1. The right of private property shall be protected by law.

2. Everyone shall have the right to have property and to possess, use and dispose of it both individually and jointly with other persons.

3. Nobody may be deprived of property except under a court order. Forced alienation of property for State requirements may take place only subject to prior and fair compensation.

4. The right of inheritance shall be guaranteed."

Russia has always had problems understanding property in general and private property in particular. Back in the 19th century, Prince Pyotr Vyazemsky wrote in his Notebooks: "Karamzin [Russian historian - A.M.] said if you could describe what is going on in Russia in one word, then you would have to say: "They steal."

Of course, the situation in the days of the USSR with property rights became even worse. When all property belongs to the state, it becomes challenging to administer and take care of it. As a result, people were not particularly shy. There were even humorous sayings like: "pull every nail from the factory — you are the owner here, not a guest."

Naturally, Putin, as a true son of the system, fully accepted this motto. His activities are monstrous theft (here and here), and he began long before he became president, about which we spoke earlier.

Obviously, the theft of public money sooner or later becomes the theft of private money.

So, the loudest case was the case of Yukos, the oil company of Mikhail Khodorkovsky. In the late 90s, Khodorkovsky was a very influential and wealthy man (at the time of his arrest, he was one of the richest people in the world with a fortune of 15 billion dollars) with an extraordinary approach to business. At some point, he showed his political ambitions, and of course, this crossed the road to Putin (here, here and here).

In 2003, the Russian authorities rolled out astronomical tax claims on the company, despite Yukos being the leading taxpayer in the country at that time, ahead of Lukoil and Rosneft. Yukos could not pay off the huge artificially accrued sums, went bankrupt, and was liquidated in 2007. Subsequently, it turned out that the company not only "did not pay taxes" but also "stole oil" (all of it) from itself, which allowed Mikhail Khodorkovsky and Platon Lebedev to be convicted again.

As for the assets of Yukos, once the largest oil company in the country, they almost immediately went to the state-owned Rosneft, owned by Igor Sechin, a friend of Putin, through the Yuganskneftegaz company at a price below the market price. Since 2005, the Yukos shareholders who managed to leave the country, united in the holding company Group Menatep Limited (GML), initiated international proceedings to recover compensation from Russia for the illegal expropriation of the company (you can read case materials here). Proceedings are ongoing to this day, with mixed success.

However, the Constitutional Court of Russia (sic!), for the first time in the history of Europe, decided to prohibit the national government from paying compensation following the decision of the international court in the Yukos case. Execution of the decision of the ECHR on compensation to the former shareholders of Yukos in the amount of €1.8 billion was considered impossible by the Constitutional Court since such a payment would violate, for some reason, the constitutional principles of the "welfare state, equality, and justice." Unquestionably, it's socially unfair to take away from Putin's friend, Sechin, what he so honestly stole!

That is, the entire system of Russian authorities was aimed at seizing assets from individuals (YUKOS shareholders) and transferring them to Putin's friend, Sechin. Now they are busy protecting what was stolen from the previous owners!

We have already said earlier that the security forces are not at all shy about initiating cases against entrepreneurs; this is an effective way to extort bribes or seize property. And 86% of the initiated cases completely or partially ruin the business.

Open robbery is also used by Putin's security forces during "searches," when the security forces seize everything that is not screwed to the floor. Searches can be carried out not even by those accused of a crime but by their relatives or even witnesses (as in the case of Irina Slavina). According to the Judicial Department at the Supreme Court of the Russian Federation, over the past 14 years, the number of searches has increased by almost 40%: if, in 2007, the courts granted about 156,000 requests for a search in an apartment, then in 2020, more than 212,000—that is, in Russia, 600 searches are carried out daily.

Moreover, searches are carried out even in those cases that do not require material evidence, for example, about comments and likes on the network (now we do not take the absurdity of these cases at all).

Property seized during a search is almost never returned. The security forces often came to Navalny's headquarters and confiscated equipment, leaflets, and campaign materials, paralyzing the work of the headquarters. Do I need to say that they never returned the equipment?

For some reason, the following cases fell out of the attention of the press. After the annexation of Crimea, Russia also appropriated more than 250 Ukrainian companies that were located on the peninsula. They are not at all shy about this, disclosing it in the newspaper. Here, we must understand that regardless of whose land the enterprise is located on, it belongs to those who founded it. In any country, there are foreign enterprises, and being in the territory of another state does not make this enterprise domestic. Therefore, when changing boundaries, the property does not change. However, since 2014, the Russian government has been seizing enterprises and lands owned by Ukrainian citizens, and this holiday of lawlessness continues to this day.

In violation of paragraph 3 of the commented article, I note that such a seizure is carried out not by a court decision but in an administrative manner. A special "Law" of the Republic of Crimea dated July 31, 2014, No. 38-ZRK "On the Peculiarities of Regulation of Property and Land Relations on the Territory of the Republic of Crimea" was issued. An attempt by the political party "Yabloko" to cancel it was unsuccessful.

But if you think that the dodgy mind of Russian officials stopped there or that there are no other examples, then you are mistaken.

So, in the capital, a whole "renovation" program is underway, where residents of houses are forcibly evicted from old homes to new ones. The problem is not even that sometimes the area is reserved for them, and the cost of housing can be approximately the same. The problem lies precisely in the fact that no one asks for the opinion of the residents, and the property is confiscated in violation of paragraph 3 without trial by the decision of ▌ of the owners of the apartment building. But if everything is clear with those who voted for it, then problems arise with those who voted against it. For someone, an apartment or a yard off the road can be like a memory, and it's generally strange to say this, but you can't treat a person like a slave and say whether he lives in his own house or not. Of course, this attitude caused some dissatisfaction among Muscovites.

It is not surprising that with such an approach, the war in Ukraine turned into a total robbery. In 2014, entire equipment factories were taken from the occupied Donetsk and Lugansk regions to Russia. Such plants were: Stakhanov Ferroalloy Plant, Stakhanov Carriage Works, Yasinovatsky Machine-Building Plant, Topaz Holding Company, Lutuginsky Research and Production Roll Plant, Lugansk Cartridge Plant, Mashzavod-100 Electronic Machine Building Plant, Yunost Plant, Lugansk Pharmaceutical Plant, "LugaTerm," Autovalve Plant.

Already in 2022, Russia was engaged in the direct theft of Ukrainian grain. The most disgusting thing is that this is done not even for enrichment (or rather, not only for it), but to artificially create hunger and to create additional blackmail leverage for Western countries that may face another wave of refugees fleeing from famine to Europe. Naturally, Putin does not give a damn about people; he is ready to kill even his citizens by the hundreds of thousands, why would he be worried about the fate of people even more distant from him at all?

The looting of Ukraine is also taking place at the grassroots level. The Internet has circulated footage of Russian soldiers engaged in total looting of everything that could be carried, up to children's train. Yes, one could talk about the fact that these are individual excesses of some soldiers, and the state has nothing to do with it. However, the Russian Criminal Code does not even have an article on "marauder," and despite the presence of a military prosecutor's office, not a single soldier was charged with theft, and of course, no one was punished. As we said earlier, without stopping the crime, the state becomes its participant.

I have no comments on point 4. The right to inherit is indeed present in the remnants of the Russian legal field.

As a result, it can be said with certainty that the Russian state practically does not comply with or even understand property rights. If it wants to take something, it calmly takes it. It takes companies, ruins entrepreneurs and ordinary people, puts them in jail; it robs property in other countries and on the occupied territories. In my opinion, this is not even the state's action but the actions of a genuine criminal group.

This situation has been going on for a long time. Still, many foreign companies have been and are (!) doing business in Russia. In 2022, many companies were forced to leave Russia, fixing huge losses. To be honest, I have no words to assess the naivete of companies that have entered a market where the right to private property has not been respected for decades.

ARTICLE 36 OF THE CONSTITUTION

"1. Citizens and their associations shall have the right to possess land as private property.

2. Possession, utilisation and disposal of land and other natural resources shall be exercised by the owners freely provided that this is not detrimental to the environment and does not violate the rights and lawful interests of other people.

3. The conditions and procedure for the use of land shall be determined by federal law."

I have no comments on the first paragraph of the commented article. Unlike the USSR, in Russia, there is a right to private land ownership.

The second point raises a lot of questions for me. When analyzing Article 6 of the Constitution, I have already examined the case of Tkachev's dacha.

Let me remind you that it is also a common practice for officials to fence off plots of land contrary to the requirements of the law (for example, paragraph 8 of Article 11 of the Forest Code prohibits preventing citizens from accessing the forest; and Article 6 of the Water Code, to water bodies; moreover, paragraph 6 and paragraph 8 article 6 of the Water Code of the Russian Federation, establish a sanitary zone in which buildings should not be located in principle). However, the authorities not only persecute officials for such violations but, on the contrary, protect their lawlessness. So, the governor of the Krasnodar Territory, Tkachev, illegally fenced off a 5.3 hectare forest plot. At the end of 2011, Suren Ghazaryan, a member of the Ecological Watch Council, wrote an official letter to the Forestry Department in which he demanded that action be taken against the illegally installed fence. Curiously, this letter was later attached to the materials of the criminal case on the "damage" to the governor's wall.

As a result, the ecologist was sentenced to three years in prison for "damaging the fence" (details here).

Of course, the case with Tkachev's dacha is not the only one. So, a no-fly zone and a ban on access to the beach have been declared over Putin's palace in Gelendzhik. And Medvedev's dacha, and Miller's house, and Zolotov's dacha, dachas of Shoigu and Vorobyov, and others.

The activities of officials often harm the forests. Thus, Greenpeace sent an appeal to Prosecutor General Igor Krasnov with a demand to initiate a criminal case on the fact of illegal logging and violation of the protection regime in the Volga-Akhtuba floodplain natural park, since the Volga environmental **prosecutor's office does not take any effective measures to stop the construction of the highway in the natural park.**

In principle, deforestation is a huge problem for Russia.

"Every year, clearcutting reduces the forest by 1 million hectares, and the figure will grow due to an increase in the volume of timber harvesting, which is due to an increase in forest areas withdrawn for the needs of subsoil users," Ivan Valentik, head of Rosleskhoz, said in an interview with TASS. In 2016, the 20-year record for official deforestation was broken - 213.8 million cubic meters. m. In 2018, this figure increased to 233.8 million cubic meters. m. (quote from here).

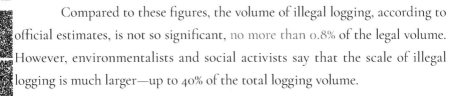

Compared to these figures, the volume of illegal logging, according to official estimates, is not so significant, no more than 0.8% of the legal volume. However, environmentalists and social activists say that the scale of illegal logging is much larger—up to 40% of the total logging volume.

Again, at one time, I worked as a lawyer in an international company with an office located near Moscow. According to the land title certificate, the company owned the land under the building, and a piece of land outside it, which the company fenced off with a barrier and used as parking for employees and customers. However, a complaint came to the local administration from other motorists, who also wanted to park their cars there and demanded that the barrier be removed. I went to understand the administration on this issue; they asked us to remove the barrier. I showed the documents and asked one question: "the company pays land tax and has all the property documents—the company has the right to do whatever it wants there; what does the company then pay money for?" And the administration just shrugged. My company also lost in court (in the Moscow region, there is a law that prohibits the installation of barriers that impede passage; but, as I said, this company only blocked the entrance to a private parking lot.

My case, of course, is casuistry. Still, the seizure of land and access to water by officials and the predatory attitude to forests and other resources is like a perfect norm, which allows us to say that paragraph 2 of Article 36 does not work.

I also have no comments on point 3. The land use order is indeed specified in the Land, Forest, and Water Codes, which are federal laws. My only question is why this provision appeared in the Constitution at all.

ARTICLE 37 OF THE
CONSTITUTION

The next article is dedicated to the labor rights.

"1. Labour shall be free. Everyone shall have the right freely to use his (her) labour skills and to choose the type of activity and occupation.

2. Compulsory labour shall be forbidden.

3. Everyone shall have the right to work in conditions, which meet safety and hygiene requirements, and to receive remuneration for labour without any discrimination whatsoever and not below the minimum wage established by federal law, as well as the right of protection against unemployment.

4. The right of individual and collective labour disputes with the use of the methods for their resolution, which are provided for by federal law, including the right to strike, shall be recognized.

5. Everyone shall have the right to rest. For those working under labour contracts the duration of work time, days of rest and public holidays and annual paid leave established by federal law shall be guaranteed."

We have already discussed the opportunity to dispose of one's abilities when analyzing Article 34 of the Constitution. We then concluded that, in Russia, a huge number of people are being persecuted and banned from their professional activities: from journalists, artists, singers, and directors to teachers. State guarantees for the free disposal of one's abilities are absent, and the state uses a ban on professional activity to deal with disagreement. I will not repeat our analysis. You can refer to the revised Article 34 of the Constitution.

The situation is more complicated with the second point.

It would be surprising if the total lack of rights of the citizens of Russia would not be used for forced labor: a slave must work; otherwise, why would one need him?

The problem with forced and slave labor in Russia has existed since the very first term of Putin. He even received a separate report from the International Labor Organization (ILO) 2004 on the state of forced labor in Russia and 2006.

The Global Report and other ILO documents identify seven main forms of forced labor:

- slavery and kidnapping;

- forced participation in public works;

- forced labor in agriculture and remote areas (forced recruitment/recruitment systems);

- forced labor of domestic workers;

- bonded labor/debt bondage;

- forced labor in the army;

- forced labor as a result of human trafficking; and

- labor of prisoners (including for rehabilitation).

These are the so-called "absolute cases." But there is also partial forced labor:

- coercion to perform additional functions;

- forced to work extra hours;

- coercion to work without pay (for example, on account of a debt);

- the compulsion to work in conditions inconsistent with the concept of decent work;

- coercion to live and work under control (control over movement, restriction of freedom, a ban on treatment, etc.); and

- sexual exploitation of workers, etc.

Firstly, in Russia, the practice of using soldier labor to construct "generals' dachas" is pervasive. The army in Russia is a draft army, an archaism inherited from Peter I. Since that time, only the terms of service have changed. And having drafted people, they use them as free labor at construction sites. More on the issue here.

Secondly, punishment in the form of corrective labor is quite officially practiced in Russia (see the above "absolute forms of forced labor") - the punishment was adopted in 2017.

Thirdly, prison labor is widely used in Russia. You can read the report on the labor of prisoners here. At the same time, the labor of prisoners can be considered slavery purely; it is forced and free. For refusing to work, punishments follow, including a prisoner will not be able to leave on parole (parole) and placing in ShiZO. Payment, if it occurs, is purely symbolic, just in violation of paragraph 2 of the commented article (here). The most notorious cases go to court, but this does not fix the system. You can read more about the slave labor of prisoners here and here. At the same time, the Federal Penitentiary Service (FSIN) receives billions of rubles as a result of using such labor.

Fourth, it is the slave labor of migrants. Immigrants from the countries of the former USSR often came to Russia for labor purposes. They agreed to work in non-prestigious and low-paid jobs that Russian citizens did not want to get. However, the legislative requirements for immigrants in Russia are unusually strict, which naturally resulted in the fact that a considerable number of labor migrants became "illegal." These " illegals" found themselves between the migration hammer and the anvil of even lower-paid labor and a disenfranchised position. Even Prosecutor General Bastrykin, who could not see signs of a crime in the poisoning of Navalny, saw the plight of migrants. However, according to Putin's tradition, he blamed business for everything. Often migrants are not paid the money they earn, and they are forced to leave without getting what they owe. This is a systemic problem, and the authorities often do not even want to deal with it.

As a result of the crisis, wages in Russia (in dollar terms) fell noticeably, almost stopping the flow of labor migrants; it no longer made sense for them to take risks and humiliation for the money they could receive at home.

The authorities have solved the problem in their way. They decided to replace one slave labor with another. And instead of solving the problem of slave labor, it is proposed to exacerbate it. Thus, there are more and more initiatives to use the labor of prisoners at Putin's construction sites, following the example of the Gulag. The most "funny thing" is that the first initiative came from the Federal Penitentiary Service itself.

I believe the situation with paragraph 2 of Article 37 of the Constitution is clear to you. I suggest turning now to the third paragraph of this article. Quote from the Open Democracy website:

"Government statistics state that there is practically no strike movement in Russia. According to Rosstat, for the entire last year, there were only two strikes in the country, in which 38 people participated. But outside this comforting and artificial reality, Russians and labor migrants are not only on strike but resort to more radical actions, including hunger strikes, suicide threats and even murders of employers...

"In Russia, the prohibitive legislation on strikes was adopted in 1993 by the neo-liberal team that then came to power. It spells out a long and complicated procedure for a collective labor dispute, which is almost impossible to complete. The most important instrument of influencing the employer has been taken out of the hands of trade unions and workers.

"As a result, over the past decade and a half, official statistics record at most five cases of legal strikes per year. At the same time, the news feed is full of information about labor protests. Therefore, fifteen years ago, our independent monitoring project was born [the link added by me - A.M.].

"Workers use various forms of protest: appeals to the authorities, pickets, rallies, stop-actions, spontaneous strikes, hunger strikes, and much more...

"Approximately in 20% of two-thirds of the cases where it is known, the labor protest ends in full or partial satisfaction of the requirements and, in about the same number—in non-compliance with the demands. In half of the cases, negotiations result in protests.

"The protest is a kind of pass to the negotiations. Before the employer starts talking to you, you must prove the seriousness of your intentions ...

"In addition, trade unions in Russia have few tools to fight. They missed their opportunity at the political level. When was the last time you heard trade union representatives in Parliament raised the issue of revising the laws on strikes?

"As a result, at collective bargaining negotiations, the employer can say: "We will raise wages when there are financial opportunities," and the trade unions agree. Otherwise, if they disagree, he will say: "Then I will not take on any obligations at all." And the point is not even that this or that trade union leader is corrupt, but that he understands: let there be at least a poor agreement than none" (the full text can be read here).

Eurasianet.org quoted trade union activist, Dmitry Kozhnev, as saying:

"Strikes in Russia are not legally prohibited (the right to strike is guaranteed by Article 37 of the Constitution). However, the Labor Code makes it difficult to carry them out. "The procedure for calling a strike is very complicated and leaves many loopholes for the employer, which makes it possible to declare a strike illegal in any case"...

"The legal procedure for declaring a strike eliminates the effect of surprise: the organizers are required to notify the employer of the upcoming action 5-7 days in advance. To suspend work legally, it is necessary to go through bureaucratic procedures to resolve a collective labor dispute, reconcile the parties with the participation of government agencies, and organize a conference of workers representing more than 50% of the workforce.

""The effect of the strike is in the damage it will cause to the employer, and the Russian legislator is doing everything to reduce these troubles. Having received notice [about the strike], the employer runs to court and files a lawsuit [whether justified or not] to declare the strike illegal. The court decides on a [temporary] ban on the strike until it decides whether it is legal. But under Russian law, a strike that has not started on time cannot be resumed. We have to go through all the procedures again," Kozhnev notes ...

""As a rule, after the start of the strike, the first to be on the job are the police. Their role is to intimidate the strikers. Officials appear next, who also try to threaten. The latest strike in Kamchatka [in November 2018 at the "Ametistovoye" Gold mine of "Gold of Kamchatka" company] is an example of how the state intervenes in the conflict on the side of employers. The peculiarity of this strike is that it occurred in a remote area where shift workers (temporary workers from other regions) are brought. They were suppressed because the neighboring enterprises had the same problems. The victory of the strike in one place would lead to a chain reaction," Dmitry Kozhnev believes.

"One of the most typical non-constructive formats in which the authorities communicate with the strikers is the "master-serf" format. This conclusion is made by analysts of the Center for Economic and Political Reforms (CEPR) in monitoring social tensions in the regions of Russia in 2016.

"An example of such a reaction was the pressure on the miners of the "Kingcoal" company in the Rostov region, who were on strike due to non-payment of wages. An attempt by protesters to leave for Moscow to appeal to the federal authorities was blocked by the announcement of the anti-terrorist operation "Anaconda" in the city. The miners received threats; there were cordons at the city's exits that delayed transport, deliberately false information was disseminated in the media, according to the monitoring" (full text of the interview here).

Concerning point 5, one can give an example of the same prisoners. According to article 104 of the Penal Code, working prisoners are provided with rest in the amount of 12 to 18 working days, which is even officially two times less than rest people who for some reason are still at large.

In general, I believe that in the presence of slave labor as such in Russia, it makes no sense to talk about the right to rest. These two rights are inextricably linked, and, I believe, there are no cases when people in a slave position are granted and fully respected the right to rest . Based on this, I see no reason to analyze this point in detail.

As you understand, I am again forced to conclude that this is another non-working article of the Constitution.

ARTICLE 38 OF THE CONSTITUTION

The full text states:

"1. Maternity, childhood and family shall be protected by the State.

2. Care for children and their upbringing shall be the equal right and duty of parents.

3. Able-bodied children over 18 years of age must take care of disabled parents."

Here, as usual, LGBT people are the most discriminated against. According to paragraph 1 of article 12 of the Family Code (SC), "marriage is the union of a man and a woman." The constitution had no such limitation. They appeared only in Putin's garbage "amendments": the exact wording was introduced by clause "g" in Article 72 of the Constitution. This fact alone renders paragraph 1 inapplicable, as we have mentioned more than once.

This is due to the primitive, dense, and archaic idea of marriage as a moral status. Note that there is no punishment for the cohabitation of people of the same sex in Russia. The state actively encourages (mostly verbally) citizens to have children, but marriage is not a moral category; it is exclusively a legal institution.

Marriage, firstly, does not oblige spouses to have children. As well as, its absence does not affect their appearance. I guess I should not explain this to adults who have children and mistresses, but officials in Russia are striking in their ignorance.

Secondly, marriage allows you to avoid many formal actions. It speeds up the resolution of some exclusively legal issues: who will the doctors call if one of the spouses has an accident and is unconscious, what is the regime of jointly acquired property, who has the right to inherit, and so on. Moreover, for two LGBT representatives in a homophobic society, their partner is often the only person close to them.

In this regard, the formal marriage restriction only for people of different sexes is a logical idiocy. Suppose we proceed from some "moral" views that sex should be only for procreation, and everything else "is a sin" and should not be encouraged, then in the same way. In that case, it is necessary to prohibit oral and anal sex. And a bailiff should be assigned to every married couple, because, from such sex, there will be no children.

When the church (because it is the ROC that is the locomotive of homophobic rhetoric) (in an allegedly secular state) and the state (in the best fascist traditions) stop inspecting the bed of two adult people acting by mutual agreement, then we can assume that this Article works. So far, I have to repeat myself; this is a sign of a totalitarian state.

This, however, is not all. Homosexual couples are also prohibited from adopting children at a completely official level. And against employees of the social protection authorities, criminal cases are initiated because of the permission to adopt a child by a gay couple.

Paragraph 2 of Article 38 is entirely declarative. Its legal essence is also not clear. If we talk about the equality of men and women in raising a child, then there were just big problems with it (see the analysis of Article 19 of the Constitution). It is even logically clear that the presence of different rights for men and women means different rights in raising children.

Well, then, let's go through family relations in connection with this issue.

The previously mentioned gender inequality immediately catches the eye: the Constitution protects only motherhood, not fatherhood.

Formally, only four articles in the Family Code of Russia (FC) explicitly declare gender inequality: 1) the right to dissolve a marriage (here a husband cannot file for divorce without his wife's consent during his wife's pregnancy and one year after the birth of a child—regardless of whether it is his child or not) (Article 17 of the FC); 2) establishing the origin of children (paternity and motherhood)—now a woman is limited here, she does not have the right to file a lawsuit to establish motherhood, only a man can file a lawsuit to establish paternity of a child (Article 49 of the FC); 3) establishing paternity for children born out of wedlock (if a child is born out of wedlock, then the father is recorded simply at the request of the woman, while the father can only submit a joint application with the woman—that is, her consent is required, which significantly complicates the issue in the event of, say, death of mother or her unknown absence); 4) the obligation of the husband to pay alimony to his wife during her pregnancy and within three years from the date of birth of a common child (Articles 89-90 of the FC).

You can read more about gender inequality in Russian family law here, but we can conclude that husband and wife have different rights and obligations in marriage and family. And the state does not even formally consider their positions to be equivalent.

The thing I want to comment on regarding paragraph 3: I am puzzled by its presence in the Constitution and the chapter on "human rights and freedoms." According to the FC, disabled parents have the right to file claims against their non-disabled children about their maintenance. Still, I don't understand what this has to do with natural human rights, perhaps because I'm not an expert in family law. Nevertheless, it is good to assume that this item works.

Based on the above, Article 38 is partially valid. However, it must be borne in mind that its "acting part" is purely declarative and is poorly applicable in practice.

ARTICLE 39 OF THE CONSTITUTION

Article 39 of the Constitution states:

"1. Everyone shall be guaranteed social security for old age, in case of illness, disability and loss of the breadwinner, for the bringing up of children and in other cases specified by law.

2. State pensions and social benefits shall be established by law.

3. Voluntary social insurance, the creation of additional forms of social security and charity shall be encouraged."

This article echoes Article 7 of the Constitution, which declares the supposedly social nature of the Russian Federation. Here, as you can see, concern for disabled citizens is stated. Well, let's dive into the numbers.

Let's start with disabled people.

According to the alternative report of the Commissioner for Human Rights in the Russian Federation within the framework of the 19th session of the UN Committee on the Rights of Persons with Disabilities, according to Rosstat, in Russia in 2017 there were 12,314,000 people with disabilities (more than 9% of the total population).

In its report, the Institute for Social Analysis and Forecasting "Disability and Social Status of the Disabled in Russia" indicates the following (you can download the full report here):

"According to the CLS-2014 survey [selective surveys conducted in 2014 - A.M.], 16% of disabled people have a paid job or an income-generating occupation (as of the week preceding the study). Among 30- and 40-year-old disabled people, the share of employed reaches 27%. At this age, disabled people with the III disability group are employed, and almost half of them have a labor income. For disabled people of group II, labor activity is less common; it is about 15% ...

"The individual income of a disabled person mainly consists of pensions and wages if they are working. The income security of a person with a disability at retirement age is essentially similar to the security of a pensioner without an officially established disability—the primary source of his income is a pension, sometimes combined with a salary. The pension assigned to people of working age due to disability in more than 90% of cases **is labor pension** [highlighted by me - A.M.] if a person ever worked...."

That is, in Russia, there is simply no disability pension. In 90% of cases, this is an old-age pension. The remaining 10% are accounted for by the disabled, who have become disabled without having a work record. The report continues:

"When a disabled person reaches the border of the official working age, he (a) automatically (without a personal application to the Pension Fund office) becomes a recipient of an old-age pension. According to the assigned disability group, they receive only single cash payments, formally leaving the disability pension recipients (FIU, 2015). At the same time, the disability insurance pension for persons with sufficient work experience is converted into an old-age insurance pension, and the rest of the disabled are transferred to a social old-age pension ...

"In turn, the household's assessment of its financial situation also indicates the low level of monetary income of the disabled and their families. Comprehensive monitoring of the population's living conditions in 2014 showed that half (49%) of households consisting exclusively of persons with disabilities find it difficult to buy clothes and pay for housing and communal services, including 5% of such families do not have enough money for food. Among households of a mixed type, which include disabled and non-disabled people, 39% find it difficult to buy clothes and pay for housing and communal services, while in general, among all households—29.5%. The average level of family income security, when there is enough money for food and clothing, but they cannot buy the necessary durable goods (TV set, refrigerator, etc.), is typical for 44-46% of households with and without disabled people. Only 7% of households consisting only of persons with disabilities and 16% of mixed families can overcome the bar of income sufficient for necessary durable goods. Such well-to-do families are much more common among all households, 26%..."

Disabled people also face numerous domestic inconveniences:

"The problem of the absence or poor operation of an elevator in an apartment building is exceptionally acute for the disabled. About 52% of people with disabilities living on the second floor and above cannot use an elevator since there is none in the house ... Given poorly functioning elevators, up to 55% of people with disabilities living in apartment blocks have limited access to the street. In addition, as the study of the Institute of Social Analysis and Prognosis showed, a significant group of citizens **does not have an officially established disability group** [highlighted by me - A.M.], but they experience severe restrictions in fundamental areas of life, including movement. Especially many of these are expected among people of the most advanced age ...

"Housing for families with disabilities is physically worse than average. Such families more often rate their accommodation as poor or very poor.

They more often say that they experience a lack of heat or high humidity in an apartment or house .... The cramped living conditions for households with disabilities are less typical than for other families due to the smaller size of these households. The difficult housing situation is a direct consequence of the low housing mobility of the population when many households continue to live in the same place as 25 years ago. It is often associated with a lack of family funds, but also with attachment to a place, fear of change or the process of buying / exchanging a home, which is especially true for the elderly."

How many disabled people, in principle, consider state assistance sufficient? The report addresses this issue as well:

"At the same time, according to the survey, the majority of officially disabled people consider the assistance received from the state insufficient—63%.

- interruptions in the provision of technical means of rehabilitation (wheelchairs, diapers, napkins, etc., hygiene products, etc.);

- the impossibility of obtaining technical means of rehabilitation that would improve the quality of life (for example, special keyboards, orthoses, walkers), the low quality of the proposed means of rehabilitation (wheelchairs, diapers, etc.); and claims for them usually ignored;

- lack of rehabilitation centers, correctional kindergartens, and schools for the profile of health disorders in the area of transport accessibility;

- it is challenging to find teachers for a child at home;

- lack of psychological support for the disabled themselves and their relatives, which would help to cope with the constant stress and pressure of society;

- extremely uncomfortable, time-consuming, and psychologically expensive process of registration and re-registration of disability, the need to solve organizational problems in this area;

- inability to use public transport, the need for a social taxi;

- social isolation (lack of communication, close relationships); lack of leisure and development centers for adults with disabilities...

"Respondents to Institute of Social Analysis and Prognosis surveys said that they lacked specific types of social support: improved living conditions; help with home renovation assistance with paying utility bills and firewood; in-kind assistance (provision of household appliances, products); travel expenses for an accompanying child with a disability; provision of a car; transportation services for the disabled; travel concessions; legal support. Respondents also talked about the insufficiency of home care—that they need a home helper, a person who would provide care, and those who already use the services of social workers noted that they have too high a workload and cannot give them enough attention.

"It should also be mentioned that several respondents noted that they had problems receiving treatment and social support due to the lack of registration at the residence or residence not at the place of registration" (ibid.). The last point is about the issue of registration at the place of residence, which we spoke about when analyzing Article 27 of the Constitution.

I think the issue of disabled people can be closed: they are limited both physically and financially (no more than 16% have a job), there is literally no disability pension, and the environment is practically inaccessible for them, forcing them to stay within four walls in apartments, below average quality. Such is the support.

Maybe the situation with pensioners is better? Moreover, we have already quoted the report, which indicates that 90% of disabled people receive old-age labor pensions.

In part, we touched on this issue when analyzing Article 7 of the Constitution. I cited footage of pensioners rummaging through the garbage, which, as you might guess, does not come from a good and decent life.

But maybe I'm exaggerating, and these are isolated cases? Then let's find out.

I want to note right away that the pension system in Russia is a distribution system. This means that the money that the state collects from the salary of each working person does not go to his pension account and accumulates there until old age. They go to the Pension Fund of Russia and are distributed among current pensioners. The worker is promised that sometime in the future, he will receive his pension, but from the next generation.

This system was inherited by Russia from the USSR and has several significant drawbacks. The most important of which is its structure of the financial pyramid: 1) everything is relatively good when the number of paying people is more than those consuming pensions; 2) pension money is not invested but immediately distributed among current pensioners.

As a result of the natural processes of urbanization and thanks to the numerous wars waged by the USSR and Russia, the so-called "demographic pits" were formed, a significant decrease in those born in specific years. As a result, contributions from working persons to the pension fund are not enough to support the minimum pensions that the state guarantees to pensioners, and the budget is forced to close the shortcomings (and this is despite the fact that the contribution to the Pension Fund is 22% of the employee's salary (part 1 of article 2 article 425 of the Tax Code of the Russian Federation; at the same time, for salaries above the established limit (depending on the year, but about 80,000 rubles per month (about $1,250)), an additional 10%).

The authorities tried to solve this problem, and in 2005, they allowed 6% of this 22% to be directed to a person's accumulative pension account. In this case, the employer could double this amount. Everything was going relatively well until the capture of Crimea and sanctions for its annexation. At some point, the government withdrew these pension savings, declaring they would "go to the development of Crimea." I then lost 300,000 rubles (about $9,090) accumulated over nine years of job and savings.

In 2015, the government tried once again to solve the pension problem. And it introduced a system of "cumulative pension points" (popularly known as "naebally" — a play word of a very rude Russian word for 'cheating' and 'points'). From this day on, not money, but some points are credited to a person's account. These are like candy wrappers, or come up with any other word you might find funny, like 'pebbles,' for example. How good a pebble is and how much it will cost in rubles when reaching retirement age is unknown. One can get a maximum of 10 pebbles per year (that is, the amount is also limited and does not depend on salary or contributions to the Pension Fund, no matter how one tries to increase

it). The government sets the exchange rate of pebbles. Accordingly, an unknown and arbitrary value is present when calculating the future pension, which makes such calculations impossible.

In 2018, Putin also announced an increase in the retirement age by five years (for men and women). This was done under the pretext of increasing pensions. However, the Minister of Finance admitted that this was only a measure aimed at saving the budget: "Both documents propose to establish an indexation of pensions up to 4% for three years, which will save from 84.5 to 240.5 billion rubles."

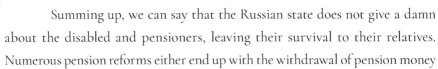

As a result, the average pension in 2019 was 15,500 rubles (about $250), and we can see numerous shots of pensioners looking for food in trash cans (additional details can be read here.

Summing up, we can say that the Russian state does not give a damn about the disabled and pensioners, leaving their survival to their relatives. Numerous pension reforms either end up with the withdrawal of pension money or in budget savings. As a result, social security puts the needy on the brink of survival. To some extent, yes, formally, there is social support, but it is not aimed at the well-being of those in need and is only a burden for the authorities.

ARTICLE 40 OF THE CONSTITUTION

The full text is as follows:

"1. Everyone shall have the right to a home. Nobody may be arbitrarily deprived of his (her) home.

2. State government bodies and local self-government bodies shall promote housing construction and create conditions for exercising the right to a home.

3. Low-income citizens and other citizens mentioned in law who are in need of a home may receive it either free of charge or for an affordable payment from State, municipal and other housing funds according to the norms established by law."

When analyzing article 35 of the Constitution, we touched upon the deprivation of the right to housing, particularly the possibility of being deprived of housing as a result of a renovation.

Regarding providing housing to those in need, such programs exist in Russia. The problem is that many more people need to improve their living conditions than houses and apartments under construction. According to the Minister of Housing and Public Utilities Irek Fayzullin, as of the beginning of 2022, 182,000 people are on the waiting list for apartments. According to forecasts, their number will double by the end of the year. And this is only in the unified register of the needy; outside the register, 298,000 orphans are waiting for their turn. At the same time, according to the same Faizullin, in 2022, 4,900 orphans were provided with housing.

As Mishustin (Prime Minister of the Russian Federation) said, the implementation of the housing program will cost the budget 150 trillion (sic!) Rubles (about $2,5 trillion) (note that the Russian budget exceeds 22 trillion rubles ($344 billion) a year, a third of which is secret and is spent on defense). Therefore, even if the entire budget of Russia is spent exclusively on a program to provide housing for those in need, it will take more than seven years, and without touching the secret part of the budget, more than 12 years. And this is if we assume the queue would not grow. And given the unleashed war with Ukraine, I can confidently say this program will be one of the first to be curtailed by the Russian authorities.

In terms of the pace of implementation, you can look at the number of housing received by orphans this year — 4,900 out of 298,000 in need is 1.6%. Then, at such a pace, children will be provided with housing in 62 years.

In this regard, I believe that although the state recognizes certain obligations to provide housing to those in need (especially those from the police, military, and special service), it cannot fulfill these obligations. Therefore, this article is partially violated by "renovation." As mentioned above; it does not apply to a wide range of people and therefore is rather declarative.

Otherwise, I have no particular complaints about the execution of this article; a certain desire to fulfill it is visible. Still, its execution is simply impossible from a financial point of view. So that our conclusion is not entirely gloomy, we will assume that the article is partially valid.

ARTICLE 41 OF THE CONSTITUTION

The next article is dedicated to the health of citizens:

"1. Everyone shall have the right to health protection and medical care. Medical care in State and municipal health institutions shall be rendered to citizens free of charge at the expense of the appropriate budget, insurance premiums and other proceeds.

2. In the Russian Federation federal programmes for the protection and improvement of the health of the public shall be financed, measures shall be taken to develop State, municipal and private healthcare systems, and activities shall be encouraged which contribute to the improvement of human health, the development of physical education and sport, and ecological, sanitary and epidemiological well-being.

3. The concealment by officials of facts and circumstances, which pose a threat to the life and health of people, shall result in liability according to federal law."

Let's start in order.

Namely, with the assertion that medicine is free in Russia. It came to Russia from the USSR and is one of its biggest myths. This is not surprising that if money is spent on it, it means that it needs to be taken from somewhere else.

Thus, in Russia, there is a Compulsory Medical Insurance Fund (CMI). Every month, 5.1% of its size is withheld from the salary of each employee (clause 3, part 2, article 425 of the Tax Code of the Russian Federation). I note that the CMI Fund operates on the same principle as the Pension Fund: current employees pay for the treatment of patients.

The report "Healthy healthcare: a step into the future for Russian medicine" (2018) by the international Boston Consulting Group (BCG) states:

"... in its November 2017 report on the Russian economy, the World Bank estimated the public spending of the Russian Federation on health at 3.4% of GDP in 2015 and 3.6% of GDP in 2016. This is well below the EU (7.2% of GDP) and OECD (6.5% of GDP) averages." (page 5).

At the same time, the work of a Russian doctor is paid very poorly, while Rosstat greatly exaggerates the salary of doctors.

As a result, Russia in 2018 occupied the following positions in international rankings:

1. 151 out of 245 in life expectancy;

2. 141 out of 183 places in terms of the number of lost years [total time of disability of patients - A.M.];

3. 55th out of 55 in health spending efficiency;

4. 108 out of 168 in treatment effectiveness; and

5. 72% of countries are more efficient than Russia in terms of VBHC (value-based healthcare) (from here, p. 14).

At the same time, there were already no positive dynamics for that.

The full text of the report can be read here.

The situation has worsened greatly due to the COVID-19 pandemic.

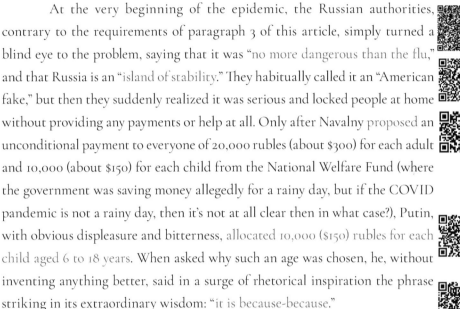

At the very beginning of the epidemic, the Russian authorities, contrary to the requirements of paragraph 3 of this article, simply turned a blind eye to the problem, saying that it was "no more dangerous than the flu," and that Russia is an "island of stability." They habitually called it an "American fake," but then they suddenly realized it was serious and locked people at home without providing any payments or help at all. Only after Navalny proposed an unconditional payment to everyone of 20,000 rubles (about $300) for each adult and 10,000 (about $150) for each child from the National Welfare Fund (where the government was saving money allegedly for a rainy day, but if the COVID pandemic is not a rainy day, then it's not at all clear then in what case?), Putin, with obvious displeasure and bitterness, allocated 10,000 ($150) rubles for each child aged 6 to 18 years. When asked why such an age was chosen, he, without inventing anything better, said in a surge of rhetorical inspiration the phrase striking in its extraordinary wisdom: "it is because-because."

But the Russian authorities would not be like this if they weren't trying to make money on COVID. They introduced fines for violating the regime by leaving people locked up at home in "self-isolation." Authorities banned all conventions and meetings (of course, only for those who disagree with the regime). For example, at this time, COVID did not prevent Putin from gathering thousands of people without masks (according to propaganda, more than 100,000 people) in stadiums to "celebrate the annexation of Crimea." Obviously, Putin, being on his intellectual level subpar with the virus, somehow agreed with it not to infect his "followers."

However, for example, when the leader of the Alliance of Doctors, Anastasia Vasilyeva, arrived in the Novgorod region with masks for doctors

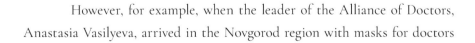

(who didn't even have enough masks for their work!), she was detained by the police twice, beaten, and in the end fined.

 A whole heap of cases was even initiated, collectively nicknamed "The Sanitary Case." Allegedly, in the protests on January 23, 2021, some people infected with COVID were among the protesters against Putin's 'amendments to Constitution.'

As a result, the government used COVID to put even more pressure on civil society instead of dealing with the pandemic.

Covid restrictions have also allowed Putin to "vote" for amendments to the Constitution, which we will discuss further.

 At the same time, attempts to force propaganda to switch from the mode "covid is an American fake" to the pro-vaccination mode failed miserably . They simultaneously tried to agitate people to get vaccinated with the domestic SPUTNIK V vaccine and lie about poor-quality foreign vaccinations from which people die. But in the minds of Russians, the West is associated with quality, and all the "horror stories" were automatically transferred to SPUTNIK V itself. Putin himself did not add confidence to the domestic vaccine. He liked to flaunt his senile boobs on camera, but for some reason, he was embarrassed to show how he was vaccinated. Still, he grew himself a table of incredible length, which inspired a bunch of memes (if you don't use Google chrome, you need to switch to 'pictures' menu for this link). The people were doubling that a country that cannot even produce its own insulin can make "the best vaccine in the world" at all.

 As a result, COVID has claimed more than 1 million (sic!) lives of Russians.

I do not know what conclusion the dear reader will draw, but in my opinion, Article 41 of the Constitution also does not work. Medicine is de facto not free; at the same time, it is very much underfunded, and the authorities constantly distort information and statistics on diseases (including on AIDS: here and here), of course, on COVID, and use the pandemic solely for repressive purposes. So the result is millions of deaths combined with a devastating blow to the economy.

Let's move on to the next article.

ARTICLE 42 OF THE CONSTITUTION

Its full text reads:

"Everyone shall have the right to a favourable environment, reliable information on the state of the environment and compensation for damage caused to his (her) health and property by violations of environmental laws."

We discussed this in sufficient detail when analyzing Article 9 of the Constitution.

In detail, the situation with the environment in Russia is depressing. Thus, the "Need Help" Charitable Foundation and the "To Be Precise" data platform, in a joint study, calculated the number of people affected by the state of the environment. Referring to Rospotrebnadzor, they point out: "According to Rospotrebnadzor, 136,000 deaths (6% of total mortality) and almost 4.3 million cases of diseases (2% of morbidity) in Russia in 2021 were due to poor ecology—poor quality of atmospheric air, drinking water, soil, unsafe food. More than 90 million people (63.6% of the country's population) experience the impact of chemical, biological, and other environmental pollution...

"...46% of Russia's urban population lives in cities with high and very high levels of air pollution. Of the 251 cities where Roshydromet conducts observations, in 2021, high and very high levels of pollution were observed in 122.

"A very high level of air pollution in 2021 was noted in 42 cities from 23 regions of Russia. Most of these cities are in the Irkutsk region and the Krasnoyarsk Territory ...

"... it is impossible not to note the change in the dynamics of all indicators related to air pollution in 2017 - 2018. Until 2017, mortality and morbidity steadily decreased, and then they grew.

"In 2014, the number of additional deaths per 100 thousand of the population from all causes associated with air pollution in residential [territories intended for housing] areas was 7.55, in 2018 - 1.6, in 2021 - 4.6.

"Ten years ago, the most significant number of environmentally related deaths and cases were caused by air pollution. In 2021, drinking water pollution leads the way in both indicators, with 11,000 deaths and 1.54 million cases of illness.

"The number of deaths related to air or soil pollution has more than halved during this time (by 53.5% and 53.8%, respectively). The number of deaths associated with contaminated drinking water decreased by only 4.4%.

"In general, the situation with drinking water in the country is gradually improving: since 2018, the share of the population provided with high-quality drinking water has increased by 1.8% - up to 87.4%, but in some regions (in particular, in Kalmykia, where high-quality drinking water from only 7.5% of the population are provided with centralized water supply systems) remains frightening.

""The quality of water in natural springs is not improving. State reports say that over the past 10-20 years, the discharge of wastewater into water bodies has been significantly reduced. But these reports consider only point sources

- discharge through pipes and other technical devices. But diffuse pollution, which accounts for at least half of the pollution in the country, is not taken into account. We have neither monitoring of diffuse pollution nor projects aimed at its reduction," says Viktor Danilov-Danilyan, scientific director of the Institute of Water Problems of the Russian Academy of Sciences...

"[At the same time,] the number of very dirty water units requiring urgent water protection measures is constantly growing. Since 2014, they have increased by 1.5 times. Experts in the report also note that the list of water bodies requiring restoration is much wider than is being implemented under the federal project. And the data of Roshydromet largely confirm this...

"According to Rospotrebnadzor, soil pollution caused 1,752 deaths and 261,000 cases of illness in 2021. Contamination of food products (chemical components—cadmium, mercury, nitrates, pesticides—microbiological and parasitological contamination) caused another 1.4 million cases of diseases ...

"According to the Institute of Global Climate and Ecology, named after academician Yu. A. Israel, in Russia 613.1 thousand km² of soils (or 3.5% of the country's area) are chronically polluted with toxicants of industrial origin. The highest proportion of chronically contaminated territories is in the Central Federal District (19.4%), and the lowest is in the Far East (0.4%). The largest total area of such territories is in the Siberian Federal District (152.4 thousand km ²), and the smallest is in the North Caucasus (14.1 thousand km ²) ...

"At the beginning of 2020, experts of the Accounts Chamber considered that while maintaining the volumes of generation and disposal of municipal solid waste (MSW) that existed at that time, already in 2022, in 17 regions of Russia, there would run out of landfill space. There will be nowhere to put waste: most regions do not have the opportunity to create new landfills. With another 15 regions by the end of 2024...

"Since the start of the pandemic, MSW generation in Russia has fallen by 20%, from 417 kg per capita in 2019 to 331 kg in 2021, but this gives the regions only a tiny respite. The situation with burial remains almost unchanged: 92% of the generated municipal solid waste went to landfills.

"The integrated municipal solid waste management system, which is part of the Ecology national project, should ensure 100% waste sorting in the country by 2030. That's just because sorting does not imply the same percentage of processing. According to Rosprirodnadzor, in 2021, 46.5% of municipal solid waste went for sorting and only 6.5% for processing. If the proportion is maintained, with a predicted 100% sorting, only 14% of the trash will be recycled..." (you can read the whole report here).

The Russian authorities issued the law on citizens' access to information only in March 2021, while in violation of this article, "secret enterprises" were withdrawn from monitoring. However, the commented article does not suggest exceptions to information about the environment.

But there is a downward trend. For example, in 2022, the government reduced environmental requirements for construction.

This situation naturally leads to environmental protests, and in general, 35% of Russians are ready to participate in eco-protests.

Given the above, it is doubtful that this article works, especially in the context of a direct ban on environmental monitoring of "secret enterprises."

ARTICLE 43 OF THE CONSTITUTION

The text of Article 43 of Constitution reads:

"1. Everyone shall have the right to education.

2. General access and free pre-school, secondary and secondary vocational education in State and municipal educational institutions and at enterprises shall be guaranteed.

3. Everyone shall have the right to receive on a competitive basis free higher education in State and municipal educational institutions and at enterprises.

4. Basic general education shall be compulsory. Parents or guardians shall ensure that children receive a basic general education.

5. The Russian Federation shall establish federal State educational standards and shall support various forms of education and self-education."

The good news is there is no special tax in Russia that would go to some kind of Compulsory Education fund which would distribute the money among educational institutions. On the other hand, like any "unimportant industry" along with the pension system or medicine, education is severely underfunded.

In addition, education has many internal problems that are only getting worse.

The first thing I would like to draw your attention to in connection with free education is the large gap between its different levels. A school program alone is not enough for a student, having graduated with honors, to enter a university immediately. Almost all parents have to hire tutors in various subjects necessary for admission to the university. Tutoring is so widespread in Russia that foreign researchers even gave it a special term, 'shadow education.' And by definition, tutoring is a paid service. At its core, tutoring is a system that is designed to hide failures in educational services, and given that from the beginning of the 2000s to 2019, the tutoring market has grown six times, the failures are getting bigger.

According to official data, a third of students are helped by repeaters, and many of them have been studying since the primary grades.

Where do these educational failures come from? There are six factors:

- Huge bureaucracy - "Any official is sure: it is worth slightly loosening control—and a lazy, negligent teacher or associate professor will immediately stop teaching. Endless reports, individual and collective plans, programs, evaluation funds, certifications, Federal State Educational Standards, accreditations, and effective contracts waste time and reduce motivation to work.";

- Inefficient and inadequate funding - "The Ministry of Education, as a regulator of creating conditions for schools, is now **absolutely not fulfilling its functional duties** [highlighted by me - A.M.]: it does not affect either the amount of funds received, or the mechanism for spending money, or its effectiveness. In this regard, there is a large gap between funding and the quality of education.

"The basis of the problem of our formation is the normalization of financial flows because now the nationalized budget is about 2.76 trillion rubles, while the required 3.6. In addition, given the number of barriers that money passes through before reaching the regions, according to various sources, about 30% of the initial figures decrease."

 Outdated knowledge and methods - "School manuals still contain tasks about Masha, who buys a jar of jam for three kopecks; From time immemorial, children write dictations with words like "obluchok" (a part of the horse cart where coachman sat). Most educators attribute this problem to the poor quality of the work of teams of authors and methodologists who compile textbooks";

 Separation from practice - "International monitoring shows that the essence of the education problem is that our school is strong in formal knowledge, but not at all strong in practical knowledge. That is, the content of the school curriculum is formally at a high level, but schoolchildren often do not know how to integrate knowledge from different areas (this is especially clearly seen in the examples of PISA). They remember the program they have completed, but they cannot extract real opportunities from it in the future; it is difficult for children to use metasubjectivity and combinatorics of knowledge from different industries regarding non-trivial tasks";

 Lack of young teachers - "Russia lacks young teachers. According to the data for 2019, which was previously cited by former Minister of Education Olga Vasilyeva, the number of teachers **who have *not* reached retirement or pre-retirement age** [highlighted by me - A.M.] ranges from 11-13% of the total share of the teaching community. As Deputy Chairman of the State Duma Committee on Education and Science Boris Chernyshov explained to Gazeta.Ru, now the problem of training and attracting young specialists to school is one of the main ones in the field of education";

- Lack of motivation and inclusion - "...the vector to emasculate the content is obvious. For example, from Efrosinina's original reading textbook for elementary school, we now see a pitiful resemblance: popular works, including the same excerpts from Harry Potter, have disappeared, but there are a lot of patriotic poems. Naturally, the interest of the modern child in this textbook is reduced. Separately, you can evaluate the illustrative series that accompany the content.

This situation is aggravated by the introduction of useless and unnecessary classes like the "foundations of Orthodoxy" (we note, in violation of Article 28 of the Constitution) or the recently proposed lessons of "initial military training." Economy? Law? What for? Let's better learn how to be baptized or assemble a machine gun.

As a result, Russia has enormous problems with science and technology. Thus, according to the Accounts Chamber, regarding patent applications, Russia is 16 times behind the United States and 38 times behind China.

Separately, I would like to go through point 5: "The Russian Federation establishes federal state educational standards, supports various forms of education and self-education."

Higher educational institutions have always been famous for their freethinking. Naturally, this could not but irritate the Russian state. Thus, the European University in St. Petersburg was closed. The government has controlled many other universities by placing members of United Russia there.

At first, the Russian authorities dealt with the country's two leading universities: Moscow State University and St. Petersburg State University. They eliminated the election of their rectors. In 2009, the State Duma passed a law according to which Moscow State University and St. Petersburg State University acquire a special status: they receive a separate line in the federal budget, and the rector is appointed by presidential decree.

The publication of the project has compiled a report on the attack on the freedom of Russian education:

"Ten years later, a few weeks before the end of the term of the rector of Moscow State University Sadovnichy, the parliament adopted an amendment abolishing the age limit for the rectors of Moscow State University and St. Petersburg State University. Time-tested people work in both universities: at Moscow State University—the scientific supervisor of Vladimir Putin's daughter Ekaterina Tikhonova, twice his confidant and member of the supreme council of the United Russia party, at St. Petersburg State University—Nikolai Kropachev, also a member of United Russia and a former teacher of Dmitry Medvedev...

"In December 2008, when the so-called "dissenters' marches" were taking place in Moscow—opposition street actions—the administration of the Higher School of Economics (HSE) received a letter from Alexander Ivanov, Major General of the Central Internal Affairs Directorate for Moscow. The officer raised the question before the university leadership about the "feasibility of further education" of six participants in political rallies, who introduced themselves to law enforcement officers as students of the HSE political faculty.

"Then HSE Rector Yaroslav Kuzminov publicly stated that the university would not expel students, and now HSE Vice-Rector Valeria Kasamara said that "the university's position is that political students are their own business." Years later, Kuzminov and Kasamara will become the personification of the political lack of freedom in Vyshka [HSE], and both will get closer to the authorities."

I want to note that the very requirement to expel students for political reasons violates paragraph 3 of the commented article.

The authors of the report continued:

"A more decisive crackdown in universities began in 2011-12 after thousands of rallies against fraud in the 2011 State Duma elections. This was the first mass participation of students in rallies, but every year more and more young people came out to protest. For example, in June 2017, at a regular rally organized by Alexei Navalny, the number of people aged 18 to 23 made up 38% of the total number of participants.

"The next step in increasing pressure on politically active students was during the summer protests of 2019 and the "Moscow case." Then the most notable case was the criminal case against Yegor Zhukov, a student of the HSE political faculty.

"The Zhukov case also involved teachers in political disputes. In August 2019, several HSE professors spoke negatively about the rallies, saying, "the university is out of politics." The dean of the Faculty of Communications, an expert close to Putin, Andrey Bystritsky, wrote the first column in Moskovsky Komsomolets. After him, professors of other faculties began to speak similarly. A few weeks later, the student magazine DOXA was denied participation in the traditional celebration of HSE Day in Gorky Park on the grounds that the publication was engaged in political activities. Soon, several academicians left the HSE for political reasons, and over the past ten years, the university has lost 28 employees for the same reason. Among them were Novaya Gazeta editor Kirill Martynov, Transparency International Russia co-founder Elena Panfilova, municipal deputy Yulia Galyamina, political scientist Alexander Kynev...

"In December 2019, DOXA magazine was stripped of the status of a student organization, and then the HSE stopped issuing such status to any journalistic organization altogether. Finally, in the winter of 2020, HSE changed its internal rules, prohibiting staff and students from using the HSE affiliation when making public political statements.

"The same thing happened at other universities, with the only difference being that by 2019 most of them had been "cleansed" much more strongly than HSE. In October 2019, the leadership of Moscow State University threatened to expel journalism students Marina Kim and Fariza Dudarova for collecting guarantees in support of the arrested mathematics graduate student Azat Miftakhov. And at the Russian Social University (RSSU), a Faculty of

International Relations student was summoned to the security service because he participated in one of the summer rallies. In October 2019, several more students, who were detained for participation in the summer protests, went through preventive conversations with the RSSU security service...

"Having studied the biographies of 559 leaders—rectors, presidents and vice-rectors (the first, as well as for security, educational and educational work) of the 100 best universities in Russia according to Forbes magazine — "the Project" and DOXA found that 74% of rectors are somehow connected with the government, 47%— with the ruling United Russia party (including those having the status of a deputy). 24% of university managers held the positions of deputies of various levels; they are now or were candidates for deputies or participated in the primaries, at least 2% are former security officials, 14% were formerly confidants of Putin, Sergey Sobyanin and Dmitry Medvedev..."

Accordingly, the state, having taken complete control over universities and expelling students who disagree with the authorities' policy, deliberately violates paragraphs 3 and 5 of Article 43 of the Constitution.

I also remind you that the state excludes "foreign agents" from the educational process, which directly contradicts paragraph 5 of Article 43 of the Constitution.

Based on the above, I believe that Article 43 of the Constitution is valid only in parts of paragraphs 2 and 4 (compulsory secondary education). If it is free is a big question, the state directly interferes with obtaining higher education for "objectionable" students and directly interferes in the educational process, eliminating student independence.

ARTICLE 44 OF THE CONSTITUTION

The full text states:

"1. Everyone shall be guaranteed the freedom of literary, artistic, scientific, technical and other types of creative activity and teaching. Intellectual property shall be protected by law.

2. Everyone shall have the right to participate in cultural life and use cultural establishments, and the right of access to cultural valuables.

3. Everyone shall be obliged to care for the preservation of the cultural and historical heritage, and to protect monuments of history and culture."

We spoke about freedom of creativity in connection with the analysis of Article 37 of the Constitution; it does not exist in Russia, and any expression of thought that differs from the state is persecuted and directly prohibited. Teaching is also forbidden for "foreign agents," as discussed in the previous article's analysis.

Point 2 goes hand in hand with point 1; it is difficult to imagine "participation in cultural life" for authors and performers whose concerts, books, and films are banned.

Paragraph 3 is violated by the state's complete disregard for architectural monuments. According to a brief report of the "All-Russian Society for the Protection of Historical and Cultural Monuments," "Over the past 10 years, more than 2.5 thousand monuments have perished in the Russian Federation. Annual losses amount to 150-200 monuments...

"Recently, **155 archeological monuments** have been lost on the territory of the Russian Federation.

"Total:

155 monuments.

Including:

- 17 - due to hydro technical construction
- 35 - due to plowing
- 8 - due to industrial and road construction
- 55 - due to various kinds of anthropogenic interference.

"Keep on breaking down:

More than **17 thousand monuments** in total

Including:

- 3.3 thousand - due to hydraulic engineering construction
- 8.7 thousand - as a result of plowing
- 0.8 thousand - industrial and road construction
- 2.3 thousand - as a result of other types of anthropogenic interference (mainly predatory excavations)

- 2 thousand - under the influence of natural processes.

"Most of the archeological monuments are in unsatisfactory or emergency condition. The reasons for this are not only external natural factors but also the lack of definition of the boundaries of their territory for most archeological monuments and, accordingly, the assignment of the lands occupied by them to the lands of historical and cultural purpose.

"Historic cities and settlements.

"Until now, not a single historical settlement has been put under state protection in accordance with the current legislation. One of the most critical problems of preserving the complex cultural and natural heritage of historical settlements is the uncertainty of the status of the "historical city." This "honorary title" does not give any special rights and does not impose specific obligations in comparison with other administrative-territorial entities. When declaring the city "historical," no economic and social conditions were stipulated that would contribute to both the revival of the heritage of the historical settlement and the special conduct of economic activities on its territory, within which the preservation of historical economic and cultural traditions would be encouraged, old quarters were not destroyed, the landscape originality of the urban environment was preserved. There is no legislatively defined economic mechanism to help restore architectural monuments and the historical environment, and attract additional investment flows in this area.

"Moreover, often the work on the real restoration of historic buildings and the preservation of cultural and natural heritage is in direct conflict with any historical city's economic and budgetary interests.

"The state of most historical settlements is also assessed by experts as close to critical. In recent years, the unjustified and, in many cases, illegal demolition of historic buildings and new construction in historical territories have not only not been reduced but have become genuinely massive.

"**Examples**:

"50 historical buildings (including those protected by the state) were demolished in **Ufa** during the period 1999-2004.

"The problem with **wooden buildings** in Arkhangelsk, Vologda, Nizhny Novgorod, Kazan, Ufa, Tobolsk."

You can read the full report here.

As we can see, there are a massive number of historical monuments that the state simply does not give a damn about and it does practically nothing to preserve them.

In connection with the above, I believe it is fair to point out that Article 44 of the Constitution does not work in full.

ARTICLE 45 OF THE CONSTITUTION

The full text reads:

"1. State protection of human and civil rights and freedoms in the Russian Federation shall be guaranteed.

2. Everyone shall have the right to protect his (her) rights and freedoms by all means not prohibited by law."

As we have repeatedly mentioned, there is nothing more secondary and insignificant for the Russian state than the rights and freedoms of man and citizen. The whole point of this work is to show it in all its glory. In this regard, the answer to the first point, after two-thirds of the book, you can already formulate yourself. But perhaps it is worth referring to the second point.

First of all, I want to remind you that the rights to express one's opinion (Article 29 of the Constitution), as well as the right to rallies, meetings, and peaceful marches (Article 31 of the Constitution), which are also de jure permitted, but de facto prohibited, are the methods of protecting one's rights and freedoms. We spoke about the situation with these rights when analyzing the relevant articles. We have also already examined cases of the Russian authorities deliberately refusing to accept claims or ignoring problems, which results in a contest on the topic of "how to draw the attention of officials to the problem in a more original way" (we talked about this when analyzing Article 33 of the Constitution). Also, I want to note that the right to associations and unions is also the right to protect a particular group of people, and we also talked about the violation of this right when analyzing Article 30 of the Constitution.

 In Russia, there is no juvenile justice—the protection of children from their parents. A bill on combating domestic violence in the family was blocked (moreover, at the personal request of the highest dignitaries from the Russian Orthodox Church (say hello again to the "secularism" of the Russian state.) And the protection of a person who has committed acts similar to crimes as a result of a self-defense is an unusually complex process, at the same time, article 108 of the Criminal Code of the Russian Federation (on exceeding the limits of self-defense) is not included in the circle of articles under which a jury can try the case.

We have also considered how Russia violates the rights of its citizens in terms of the report of the ECHR, the body that monitored the implementation of the Convention for the Protection of Human Rights and Fundamental Freedoms until the shameful exclusion of Russia from PACE in 2022. Remember when analyzing Article 15, we said that Russian lawyers sadly joked: "What is the best Russian court? ECHR!"? Let me remind you what we talked about then. The judicial system in Russia is terrible. And practically only through the ECHR could an ordinary Russian get at least some truth in the absence of Russian courts. In 2021 alone, the ECHR had 9,432 cases from Russia pending, only slightly behind Turkey with 9,548 cases and well ahead of Ukraine, which had 3,721 cases.

Moreover, Russia was the primary violator of the Convention. In the vast majority of court rulings in 2021, 986 out of 1,105, the ECHR found at least one violation of the Convention. The Strasbourg Court issued the most such orders concerning Russia; 219. For example, in Turkey, only 78.

Moreover, if initially, Russia tried to take measures to correct the situation with violations of the Convention, then it limited itself to simply paying compensation to the victims according to the decisions of the ECHR. Then the State Duma adopted a law to which it could not pay these compensations. In 2022, Russia, due to gross violations of international law, was expelled from PACE, and its citizens were deprived of the opportunity to apply to the "only fair Russian court."

The Higher School of Economics analyzed the work of the Russian courts and found the following:

"A Russian judge, on average, considers up to 180 cases and materials per month, and 62% of judges process more than twice, follows from the report of the Higher School of Economics (HSE) on the workload of judges (available to RBC). To process the number of documents that are annually received only by district courts, the staffing of judges throughout Russia should be increased by 2.1 times, experts say ...

"Russian judges try an average of two cases daily "at a pace three to five times faster than recommended," the report says. On average, a judge of a court of general jurisdiction tries 46.6 cases or material per month, and of an arbitration court—68 cases. The pace of work depends on the court level and varies depending on the region. In many subjects, it is much higher than the average values.

"For example, a Moscow district court judge reviews, on average, 99 cases and materials per month. And in the arbitration courts of the capital, judges hear up to 180 cases per month, which is the maximum among the regions ...

"Only 24% of judges fit into their standard work schedule or exceed it by less than 20%; the rest are overworked, as follows from the HSE report. These figures are derived from a collection of data provided to the researchers by 449 Russian judges. In total, 62% of judges work over the clock twice or more times, and 5%—five times. This is not about working time, although most judges regularly stay late at work and miss their lunch break, but about "acceptable labor productivity," the researchers specify. "When there is not enough time, the process of legal proceedings is accelerated. Instead of devoting half an hour to a meeting, it is held in 15 minutes," explained Maxim Davydov, head of the study, head of the Department of Public Sector Economics at the Institute of State and Municipal Administration of the National Research University Higher School of Economics, to RBC.

"The situation is aggravated by the fact that the number of cases and materials in courts is growing every year. Between 2014 and 2016, in the courts of general jurisdiction, it increased by more than 13% (from 11 million to 12.4 million materials), according to statistics from the judicial department of the Supreme Court. In arbitration courts, the volume of cases over the same period increased by almost 22% (from 2.5 million to 3 million cases) annually ...

"However, the number of judges and court staff during this time almost stayed the same. According to the Court Department of the Supreme Court, between 2014 and 2016, the number of judicial positions throughout Russia increased by half a thousand and approached 30 thousand (of which 25.4 thousand were in courts of general jurisdiction, another 4.5 thousand were in arbitration courts). The actual number of the judiciary has even decreased over this period. As of 2016, the staff of judges was less than 87%...

""Judges are adapting to the increased workload by increasing productivity and compressing the time needed to consider one court case. Justice is consistently turning into assembly line production** [highlighted by me - A.M.]," the report's authors said. Instead of protecting or restoring violated rights, courts are increasingly pursuing the goal of completing the process as soon as possible and making a decision according to a well-established template," the study says. At the same time, the judicial department of the Supreme Court "avoids responsibility" for managing human resources—only this can explain the use of long-outdated workload norms, the report says" (For more details on RBC: you can read here).

Additionally, the courts limited the right to protection during the pandemic. In particular, the deadline for filing complaints was not changed, even despite the fines introduced for finding people on the streets, access to court sessions was limited for journalists, lawyers could not access courts, etc. (You can read more on the topic here).

Here, it is also necessary to keep in mind that to protect one's rights, a person must first have these rights. One cannot defend his right to be an emperor; a person does not have such a natural right. Therefore, to analyze the possibility of "protecting one's rights in any legal way," it must be borne in mind that a Russian citizen has no rights left (which I have repeatedly mentioned and this work is devoted to), and, therefore, their protection is significantly complicated.

Based on the above, I believe it is clear that Article 45 of the Constitution also does not work in full.

ARTICLE 46 OF THE CONSTITUTION

The full text is written as:

"1. Everyone shall be guaranteed protection in court of his (her) rights and freedoms.

2. Decisions and actions (or inaction) of State government bodies, local self-government bodies, public organizations and officials may be appealed against in court.

3. Everyone shall have the right in accordance with international treaties of the Russian Federation to appeal to interstate bodies for the protection of human rights and freedoms if all available internal means of legal protection have been exhausted."

We have repeatedly mentioned the judicial protection of rights and freedoms in Russia. We talked about their monstrous inefficiency (when analyzing Article 45), the servility of the Constitutional Court (when analyzing Article 9), and the virtual absence of jury trials, which are entirely excluded from civil cases and limited to a narrow list of criminal articles (when analyzing Article 32 of the Constitution). Everything is so bad that the chairman of the Constitutional Court (sic!), Zorkin, openly speaks in his interview about the positive impact of serfdom (actual peasant slavery), the inequality of men and women, and the positive effect of the ban on LGBT rights. No wonder the judicial system in Russia works so poorly.

In Russia, the court is not independent. If adequate decisions can sometimes be made at the lowest level, then with the transition to a higher level, the class character of Russian society is included in the matter. Win a trial against the Patriarch? I am begging you. "Nanodust" penetrated into his apartment from the apartment above, where repairs were carried out, and the court awarded, with God's help, almost 20 million rubles to the poor non- possessor. Of course, this holy man did not forgive anything.

Win the case where Prigozhin (a criminal and a friend of Putin) filed a defamation lawsuit to the journalist who revealed he was the owner of the illegal armed formation "PMC "Wagner"? Of course not! The most "funny thing" is that Prigozhin himself is now talking about this and even bragging with it.

Or against a journalist for saying Prigozhin is a criminal, having a court decision in his hands? Of course not (here and here).

Of course, civil cases against Navalny can also be included here (here and here). As we can conclude, the court here is not a means of protecting rights but is only a means for repression and a screen for absolute lawlessness.

And there are thousands of such cases. They concern mainly journalists and their investigative activities; this is a way to hide corruption and other crimes of Putin's guardsmen. Ruin, so that would intimidate the "offender" and the rest, is a common practice in Russia. In particular, including journalists in the register of "foreign agents" is a direct method of financial strangulation.

Protecting your rights, for example, against being declared a "foreign agent," through Russian courts is a waste of time (here and here). The only exclusion in the history of Russia of two persons from the register of "foreign agents" was carried out only by the Ministry of Justice itself and was done by a procedure not found in the law.

According to some lawyers, in Russia, there is no request for the independence of the courts at all.

Regarding paragraph 3, we have already mentioned the "best Russian court," the ECHR. With Russia's expulsion from the Council of Europe in 2022, this remedy is closed to Russian citizens. So this item is no longer valid. In fairness, it must be said that even before the exclusion, Russia was extremely

reluctant to comply with the decisions of the ECHR. Thus, according to the report of the Committee of Ministers of the Council of Europe on the implementation of decisions of the European Court of Human Rights in 2020, "... Russia remains the leader in non-execution of ECHR judgments ... the

Russian Federation accounts for 34% of all pending cases..." You can read the full report here.

Given the foregoing, I am also forced to conclude that Article 46 does not work.

ARTICLE 47 OF THE CONSTITUTION

Article 47 states:

"1. Nobody may be deprived of the right to have his (her) case heard in the court and by the judge within whose competence the case is placed by law.

2. Any person accused of committing a crime shall have the right to have his (her) case examined by a court with the participation of a jury in the cases envisaged by federal law."

I would not say that there is some kind of consistency in the violation of paragraph one of this article. As usual, it is violated in relation to one of the two people to whom the Russian Constitution de facto does not apply, Navalny. So, after his return to Russia from Germany, where he underwent treatment and rehabilitation of the consequences of poisoning with the Novichok chemical warfare agent, he was tried, contrary to all the rules of the Code of Criminal Procedure, by a "visit court" right in the Khimki police department. So, in Russian practice, not only call girls appeared but even call judges.

Regarding the trial by jury, we have already analyzed it when discussing Article 32 of the Constitution. If you want to refresh your memory, you can see information about them on page 257.

Thus, I cannot show the systematic nature of the violation of the first paragraph of Article 47 of the Constitution. But given the generally low level of the judicial system, this is unlikely to affect anything substantially. The second paragraph does not work almost completely; therefore, Article 47 of the Constitution is only partially effective.

ARTICLE 48 OF THE CONSTITUTION

The full text reads:

"1. Everyone shall be guaranteed the right to qualified legal assistance. In the cases envisaged by law, legal assistance shall be provided free of charge.

2. Any person detained, taken into custody or accused of committing a crime shall have the right to use the assistance of a lawyer (counsel for the defence) from the moment of being detained, placed in custody or accused."

The Federal Union of Lawyers of Russia (FPA) prepared a summary of violations of the professional rights of lawyers in 2019-2020, where they indicated the following main problems that affect the work of lawyers in criminal proceedings:

"– illegal summons by investigators and judges of lawyers for interrogation as witnesses on circumstances that became known in connection with the provision of legal assistance, despite the existing legislative prohibitions;

- unlawful removal of a defense counsel previously interrogated as a witness from participation in a criminal case in violation of the right to defense through a chosen lawyer, as well as groundless removal of lawyers from court hearings for procedural activity and criticism of the court in the process of advocacy;

- obstruction by investigators and employees of remand prisons to lawyers in access to their client in custody, requirements not provided for by law to present the investigator's permission, despite the amendments made to the Code of Criminal Procedure of the Russian Federation;

– Lack of proper conditions for the work of lawyers in many pre-trial detention centers, long queues, and long waiting times; and

- the absence of real equality and competition of the parties in criminal proceedings, which is confirmed by the data of the Judicial Department at the Supreme Court of the Russian Federation, characterized by an extremely low percentage of acquittals and an extremely high percentage of satisfied applications for detention, an extension of detention, etc."

However, the work of lawyers is not limited to these problems. The following is a quote from the site:

"As noted in the explanatory note to the certificate of violations of the professional rights of lawyers prepared by the FSAR (available in the editorial office of the website of the FPA of the Russian Federation. - Note ed.), the most common violations of the professional rights of lawyers are the non-admission of a lawyer to a client, as well as physical violence against a lawyer. In particular, a link is provided to recent events in the Kabardino-Balkarian Republic, when female lawyers were first not allowed to see a client, then used violence and special equipment against them, and then opened a criminal case against the lawyers.

"The document states that the information provided by the Chambers of Lawyers with the active support of the FPA of the Russian Federation on violations of the rights of lawyers that have become known allows us to conclude that **such violations are systemic** [highlighted by me - A.M.], calling into question the fairness and legitimacy of the entire process of criminal prosecution and justice in general...

"Vice-President of the FPA of the Russian Federation and Vice-President of the FSAR Mikhail Tolcheev noted that the lack of a tough reaction from the judiciary to violations of the law and the right to defense gives rise to a sense of permissiveness. According to him, the indignation of the legal community is caused by the fact that lawyers understand better than others the danger of such a development of the situation: a weak and lacking effective mechanisms for protecting the legal profession, the connivance of the judiciary to violations of the right to defense, no matter what they are, lead to an increase in abuses, rooting imitation of compliance with legal procedures.

"Vadim Klyuvgant, Vice-President of the Moscow Chamber of Lawyers, Deputy Chairman of the Commission of the Council of the Federal Chamber of Lawyers of the Russian Federation for the Protection of the Rights of Lawyers, drew attention to the fact that the impunity of officials contributes to the increase in the number of cases of obstruction of the practice of law and their impudence, especially since there is no legally established responsibility for such actions does not exist (unlike, for example, obstructing the activities of journalists, election commissions, and even religious organizations). As Vadim Klyuvgant emphasized, the absence of such responsibility is a flagrant disgrace, given that lawyers, in the course of their professional activities, ensure nothing less than the implementation of the constitutional guarantee of the right of everyone to receive qualified legal assistance. This means that the violation of the professional rights of lawyers violates the constitutional right of every person who, because of this, did not receive the assistance of a lawyer in an acute situation when he especially needed it ...

"Vice-President of the Federal Union of Lawyers of Russia, lawyer Aleksey Ivanov stated that in 2020 the number of violations of the professional rights of lawyers and obstruction of the practice of law has **increased significantly** [highlighted by me - A.M.]."

As we can see, the situation is getting more and more serious. So much so that the problem was noticed even by the media biased towards the state, in particular, TASS. They also cite the above report, adding some details:

"...FPA stated that in the Russian Federation, illegal interrogations of lawyers and searches of them, as well as violations of lawyer secrecy, occur on a massive scale. "Massive violations of the professional rights of lawyers continue to remain: infringement of lawyer's secrecy, **illegal interrogations of a lawyer as a witness with the aim of further disqualification as a defender (representative)** [pay attention to this "interesting" scheme - A.M.], illegal searches of lawyers' formations, lawyers and their places of residence, illegal conduct of operational-search actions against lawyers," the document says.

"At the same time, it is noted that officials are not responsible for these violations. "Despite repeated appeals from the legal community, as well as other civil society institutions, so far no special rules of responsibility for obstructing the practice of lawyers have been introduced," the report says.

"In just two years, 483 cases of infringement of lawyer secrecy were registered, including 306 cases of illegal interrogation of a lawyer as a witness, 78 searches of lawyers' homes and workplaces, 34 operational search activities, and 65 cases of violation of the confidentiality of a conversation with a client. In addition, 1,321 cases of interference with or obstruction of the practice of law were recorded, including 360 cases of non-admission to courts, law enforcement agencies, and the Federal Penitentiary Service. The total number of violations of the professional rights of lawyers has increased over the past two years and amounted to 2,142 violations.

"The FPA of Russia also noted a negative trend in bringing lawyers to criminal responsibility in connection with allegedly overpriced, non-market, from the point of view of the prosecution, remuneration, as well as for falsifying evidence, opposing the activities of the preliminary investigation bodies and interfering in the activities of the preliminary investigation bodies and the court. In two years, 126 criminal cases were initiated against lawyers, of which 20 were dropped" (quote from here).

You can read (and watch) more about the state of the legal profession in Russia here.

As you understand, the pressure on the legal profession from the state is only growing since it is the lawyer who stands between the security official and his new shoulder straps or money for a closed case. I will separately note for those who are not aware of the system of work of the Russian police (and before that, the police). Their "KPI" has always been measured in terms of the number of "cases closed"; this is the so-called "stick system." You can read more about that, for example, here. The problem is recognized at the highest level, for example, here. How does it work? For each security officer, indicators are descended from above that must be achieved over a period of time (for example, per month), like solving a certain number of cases. No conclusion is made about good crime prevention if there are no cases. On the contrary, for the authorities, this means that such a security official "worked poorly," which threatens to reduce the budget (if there are no crimes, then such staff is not needed) or to deprive of bonuses. Therefore, no matter how honest, say, a policeman strives to be, the sword of Damocles will always hang over him for "disclosing" a certain number of cases.

This system, with its illogicality and even cruelty, causes many jokes; for example, this meme regarding the "Breaking Bad" series:

@Brodie_Bruce

Идея для сериала. Тихий учитель химии постепенно превращается в матерого наркоторговца после того, как местное отделение полиции недовыполнило план по раскрываемости за месяц

t.me/top_twit

Fig 2. "I have a series idea. Quiet school teacher of chemistry slowly turns to the major drug dealer after the local police office hasn't accomplished its plan of cases closed for the month."

But setting laughter aside, the problem is severe. Of course, in such a system, the lawyer, by his actions, prevents the security forces from earning (I have to repeat, even in the case of the very, very crystal-honorable security official). Hence the growing pressure on the lawyers.

Given the systematic and massive violations of the rights of lawyers, and as a result, the rights of citizens to defense, with a tendency to increase, I believe we can conclude that Article 48 of the Constitution also does not work.

ARTICLE 49 OF THE CONSTITUTION

The full text of Article 49 is as follows:

"1. Any person accused of committing a crime shall be considered innocent until his (her) guilt is proven in accordance with the procedure stipulated by federal law and is confirmed by a court sentence which has entered into legal force.

2. The accused shall not be obliged to prove his (her) innocence.

3. Irremovable doubts about the guilt of a person shall be interpreted in favour of the accused."

This wording (of all three points) is known in short as the "presumption of innocence." What is the problem here? The problem is that this rule was borrowed by the founders of the Constitution from English law, where the entire criminal process is conducted not by the bodies of preliminary investigation but by the court. The judge leads the case and controls the parties, thus ensuring a fair trial and equality of the parties. Hence the rule that a search requires a court sanction. An English (and American) judge does not need to delve into the whole case first to determine whether a search is really required; he is already aware.

But Russia has adopted absolutely the same system that existed in the USSR: there are bodies of inquiry and preliminary investigation that investigate the case, establish the criminal, and his motive, collect evidence and draw up the so-called "indictment," which is then filed with the court. This gives rise to a strong bias in favor of the prosecution: the defense is included in the case much later than the prosecution, and there is no longer any "presumption of innocence" at the trial since the prosecution has already formed its opinion about how the crime took place and who is guilty, and only proves its point of view. At the same time, if in the Criminal Procedure Code of the RSFSR there was an obligation for the investigation and the court to "establish the truth in the case" (Article 20 of the Code of Criminal Procedure of the RSFSR), then in the Code of Criminal Procedure of Russia court and preliminary bodies are not obliged to seek the truth.

Not that I was against the presumption of innocence, not at all, just along with it, absolutely the entire criminal process had to be changed, which was not done in Russia. As a result, some of the rules of the Constitution look completely out of this world, and their application is completely ugly (as in the case of searches, which we talked about when analyzing Article 25 of the Constitution).

What is the difference?

According to Western law, a person retains all rights as long as there is no court verdict. The court imposes an obligation on him to come to court sessions. To guarantee this, there is an institution of bail, depositing a certain amount (sometimes very significant) on a court deposit to guarantee an appearance. But, otherwise, the person remains free and continues his activities.

In Russia, most of those accused of criminal offenses are kept in pre-trial detention centers in near-torture conditions (remember about 84% of enterprises that went bankrupt due to criminal prosecution? So this is one of the reasons of the system's bias in favor of the prosecution and the virtual absence of the "presumption of innocence"). At the same time, a person may not even have the status of "accusing" in a criminal case but only be "suspected of committing a crime" (in the case of the latter, no more than 48 hours, but the fact remains; this is relatively poor recognition of "innocence"). At the same time, in the legislation, there is no maximum period of detention in a pre-trial detention center. Even the prosecutor's office points to this.

In addition, the defense is very limited in the right to collect evidence. The legislator assumed that the lawyer would manipulate the evidence: and destroy those that proved the guilt of the client. At the same time, the falsification of evidence by the prosecution does not mainly concern him. "[So], according to par. 2, 3, 4 hours 3 tbsp. 6 of the Federal Law "On Advocacy and the Advocacy of the Russian Federation," a defense lawyer—a lawyer—has the right "to interrogate, with their consent, persons who allegedly possess information related to the case ... collect and present objects and documents that can be recognized as material, and other evidence, in the manner prescribed by the legislation of the Russian Federation ... to involve specialists on a contractual basis" (the same in subparagraphs 2, 3 parts 1 article 53, subparagraphs 1, 2 parts 3 art. 86 Code of Criminal Procedure). However, the law does not define the rules for collecting evidence; moreover, in order for the collected information to become evidence, it must be attached to the materials of the criminal case, which, again, **directly depends on the will of the investigator and the court** [highlighted by me - A.M.]...

"At the moment, the courts turn a blind eye to the fact that the investigators in violation of the provisions of Art. 159 of the Code of Criminal Procedure of the Russian Federation refuse to interrogate important eyewitnesses, conduct examinations proving the innocence of the accused, to conduct confrontations that cannot be carried out during the trial due to the specifics of this investigative action. And although the Constitutional Court of the Russian Federation, in its Resolution of December 8, 2003, No. 18-P, "On the case of checking the constitutionality of the provisions of Articles 125, 219, 227, 229, 236, 237, 239, 246, 254, 271, 378, 405 and 408, as well as chapters 35 and 39 of the Code of Criminal Procedure of the Russian Federation in connection with requests from courts of general jurisdiction and complaints from citizens" expressly indicates that such violations of the rights of the accused to defense should entail the return of the criminal case for additional investigation, the appropriate changes to Article 237 of the Code of Criminal Procedure of the Russian Federation have not yet been made even now. Which gives the courts grounds in most cases to unreasonably refuse the defense's petitions to return the case" (quote from here).

I would also like to draw attention to the fact that if the appellate court finds significant violations of the law during the criminal process, it does not release the accused; it "returns the case for additional investigation." At the same time, the accused may continue to be in the pre-trial detention center, paradoxically, but he was not found not guilty by the court.

Accordingly, this leads to a tiny number of acquittals of less than 1%, which the investigation takes credit for as an "example of effective work." At the same time, in jury trials (where they exist), the percentage of acquittals is almost 20%, which is explained precisely by ignoring the presumption of innocence of the court without a jury).

The situation even comes to an utterly egregious fact. Thus, the accused in the criminal process are kept in the courtroom in special cells, regardless of the severity of the alleged crime. I think this is necessary in order to emphasize the innocence of a person before sentencing.

As you understand, the presumption of innocence (despite numerous violations) is still a barrier between a security official and shoulder straps or power and money. It is not surprising that it is officially proposed to be canceled in part of the articles of the Code of Administrative Offenses (Code of Administrative Offenses): in particular, several articles of chapter 12 relating to driving violations. Once again, you can appreciate the intellectual and legal level of the Duma, elected with huge falsifications.

Under such conditions, I believe it is clear that the principle of the presumption of innocence in Russia practically does not work. An exception, when the Russian government loves it very much, is the justification for not ratifying Article 20 of the UN Convention against Corruption. This article says that if the official's assets significantly exceed his income, it is assumed that he is guilty of corruption and must provide evidence of the legality of obtaining these assets. It is not surprising that in Russia, where corruption is the backbone of Putin's vertical, such a position is not accepted. Officials refer specifically to the "presumption of innocence", which in other cases is, frankly, not so effective.

ARTICLE 50 OF THE CONSTITUTION

The next article goes on the circle of articles dedicated to justice. It states:

"1. Nobody may be convicted twice for one and the same crime.

2. In administering justice it shall not be permitted to use evidence received through violating federal law.

3. Any person convicted of a crime shall have the right to appeal against the verdict to a higher court in accordance with the procedure established by federal law, as well as to request pardon or mitigation of the punishment."

The first point is known even to Roman law. Then it sounded like "non bis in idem." It is simple and straightforward: one cannot constantly punish a person for what he once already had been punished. Hence, the conclusion follows: as soon as the guilty person has been punished, he is considered to have redeemed his guilt and should not be persecuted by the state.

The most frequent violation of this principle in Russian law lies at the intersection of several types of liability: disciplinary, administrative, and criminal.

Moreover, the violation of the principle exists in several official documents. The first is the Ruling of Supreme Court No. 51-КАД21-12-К8 dated March 2, in which the Supreme Court explicitly stated that the principle set forth in Part 1 of Article 50 of the Constitution could not unconditionally extend to legislation on bringing suspects (accused) to disciplinary liability.

The situation itself looked like this (quote from the site: https://www. advgazeta.ru)):

"Eldar Huseynov was kept in the FKU SIZO-1 of the Federal Penitentiary Service of Russia in the Altai Territory as an accused of committing crimes under paragraphs "a," "c," part 2 of Art. 163, paragraph "a" part 2 of Art. 163, paragraph "a" part 2 of Art. 163 of the Criminal Code ...

"On December 6, 2019, after the announcement of the accusive decision Eldar Huseynov began to speak in a rude, obscene manner to the judge and the prosecutor. For this, the head of the pre-trial detention center issued a resolution on bringing Eldar Huseynov to **disciplinary responsibility and placing him in a punishment cell for seven days** [highlighted by me - A.M.] for violating the provisions of clauses 1, 7, part 1 of Art. 36 of the law on the Detention of Suspected and Accused of Committing Crimes, paragraph 4 of the Rules of the internal order of pre-trial detention centers of the penitentiary system. In addition, Huseynov was prosecuted [highlighted by me - A.M.] for committing a crime under Parts 1, 2 of Art. 297 "Contempt of court" **of the Criminal Code**.

"Considering the decision of the pre-trial detention center unlawful, Eldar Huseynov applied to the Central District Court of the city of Barnaul, Altai Territory, with an administrative claim to recognize the decision and actions of the official as illegal.

"Refusing to satisfy the demands, the court of the first instance proceeded from the fact that Huseynov, having insulted the judge, violated both the court's order and conditions of detention. The penalty in the form of placement in a punishment cell was deemed to be legal, corresponded to the severity of the offense committed, an authorized official imposed the disciplinary sanction, and the procedure for bringing to disciplinary responsibility was observed. At the same time, the court pointed out that bringing Eldar Huseynov to criminal liability for insulting a judge does not affect the legality of the decision to place him in a punishment cell. The Altai Regional Court agreed with these conclusions.

"In turn, the Eighth Cassation Court of General Jurisdiction concluded that the administrative claim was justified. They were referring to the provisions of point 1 of Article 258 of the Code of Criminal Procedure, according to which, in case of violation of the order in a court session, disobedience to the orders of the chairperson or an employee of the enforcement authorities of the Russian Federation, **a person present in the courtroom is warned about the inadmissibility of such behavior or is removed from the courtroom, or a monetary penalty is imposed on him in in the manner prescribed by Art. 117 and 118 of this Code. The cassation concluded that the object of the unlawful actions of the administrative plaintiff was not the procedure and conditions of his detention but the established procedure in the court session** [highlighted by me - A.M.]. Taking into account the fact of bringing Huseynov to criminal responsibility for committing a crime under Parts 1, 2 of Art. 297 of the Criminal Code, the court of cassation declared the decision to place in a punishment cell illegal ...

"The Supreme Court pointed out that ... [s]ince administrative and criminal liability, being varieties of legal liability for committing acts that pose a public danger, have similar tasks, are based on several principles, pursue the common goal of protecting the rights and freedoms of man and citizen, ensuring the rule of law and order and, in fact, largely complement each other, this rule has a general meaning and applies to legislation on administrative offenses (decrees of July 14, 2015 No. 20-P and February 4, 2019 No. 8-P).

"Based on the preceding, the Supreme Court noted, as a general rule, the principle "there is no double punishment for the same offense" operates in the field of criminal law relations, as well as relations related to bringing the perpetrators to administrative responsibility. Meanwhile, bringing to disciplinary responsibility persons suspected and (or) accused of committing crimes to pursue a goal different from other types of responsibility: ensuring the regime established by law in places of detention. Therefore, the principle set out in Part 1 of Art. 50 of the Constitution, cannot unconditionally apply to legislation on bringing the named persons to disciplinary responsibility, is indicated in the definition ..." (quote from here).

In my opinion, the Supreme Court is wrong here. It does not matter what category of cases the punishment for an action belongs to, this is an exclusively formal justification. The same "deed" can, at different times, be either an administrative offense or a criminal act (especially in Russian law!). So it was, for example, with slander, where initially it was a criminal offense. Medvedev decriminalized it into an administrative one, and then Putin returned it to the Criminal Code again. The only important thing is that for one action, a person is punished several times. In our case, he was first placed in a punishment cell (let me remind you that the conditions there are almost torture), and then a criminal case was initiated. Note also that the Constitution does not provide for the restriction of the rule on non-punishment twice for one act to different areas of law. The court had to choose either to initiate a criminal case, or put him in a punishment cell, but not all at once.

This is not a separate case. This is the opinion of the Supreme Court, the highest court of appeal; the lower courts do not just take into account its opinion; they execute it (what is the point of not executing if the case can again reach the same Supreme Court, which will make exactly the same decision and cancel any decision, which would contradict it?).

Well, let's say at the junction of disciplinary and other types of responsibility, such a rule applies. What about the intersection of administrative and criminal law? And here, too, it is not at all smooth.

Another violation of paragraph 1 of Article 50 of the Constitution is the so-called "Dadin's Article" (named after Ildar Dadin, the first person convicted under it). Officially, this is article 212.1 of the Criminal Code ("repeated violation of the rules of rallies and pickets (sic!)").

The history of the case is as follows: in December 2015, the opposition civil activist Ildar Dadin was the first in Russia to be convicted under article 212.1 of the Criminal Code of the Russian Federation for repeated violations of the rules for holding rallies and pickets.

The conviction was preceded by a long story from administrative protocols on protest articles. In 2014, the court fined Dadin twice under Article 20.2 of the Code of Administrative Offenses of the Russian Federation for pickets and participation in a rally on Manezhnaya Square. For participation in two subsequent actions in the capital—in 2014 and early 2015—two more administrative protocols were drawn up against Dadin. They resulted in a couple of criminal cases, which were later combined into one. In one of these episodes, the case was later dismissed due to the imposition of an administrative fine. Considering the criminal case's materials, the Basmanny Court sentenced Dadin to three years in prison. In March 2016, following an appeal, the sentence was reduced to two and a half years.

That is, for one act, "violation of the rules for holding rallies," Ildar Dadin was immediately punished in an administrative and criminal case.

Accordingly, Dadin and his lawyers filed a complaint with the Russian Constitutional Court. In their opinion, Article 212.1 of the Criminal Code of the Russian Federation, which appeared in 2014 as a reaction to protest activity, allows a person to be punished several times for the same offense. Responsibility for it comes if the protester commits three or more violations of Article 20.2

of the Code of Administrative Offenses within six months. Moreover, the rule allows the initiation of a criminal case before the entry into force of court decisions in administrative cases. At the same time, the article allows for the possibility of imposing a sentence of imprisonment for up to five years for actions that did not cause harm to human health or property and did not threaten the safety of the people and the environment.

Surprisingly, the Constitutional Court agreed with the defense's arguments, pointing out that criminal liability is possible only if an administrative case has not been initiated under this article.

But if you think this is the story's end, you are wrong.

On February 22, 2017, the Presidium of the Supreme Court of the Russian Federation canceled the sentence against Ildar Dadin, decided to dismiss the case against him, release him from custody and recognize his right for rehabilitation. So, among the people and among lawyers Art. 212.1 of the Criminal Code became known as "Dadin's article."

However, in August 2019, under article 212.1 of the Criminal Code of the Russian Federation, a new case was again opened against activist Konstantin Kotov for participating in protests against the exclusion of candidates for elections to the Moscow City Duma. On September 5, 2019, Kotov was sentenced to 4 years in prison. At the same time, the court completely ignored (sic!) the binding decision of the Constitutional Court on Dadin's complaint.

Kotov's defense filed a complaint with the Constitutional Court. In January 2020, the Constitutional Court issued a ruling on the need to review the sentence for Kotov, emphasizing once again that criminal liability under Art. 212.1 of the Criminal Code of the Russian Federation should only attack in the event of causing severe harm to someone.

However, the court of cassation simply instructed the Moscow City Court to once again check the legality of the decision made by the court of the first instance. On April 20, the Moscow City Court, following an appeal review of Kotov's case, commuted his sentence to 1.5 years in prison (that is, it did not even cancel it). You can read more about the "Dadin's article" here and here.

Regarding paragraph 2, we had already mentioned in passing when we talked about surveillance and wiretapping of the opposition and searches.

However, the problem is much deeper, and, like the violation of paragraph 1 of Article 50 of the Constitution, it is directly enshrined in Russian law. Namely, in the Decree of the Plenum of the Supreme Court of the Russian Federation of December 19, 2017, No. 51, "On the practice of applying legislation in criminal cases in the court of the first instance (general procedure for legal proceedings)" (quote from here).

According to clause 13 of the said resolution: "Evidence is recognized as inadmissible, in particular, if there were **significant** [highlighted by me - A.M.] violations of the procedure for collecting and securing them established by the criminal procedural legislation, and also if the collection and consolidation of evidence were carried out by an improper person or body or as a result of actions not provided for by the procedural rules.

As Gasparyan Nver (Attorney at the Bar of the Stavropol Territory) notes: "... The main problem is that the Plenum of the Supreme Court of the Russian Federation did not give criteria for distinguishing a material violation from an ordinary violation, which means that the resolution of this issue is at the mercy of the judges, who, in the last years, have not satisfied and practically did not justify almost anyone..."

It is difficult to disagree with this point of view. First, paragraph 2 of Article 50 of the Constitution does not establish the degree of violation of the law at which evidence can be considered admissible. It even sounds absurd: "we broke the law a little, but we have evidence." Secondly, the assessment of the materiality of the violation is very vague and will directly lead to judicial arbitrariness. Thirdly, such a law raises questions about articles that become "unimportant" when evidence is collected. Formally, if there are such provisions, then they are as important as the rest. And the violation of some procedural articles cannot be more or less severe than others. This state of affairs simply leads to the annihilation of some of the articles of the Code of Criminal Procedure, which, in their essence, gave additional guarantees of the rights and freedoms of the accused.

You can read more here and here.

I have no significant objections to the third point. However, I would like to make one remark. Before Russian citizens were deprived of the right to apply to the ECtHR, the condition for filing complaints was "the use of all effective methods of appeal within the country." This is logical; if you have an effective internal method for solving your problems, there is no point in applying to the ECtHR. There are a lot of appeal bodies in Russia, and, accordingly, the question arose of which methods of appeal in Russia are effective and which are not. And it was possible to miss the deadline for filing a complaint with the ECtHR, getting involved in a challenge in an "ineffective instance." So, civil cases were considered only after the decision of the Supreme Court, and administrative cases after the second cassation.

A complete list of "effective" appeal methods can be found here.

As you, I think, understand, Article 50 of the Constitution does not work not only at the actual but also at the legislative level. We can stop our analysis here. Let's move on to the next article.

ARTICLE 51 OF THE CONSTITUTION

The full text states, and corresponds to the 5th amendment of the US Constitution:

"1. Nobody shall be obliged to testify against himself, his (her) spouse or close relatives, the range of whom shall be determined by federal law.

2. Federal law may establish other cases where the obligation to give evidence may be lifted."

This right did not come about by accident. In ancient times and the Middle Ages, one of the key pieces of evidence was a person's confession of a crime. It was called Regina probationum; confession is the queen of evidence. And torture was used to obtain such a confession. At the same time, it doesn't matter who was tortured: the "suspect" himself or members of his family—in any case, this is unbearable for a person and led to self-incrimination and a significant distortion of the truth in the case.

To significantly reduce such a distortion of the truth during the investigation, not only the rules on the prohibition of torture but also provisions similar to those indicated in this article were almost universally adopted. I want to emphasize that this is the right of the individual. He retains the opportunity to make a confession, and this is the essential vulnerability of this rule.

And here, the torture comes back on the scene! We have already discussed it in the analysis of Article 21 of the Constitution. And although there is a rule in the Criminal Procedure Code that if a confession of guilt is not supported by other evidence in the case, then it cannot serve as the basis for a guilty verdict, the practice went in a completely different way. The Supreme Court even had to issue a separate ruling. However, the Supreme Court itself indicates in paragraph 13 of the Decree of the Plenum of the Supreme Court of the Russian Federation of November 29, 2016, No. 55 "On the Judgment": "If there are grounds for verifying the defendant's statement in the manner prescribed by Article 144 of the Criminal Procedure Code of the Russian Federation, the court sends it to the head the relevant body of preliminary investigation. **Carrying out such a check does not relieve the court from the obligation to assess the materials presented on its results and reflect its findings in the verdict** [emphasis mine - A.M.]." That is, the Supreme Court officially stated that despite the report of torture (a violation of Article 21 of the Constitution), an illegal gathering of evidence (a violation of Article 50 of the Constitution), and a violation of the right not to testify against oneself (violation of Article 51), such evidence must be reflected in the verdict. It seems that the Supreme Court here established a certain combo in the nomination "how to violate the maximum number of articles of the Constitution with one phrase."

I note that "to testify against oneself" means not only a confession of committing a crime but any other information that can help the prosecution. And it includes the right to remain silent (which is called "Miranda's rule" in American law) or to take any action. This interpretation is expressed in the decisions of the ECtHR - in particular in the case of Saunders v. the United Kingdom. In this case, the government insisted that paragraph 1 of Art. 6 of the

Convention for the Protection of Human Rights and Fundamental Freedoms was not violated since "from what the applicant said during the interviews, nothing was in the nature of self-accusation, <...> he only gave explanations testifying in his favor <...> Only testimonies testifying against the accused are subjects to the privilege." However, the ECtHR recognized this argument as untenable, emphasizing that the right not to incriminate oneself cannot be reasonably limited to a confession of an offense or evidence that is directly incriminating. The European Court noted, in particular, that coerced testimony that does not outwardly appear incriminating can be subsequently deployed in the course of a criminal trial in support of the prosecution; for example, to contrast it with other statements of the defendant, to cast doubt on the testimony or otherwise undermine its credibility. Which, in general, is completely logical.

However, in Russia, even the Constitutional Court understands the right provided by the commented article differently. In its ruling dated February 27 No. 320-O, it did not see any grounds for accepting for consideration the applicant's complaint that the receipt of voice samples for a comparative study during a conversation conducted on behalf of the investigator by an operational officer with a suspect (accused) violates the right of a person to defense, as well as the right not to incriminate himself. That is, as we see, in Russia, contrary to the interpretation of the ECtHR and the meaning of Article 51 of the Constitution, quite officially, the right not to incriminate oneself applies only to incriminating information. Moreover, the position was taken at the highest level.

As a result, torture is an integral attribute of the Russian investigation. You can read about what kind of torture is used in Russia here. You can read more about torture for obtaining testimony here.

Based on the above, I believe Article 51 is also not valid, even partially at the official level.

Articles 52 and 53 of the Constitution

The full text of Article 52 reads: "The rights of victims of crimes and of abuses of office shall be protected by law. The State shall provide the victims with access to justice and compensation for damage sustained."

And Article 53 says: "Everyone shall have the right to State compensation for damage caused by unlawful actions (inaction) of State government bodies and their officials."

They are talking about the same thing: compensation for harm. Only in the case of Article 52 is it about damage in general. In the case of Article 53, specifically about the harm caused by public authorities and officials.

We have already partially dealt with this issue from several sides. Firstly, when we talked about the effectiveness of the Russian courts and the ECHR (when analyzing Article 46 of the Constitution), and secondly when we talked about the attempts of Navalny and his team to initiate a criminal case on the fact of his poisoning.

The situation, however, is much broader. In particular, to compensate for the harm caused by illegal actions, Russian law uses the concept of "compensation for moral damage." However, the sums awarded by the courts are tiny. This is recognized even at the official level. According to the statistics of the Judicial Department at the Supreme Court of the Russian Federation, the **average** amount of compensation for life and health in 2018 amounted to 84,000 rubles (about $1,300). Generally, the average amount of moral damages collected is 15,000 rubles (about $230).

Of course, such an amount of recovered moral damage cannot be considered "compensation" in total. In most cases, people do not even go to court. The costs of legal assistance, representation, and time spent may not even pay off but exceed the amount awarded.

On the other hand, the meager income of the majority of the Russian population is unlikely to quickly correct this situation: the award of large sums does not guarantee that the culprit will be able to pay such an amount.

Also, a tiny amount of compensation is generally not taken into account by the criminal when planning and committing a crime. That is, it is entirely devoid of a preventive function. This is especially true of compensation for illegal actions of authorities, which we will discuss below.

I want to point out separately that only persons whom the court has acquitted, or in respect of whom the case was dismissed, have the right to compensation in criminal cases (paragraph 3 of the decision of the Plenum of the Supreme Court No. 17 of 09.11.2011 of the Code of Criminal Procedure of the Russian Federation, regulating rehabilitation in criminal proceedings." If you remember, we spoke several times about the extremely low number of acquittals in Russia — less than 1%. The court prefers to give the accused a suspended sentence (without actually serving a sentence) than to recognize the person as innocent. And even such a sentence is already considered a great success. But, as you understand, the accused does not receive any right to compensation.

A similar situation applies to copyrights. The compensation offered by the law is ridiculous: it amounts to 10,000 rubles (about $150) for one violation. However, in 2016, the Constitutional Court additionally allowed the courts to reduce compensation for breach of exclusive rights below the minimum legal limit of 10,000 rubles (in case of violation of rights to several objects of intellectual property by one action).

I once represented a photographer friend who was suing "Maxim" magazine for simply stealing his photographs and using them in one of their issues. We went to court with a demand to pay for the work at a fixed rate of 10,000 rubles for each violation (use of a photo, failure to indicate the author's name, change of an image) for three of his photographs. In violation of the Code of Civil Procedure, the court changed our requirements to the "average cost of services," randomly taking the figure of 3,000 rubles (about $45) (!) and multiplying by 6. At the same time, the appeal court agreed with the lower court... Well, in any case, I have proof of the theft, approved by a court decision that has entered into force. And since then, I openly called "Maxim" magazine what they are — thieves (I wrote more here).

However, as you can see, the state does not seek to protect violated rights. The amounts awarded are ridiculous and only contribute to the violation of rights: why pay a photographer when you can steal his photographs? If he sues, he can be paid below the average rate or below the amount specified in the law.

In any case, compensation for damages caused by wrongdoing is carried out and guaranteed in a completely formal way (and this is provided that one can get through an inefficient judicial system or (in the past) through international courts). At the same time, an insignificant number of acquittals also come into play to compensate for illegal criminal prosecution. I will not dwell on the problem in detail; if you are interested in this topic, you can read about the problem here.

ARTICLE 54 OF THE CONSTITUTION

Article 54 states:

"1. A law, which introduces or increases liability, shall not have retroactive force.

2. Nobody may bear liability for an action, which was not regarded as a crime when it was committed. If, after an offense has been committed, the extent of liability for it is lifted or mitigated, the new law shall be applied."

Retroactive force is the extension of the effect of the law on those actions that a person committed before the law came into force. Simply put, if something was not previously considered punishable, and then it suddenly became an offense, one cannot convict a person for all his past deeds, which suddenly became a crime. The same applies, for example, to taxes.

However, this article is also violated in Russia. The most scandalous was the law once again changing the electoral legislation (namely: Federal Law No. 157-FZ of 04.06.2021 "On Amendments to Article 4 of the Federal Law "On Basic

Guarantees of Electoral Rights and the Right to Participate in a Referendum of Citizens of the Russian Federation" and Article 4 of the Federal Law "On Elections of Deputies of the State Duma of the Federal Assembly of the Russian Federation"). It established a ban on the participation in elections of persons "involved in the activities of extremist or terrorist organizations." Please, note the word "involved." It is not even necessary to participate in such organizations.

Naturally, this is connected with the fight against the opposition: none of the terrorists has ever participated in the Russian "elections," but the adoption of the law, by an utterly incomprehensible coincidence of circumstances, coincided with the recognition of Alexei Navalny's Anti-Corruption Foundation as an "extremist" organization.

The case itself is absurd and is just a lump of violations of the law and even common sense. So, in particular, the hearings were made unpublic because it "concerned state secrets," and the declassification claim was rejected. "The classified documents are four volumes that lawyer Ivan Pavlov, who heads Team 29, described as "information and reference material, which is a chronicle of repression against everything related to Navalny" (quote from here). The full interview of Team 29 lawyer Valeria Vetoshkina regarding this case can be read here.

I want to note that the very recognition of FBK and Navalny's Headquarters as extremists caused an avalanche of criminal prosecution of people who worked in these organizations. That is, they are tried for activities that were not (and in principle could not be) prohibited, which is clearly a violation of commented article. In particular, we are talking about Lilia Chanysheva, but she is far from the only one. The authorities are persecuting even for the symbols of Navalny and Smart Voting.

Thus, "On February 9, fem-activist and writer Daria Serenko was arrested for 15 days just for such a post. In it, Serenko spoke critically about the United Russia candidate for the State Duma, Tatyana Butskaya. The activist used a screenshot from a video by opposition activist Lyubov Sobol, which

369

shows the "Smart Voting logo"—a red exclamation mark in a white square with a blue border. As a result, Serenko was found guilty of **demonstrating extremist symbols**.

The day after the arrest of the femme activist, the police in Pskov drew up a report on the demonstration of extremist symbols on the local municipal deputy Nikolai Kuzmin. The reason was two publications on VKontakte. One of the posts is a photograph of Kuzmin standing with Alexei Navalny in front of a banner that reads "Navalny 20!8" and 2018.navalny.com. The other is an instruction explaining how to get to a meeting with a politician that took place as part of the oppositionist election campaign in December 2017 in Pskov. The instructions had the inscriptions "Navalny 20!8" and "It's time to choose." (details here).

I think it is clear that if there is a law in force that directly violates this article (not counting even numerous court decisions), it seems we cannot talk about the effect of this article.

ARTICLE 55 OF THE CONSTITUTION

Article 55 is quite declarative:

"1. The enumeration in the Constitution of the Russian Federation of the basic rights and freedoms should not be interpreted as a denial or diminution of other universally recognized human and civil rights and freedoms.

2. In the Russian Federation no laws must be adopted which abolish or diminish human and civil rights and freedoms.

3. Human and civil rights and freedoms may be limited by federal law only to the extent necessary for the protection of the basis of the constitutional order, morality, health, rights and lawful interests of other people, and for ensuring the defence of the country and the security of the State."

It is trying to say that the list of rights and freedoms listed in the second chapter of the Constitution is not limited. In fact, as you probably already understood, it is not only not limited; it does not exist at all.

I have already cited many laws, regulations, court decisions, and simply actions of the authorities that ignore the Constitution. And therefore, it makes no sense to analyze the third paragraph of this article since, in a state of lawlessness, there is no need for any grounds for restricting the rights and freedoms of citizens; Putin is no longer embarrassed to restrict rights simply because he wants to.

Based on this (and what was written in the analysis of other articles of the Constitution), I believe that this article does not work in full.

ARTICLE 56 OF THE CONSTITUTION

Article 56 also speaks of cases where human rights and freedoms may be restricted. In this case, in an emergency.

"1. In the conditions of a state of emergency, in order to ensure the safety of citizens and the protection of the constitutional order and in accordance with federal constitutional law, certain restrictions may be imposed on human rights and freedoms with an indication of their limits and the period for which they have effect.

2. A state of emergency on the entire territory of the Russian Federation and in certain areas thereof may be introduced subject to the circumstances and in accordance with the procedure stipulated by federal constitutional law.

3. The rights and freedoms specified in Articles 20, 21, 23 (part 1), 24, 28, 34 (part 1), 40 (part 1), and 46-54 of the Constitution of the Russian Federation might not be restricted."

However, my argument remains the same as it was in the analysis of the previous article. In a situation of lawlessness, the authorities do not need to introduce a state of emergency to violate citizens' rights. Moreover, introducing such a position to a handful of these stupid and spineless people seems to be an admission that "not everything is so smooth and beautiful" in the country and will highlight their total incompetence.

For example, a state of emergency was not introduced in Russia during the COVID 2019 pandemic. At the same time, nothing prevented the authorities from locking people in their homes and fining them for appearing on the street, restricting entry and exit, etc. (You can read more here).

Martial law was not introduced in connection with the war in Ukraine. Putin coquettishly called it "Special Military Operation," a term that does not exist in Russian law at all. But for the uttered word "war," they give a term of seven years, which, of course, does not apply to propagandists. However, in Russia, authorities also fine people for the word "peace."

I will not delve too deeply into the topic of Russian aggression in Ukraine; there is material for a separate book. Still, I will repeat my thesis that the Russian authorities do not even need to introduce a state of emergency to restrict the rights and freedoms of citizens. The desire of Putin's left heel is enough. In this regard, I believe that this article simply does not work since it does not establish any restrictions on power.

ARTICLE 57 OF THE CONSTITUTION

The text of the Article 57 reads: "Everyone shall be obliged to pay legally established taxes and levies. Laws, which establish new taxes or deteriorate the position of taxpayers, shall not have retroactive force."

I have no particular objection to this article. Of course, you can call citizens' attempts to evade taxes a specific sport, but I think this is hardly interesting to the reader.

I just want to note a separate abundance of various taxes and councils in Russia, reaching up to 63% of an employee's salary (including VAT). All of them have a significant impact not only on the well-being of citizens but also on businesses that are trying to comply with all laws: it becomes at a distinct disadvantage compared to businesses that do not make deductions from employees' salaries (black scheme) or do it partially (gray scheme). It is easier for such companies to bribe numerous inspectors; it also more efficient, and often, much cheaper.

Nevertheless, let's say this article is working. I have no objections.

ARTICLE 58 OF THE CONSTITUTION

"Everyone shall have a duty to preserve nature and the environment and to treat natural resources with care."

And again, an inevitable repetition. We have already discussed the situation with the environment in the analysis of Articles 7 and 36.

And I won't repeat myself here. You can refresh your memory by referring to these articles.

ARTICLE 59 OF THE CONSTITUTION

The full text of the article reads:

"1. Defence of the Fatherland shall be the duty and obligation of a citizen of the Russian Federation.

2. Citizens of the Russian Federation shall perform military service in accordance with federal law.

3. In the event that their convictions or religious beliefs run counter to military service and in other cases established by federal law, citizens of the Russian Federation shall have the right to replace it with alternative civilian service."

I note that in such a formulation as this, in combination with complete lawlessness, this article in itself violates the right to life. Who supposed that by "protection," Putin would mean "waging an aggressive war"?

If you remember, we talked about the conscript army in Russia when analyzing Article 37 in the context of slave labor, which was done by citizens drafted into the military. There were attempts to transfer the army to a contract basis, but they failed: after all, free labor is free labor.

However, the situation worsened six months after Russia's aggression against Ukraine. The almost wholly plundered "professional army" could not fulfill the tasks set by Putin to seize Ukraine. Ironically, all the journalists and lawyers who investigated the theft in the Russian army were persecuted by Putin (the same Ivan Safronov, sentenced to 20 years, or Navalny and his team. And for the third time in history (I don't want to say "Russia"—it's a little over 30 years old as a state—but rather Moscow), mobilization was carried out (the other two were during the first and second world wars). According to Putin, who never learned how to tell the truth—"partial."

Moreover, in the decree itself, no restrictions on mobilization are given. Even the figures he voiced of 300,000 people are not found there. I believe that it is indicated in paragraph 7, which, contrary to Article 24 of the Constitution, is hidden by the mark "dsp" ("for internal purposes"), that is, it is classified, although the information in it does not belong to state secrets. We have already talked about this phenomenon in the analysis of the same article 7. Since Putin is physically incapable of telling the truth, I believe the amount he announced to be mobilized is greatly underestimated. Otherwise, why hide it?

Yet, thousands of untrained unequipped citizens were not only taken out of the economy and separated from their families but worst of all, they were literally sent to their deaths for the sole purpose of buying Putin time while he terrorizes the Ukrainian population and "forces them into negotiations" and the actual abandonment of part of their territories (you can read a series of articles about the situation with the mobilized here). At the same time, after the announcement of mobilization in Russia, thousands of citizens fled abroad.

I note that mobilization was carried out even in the occupied "DPR" and "LPR", which is a military a crime and is prohibited by Article 51 of the Geneva Convention. However, Putin's actions in Ukraine generally consist of continuous war crimes, starting right from the beginning. I cannot list them all; for this, I need to write a separate book. Instead, it is difficult to enumerate what Putin does non-criminally in this regard.

In any case, it cannot be directly and firmly said that this article is violated. Indeed, the creators of the Constitution provided for the obligation to, and I want to emphasize it, the defense of the motherland. However, Putin, under Article 353 of the Criminal Code of Russia, unleashed an aggressive war, and more than once. He added a whole cycle of military crimes to the already long list of crimes he committed. As a result, Putin perverted the meaning of this article, forcing hundreds of thousands of his citizens **to die** in a war of aggression. Therefore, I propose to move on to the next article. If you want to read more about Putin's crimes in Ukraine, you can do so here and here.

ARTICLE 60 OF THE CONSTITUTION

I have no objection to this article. It simply sets the age of full capacity. "A citizen of the Russian Federation can independently exercise his rights and obligations in full from the age of 18."

ARTICLE 61 OF THE CONSTITUTION

But I have a few comments about this article. Its full text is as follows:

"1. A citizen of the Russian Federation may not be deported from the Russian Federation or extradited to another state.

2. The Russian Federation shall guarantee its citizens protection and patronage abroad."

I don't have any particular objections to the first point either. This rule is especially true for murderers who are class close to Putin—Lugovoy (the murderer of British citizen Litvinenko), Chepiga and Mishkin (the murderers of British citizen Don Sturgess) or the murderers of Yandarbiev). However, issues arise concerning the second point.

The fact is that here again, the class character of Russian society is turned on. If it is arms dealer Viktor Bout, convicted in the United States in the early 2000s, or pilot Leonid Yaroshenko, who brought drugs to Africa (here and continued here), Russian diplomacy is trying to rescue even now. Still, somehow with the help of ordinary citizens, it turns out badly.

Two such examples are the stories of Maria Butina and Sofia Sapega.

Maria Butina was used by former Vice Speaker of the Federation Council Torshin for actual espionage (here and here (you can find video transcript here)). She plead 'guilty,' was convicted by an American court, and was sent to prison, from where she tearfully begged to collect money for her lawyer. But the Russian authorities did not help her. Even Navalny asked Russian leaders to help her, at least with legal assistance. For this, she later repaid him: upon her return to Russia, she was placed in the propaganda channel "Russia Today" and visited Navalny in prison, where she told him about her bitter experience of imprisonment in an American prison.

"Helping" citizens is another matter. The most high-profile case was with Sofia Sapega—the girlfriend of the administrator of the telegram channel NEXTA Roman Protasevich. I will remind you of the story of their detention. Roman Protasevich covered the protests in Belarus in 2020, for which he was put on the wanted list by Lukashenka's dictatorial regime. The plane he flew with his girlfriend, Sofia Sapega, from Athens to Vilnius was forcibly landed in Belarus by fighter. It is not known precisely for how long Roman was subsequently convicted. Four criminal cases were initiated against him, with a total sentence of more than 25 years. Sophia was sentenced to six years. At the time of writing, she is still serving her "punishment" in Belarus, despite promises from the Kremlin to help her.

However, my favorite case concerns the beating of Russian propagandists at the same protests in Belarus in 2020. The fact is that many Belarusian propagandists quit, and there was almost no one left to lie to the population. Putin helped his dictator friend not only with money for the security forces but also with the dispatching of propagandists. Some ended up with the protesters and were severely beaten in the now-infamous Akrestino prison. At Lukashenka's meeting, even the editor-in-chief of Russia Today, Margarita

Simonyan, remarked that it was too much. To which Lukashenka simply offered to "turn the page." And this was everything the state did to help the beaten propagandists.

I have already said that personal experience is not the criterion of truth, but I have also encountered the great help of the state in trouble abroad.

If you remember, in 2010, there was an eruption of an Icelandic volcano with the unpronounceable name Eyjafjallajokull. My wife and I were then on vacation in Berlin. However, a ban on aviation flights was introduced due to ash emissions. As citizens of Russia, the main problem was the violation of the visa regime. We simply physically could not leave on time: the planes did not fly, and the train tickets were all sold out by our comrades in misfortune. What was left for us to do? We went to the Russian embassy on Unter den Linden for advice and help. However, we were not even allowed inside. Probably, as we were neither murderers nor drug dealers. We were helped only by the Berlin police, who gave us the necessary certificate.

But the situation is not limited to the casuistry listed above. So, in Syria and Iraq, there are thousands of Russian women — the wives of the "Islamic State" militants — precisely those who were imposed with medieval values of unquestionable obedience to their husbands. The Russian state is also in no hurry to help them.

I think there are enough examples to make a conclusion. Regarding the effect of this article, the Russian state will help Russians abroad only in cases where it is not possible to cover up some crime abroad or if it is beneficial. In any other cases, the Russian authorities do not give a damn about citizens, but this is not surprising, given the general attitude towards their citizens and their rights.

ARTICLE 62 OF THE CONSTITUTION

I will only go into a little detail on this article too. It concerns dual citizenship.

"1. A citizen of the Russian Federation may have citizenship of a foreign state (dual citizenship) in accordance with federal law or an international treaty of the Russian Federation.

2. The possession of foreign citizenship by a citizen of the Russian Federation shall not diminish his (her) rights and freedoms and shall not release him from obligations stipulated for Russian citizenship, unless otherwise specified by federal law or an international treaty of the Russian Federation.

3. Foreign citizens and stateless persons shall enjoy rights and bear obligations in the Russian Federation on a par with citizens of the Russian Federation, except in those cases envisaged by federal law or by an international treaty of the Russian Federation."

It describes the general legal definition of dual citizenship adopted in international law: the recognition by one state of a person as its citizen.

On the other hand, we are already at the final stage of the analysis of the rights and freedoms of man and citizen. I think it is already clear to the dear reader that the passport of a Russian citizen is not much different from the collar of a slave: it does not give rights or protection but imposes only duties and insane administrative and criminal obligations.

In this regard, almost the entire upper class in Russia either has second citizenship or has already moved their children abroad. For example:

- Putin's daughters are in Holland and South Korea.

- Dmitry Peskov's daughter, Putin's press secretary, lives in France.

- Deputy Pekhtin is a son in the USA.

- Minister of Transport of the Moscow Region, Katsyva. With my son in the USA.

- The children of deputy Zheleznyak live in Switzerland.

- Astakhov's children: one is in France; the other is in England.

- The children and grandchildren of the "chief patriot of Russia" head of Russian Railways, Vladimir Yakunin, lives outside of the country in England and Switzerland.

- The daughter of Foreign Minister Sergei Lavrov, Ekaterina, lives and studies in the United States.

- The son of the Vice-Speaker of the State Duma A. Zhukov lived and studied in London for a long time.

- The daughter of the Deputy Speaker of the State Duma, Sergei Andenko, studies and lives in Germany.

- The eldest son of Deputy Prime Minister Dmitry Kozak, Alexei, lives abroad and is engaged in the construction business.

- Aleksey Kozak's younger brother, Alexander, works at Credit Suisse.

- The eldest son of Deputy Remezkov, Stepan, recently graduated from Valley Forge Miller College in Pennsylvania (a year of study costs 1,295,761 rubles). His youngest daughter lives in Vienna, where she does gymnastics. Masha Remezkova represented the Austrian national team (!) at children's competitions in Ljubljana.

- The daughter of deputy V. Fetisov, Anastasia, grew up and studied in the USA. Nastya never learned to write and read in Russian.

- The daughter of Svetlana Nesterova, a State Duma deputy from the United Russia faction, lives in England.

- The main fighter for "traditional Orthodox values," E. Mizulina, the son, Nikolai, studied at Oxford, received a diploma, and moved to live on a permanent basis in tolerant Belgium, where same-sex marriages are allowed.

- The daughter of Deputy Vorontsov, Anna, lives in Italy. She moved there from Germany.

- United Russia member Elena Rakhova became famous for calling Leningraders who lived less than 120 days in the blockade "non-blockade"— her daughter lives in the United States.

- The daughter of the ex-speaker of the State Duma, one of the founders of the United Russia party, and now a member of the Security Council, Boris Gryzlov, Evgeny, lives in Tallinn. And even recently received Estonian citizenship.

- The son of the former Minister of Education, Andrei Fursenko, lives permanently in the United States.

- Son of V. Nikonov (grandson of Molotov), president of the Politika Foundation, is a US citizen (quote from here).

It's funny that among Putin's garbage amendments to the 2020 Constitution, there was one banning dual citizenship for senior officials (changes to Article 71 (paragraph "e")). The State Duma, on this basis, in April

2021, adopted a law banning dual citizenship for these officials and military personnel. But "suddenly," it turned out that most of the top officials there, one way or another, have dual citizenship. And Putin had to adopt a separate decree that allowed specific officials to violate these laws (the text of the decree itself is here). Let us note, in addition, that once again, the Decree of the President, for some reason, is placed above the law and even above the Constitution, which was amended by him himself!

On this incident, I propose to leave Article 62 alone. As you can see, its use at the moment also depends on what Putin ate for breakfast and how well he squatted into his suitcase.

ARTICLE 63 OF THE CONSTITUTION

This article is de facto dead; just a few people use it. In the presence of a vast choice, almost no one wants to check it for themselves, which, as you understand, is the right choice. It concerns political asylum.

"1. The Russian Federation shall grant political asylum to foreign citizens and stateless persons in accordance with the universally recognized norms of international law.

2. In the Russian Federation persons who are persecuted for their political convictions or for actions (or inaction) not recognized as a crime in the Russian Federation may not be extradited to other states. The extradition of persons accused of a crime, as well as the surrender of convicts to serve sentence in other states, shall be carried out on the basis of federal law or an international treaty of the Russian Federation."

It is challenging to imagine a person running to Russia for political asylum. The only known person who asked for this was Edward Snowden, a former CIA agent who disclosed information about CIA surveillance worldwide and was accused in the United States of espionage. Subsequently, he even received Russian citizenship. Which, in general, is not particularly surprising, given Putin's special love for criminals of various types and sizes.

However, we can confidently say this article is in full force. I think it is clear to the dear reader that you don't even have to be a murderer or a drug dealer for this; accusations of espionage are pretty enough.

ARTICLE 64 OF THE CONSTITUTION

This is the last article in our analysis.

"The provisions of this Chapter shall constitute the fundamental principles of the legal status of the individual in the Russian Federation and may not be changed otherwise than in accordance with the procedure which is established by this Constitution."

I already spoke about the particular procedure for changing the Constitution when analyzing Article 16: it prohibits changing chapters 1, 2, and 9. And Putin had to fill in many garbage amendments to other chapters to remove the limitation of his terms somehow. It turned out poorly, and we will discuss this in the next chapter.

However, given the fact that in 2020, Putin introduced more than 200 amendments to the Constitution, in violation of not only the Constitution itself but also the laws on changing it, I believe this article no longer works. It is enough to introduce into any other article the opposite within the meaning of the provisions contained in chapters 1 and 2, and voila! You can already refer to the new article for violating any rights. That's why I call the amendments "garbage"—even this poor Constitution totally died with their adoption. And I propose to turn to how this happened.

In general, "Agora," a group of human rights activists "Coming Out" and "Civil Control" compiled a report for the OSCE on the situation with civil rights in Russia, which you can read here.

Chapter 5

CHANGES TO THE
CONSTITUTION OF 2020

I have already told the story of these changes, and I will remind you with your permission.

Putin's first term began in 2000. At that time, the presidential period was four years, and Article 81 of the Constitution limited the number of terms to two. Unfortunately, here, too, there was a significant shortcoming of the Constitution: the wording of paragraph 3 turned out to be too controversial: "The same person cannot hold the position of the President of the Russian Federation for more than two **consecutive** terms [emphasis mine - A.M.]." It was precisely the word "consecutive" that Putin used.

He had a "castling" with Medvedev. And during Medvedev's "reign," he increased the presidential term from four years to six. Accordingly, when he returned, under mass protests, his third term expired in 2018 and the fourth, in 2024. At the beginning of the fourth term, Putin was already becoming a lame duck; officials began to look around in search of a possible successor, which he wildly did not like. Besides, to give power to someone else for six years again? It was incredible. Putin is old; in 2024, he will be 72 years old, taking into account six years for the next "castling"; in 2030, he would already be 78 years old. In addition, I believe his paranoia is growing, and he can hardly find the same stupid, weak-willed, and obedient candidate to take his position and return it. No, of course, it was not an option. But he cannot retire; I think you understand that the number of violated criminal code articles under absolutely any government would cost him freedom and loot.

Consequently, it was necessary to remove the time limit in the Constitution. However, he understood that the one-time limit amendment would be sharply negatively perceived by everyone, including his loyalists. And he decided to make a whole bunch of amendments so that the amendment he needed would be lost among the rest.

At the same time, of course, a number of articles of the then formally valid Constitution were violated to the maximum. In particular, paragraph 2 of Art. 16 (on non-contradiction) and Article 64 of the Constitution (on the procedure for amendment). But I'm getting ahead of myself a little.

Putin came up with a "cunning" plan. Let's call it conditionally "zeroing the deadlines." He put forward the thesis that the changes are so significant that they reset all the previous terms of the president. Since his possible entry into office will take place according to the new rules, the old terms, for some reason, disappear and are not counted according to the rules of Article 81 of the Constitution.

Where did he get it is the big question. First, in the theory of constitutional law, there is no such provision at all. Secondly, Article 81 of the Constitution still contains (even after its amendments) requirements for time limits, and its old ones have not magically disappeared. Nobody forgot about them.

The countries where the presidential terms were reset in this manner were such beacons of democracy as Belarus, Peru, Kyrgyzstan, Venezuela, Kazakhstan, Tajikistan, Burkina Faso, Uzbekistan, Senegal, Bolivia, Burundi, Egypt (more details can be found here).

But as you probably noticed, Putin didn't have much choice here either to keep power (and freedom and property with it) or to act according to the law, which he never knew and understood.

Then again, alas, historical parallels with Ivan the Terrible arise. Here is a quote from diletant.ru:

"On December 3, 1564, hundreds of wagons stood by the Kremlin. Ivan the Terrible packed his things and his family and left Moscow. He rode with faithful servants, as in a war, and close associates and servants. And not empty-handed: the tsar took with him "holiness, icons and crosses," precious, gold and silver dishes, clothes, and most importantly, the entire treasury. No one in the city knew where he would go. The people and the nobility were perplexed—what was happening?

"Grozny went to Aleksandrovskaya Sloboda (now the town of Aleksandrov, Vladimir Region). Only on January 3, 1565, his messenger, Konstantin Polivanov, arrived in Moscow. By that time, everything in the capital was in turmoil. Orderly people began to scatter from the city, government in wartime stopped. Polivanov aggravated the situation. He brought two epistles—one to the metropolitan and one to the people (it was read out publicly). Grozny said that he "put wrath" on the clergy, boyars, courtiers, thieving clerks, and devious ones. He declared all of them disgraced for predatory crimes committed in his infancy and later for disobedience, oppression of the people, and unwillingness to fight honestly. That is why, the king explained, he left because he did not want to endure "changing deeds."

"According to foreigners, Ivan IV was so afraid of losing the throne due to his adventure that his hair began to fall out. But he didn't show it. He very accurately thought out the impact of his message to the people—Grozny told the common people, among other things, that "there is no anger at them and some disgrace"; that is, they supposedly have no claims against them, but only against the nobility and priests who prevent him from punishing traitors. This tactic worked great. A crowd gathered in the metropolitan's courtyard and, to put it mildly, urgently demanded that the tsar be returned to Moscow and that he rule as "fit him." Otherwise, the townspeople threatened, they might punish the traitors themselves.

"The nobility understood that royal wrath and executions were a hundred times less evil compared to what black people could do with them. In the face of this threat, the boyars agreed to everything and decided to tearfully beg Ivan IV to take the throne again. The metropolitan sent Archbishop Pimen and Archimandrite Chudovsky to Aleksandrovskaya Sloboda to mitigate the tsar's wrath by persuasion. Boyars, service people, merchants, and townspeople followed them to bow to the sovereign. They all begged for royal forgiveness.

"Ivan the Terrible, of course, relented. On February 2, 1565, he returned to the capital. But now he has set conditions—from now on, he has the right to punish and pardon at his discretion, even execute, even deprive anyone of their property without trial. At the same time, Ivan Vasilyevich declared part of the country to be entirely and personally belonging to him—"oprichnina" (from the word "oprich," which means "except"), all income from which relied personally on the king. The oprichnina included Moscow (partially), Mozhaisk, Vyazma, Suzdal, Galich, Vologda, Dvina, and other cities of the central and northern Russian lands. The rest was allocated to the "zemshchina.""

In general, this is excellent historical material, and you can read about all the grievances of Ivan the Terrible here.

Accordingly, Putin wanted to pull off the same trick: to make everyone "beg to return him to the kingdom." He decided to approve the amendments by "popular vote." Separately, I want to note that it was not even a referendum, which required campaigning, including against—all the campaigning was, of course, exclusively "for." The Federal Constitutional Law of 06.28.2004 N 5-FKZ "On a referendum of the Russian Federation" no one even recalled.

I emphasize that the Federal Law of March 4, 1998, N 33-FZ "On the procedure for the adoption and entry into force of amendments to the

Constitution of the Russian Federation" (with amendments and additions) does not provide for the procedure for changing the Constitution of the Russian Federation at a referendum (especially some kind of "general voting," which does not exist in Russian legislation at all).

In addition, in accordance with Article 141 of the Decree of the State Duma of the Federal Assembly of the Russian Federation of January 22, 1998, N 2134-II GD "On the Regulations of the State Duma of the Federal Assembly of the Russian Federation" (with amendments and additions), each amendment to the Constitution must be considered and discussed separately from the others. Voting must take place on each amendment separately and not be adopted as a whole package. Moreover, his lackeys did break a leg. More than 339 amendments were proposed, of which 206 were selected for adoption.

And among the commission on these amendments, Putin appointed "professional lawyers" like himself; for example, Yelena Isinbayeva, a champion in pole vaulting. The athlete thanked the president for being included in the working group and added: "I've just read the Constitution of our country; this is important because, before that, there was no reason and no need to read it. And now I understand that this is a very important book, and everyone needs to read it. I learned a lot of interesting things."

Of course, apart from laughter, this caused nothing among the people. There were jokes like:

"One day, Putin walked around the Kremlin and saw that Yelena Isinbayeva was writing something.

- Elena, what do you write? - Putin asked.

- A Constitution. - Elena answered.

- Instead of the old one? - Putin asked.

- Was there an old one? - Isinbayeva exclaimed and cried."

The amendments were "essential." I won't bore you with all of them (the full list can be found here). I will highlight only the most "important" and "necessary":

- The guarantees of the President's immunity after his resignation specified in the Federal Law of February 12, 2001 No. 12-FZ "On Guarantees to the President of the Russian Federation, who has terminated the exercise of his powers, and to his family members" were duplicated (Articles 92.1, 93);

- Obliged the President to maintain peace and harmony (clause 2, article 80);

- They allowed former Presidents and persons who have outstanding services to the country to be senators for life (paragraph 2 of article 95);

- Tighter requirements for officials. The right to be elected is a person permanently residing in Russia, without foreign citizenship and deposits abroad without foreign citizenship, residence permit, or other document allowing to live in another country; hold deposits abroad; store valuables in foreign banks (remember those very amendments that Putin urgently had to correct by his decree?) (clause 3 of article 77, clause 5 of article 78, clause 2 of article 81, part "p" of article 95, part "n" of article 97, subparagraphs "e" of paragraph 1 of article 103, paragraph 4 of article 110, article 119, paragraph 2 of article 129);

- Obliged to create economic growth and increase trust between the state and citizens (Article 75.1). Obviously, before the indication of this in the Constitution, this was not the goal at all (which, in general, is not far from reality);

- pointed out that Russia is the legal successor of the USSR and, at the same time, "retains faith in God" (Article 671). How this is combined with the materialism of Marx and Article 28; I need help understanding.

They even included in the text of the Constitution the obligation to provide students with hot breakfasts! (Article 72).

But if you think that the circus gathered its clowns on this and rode, then you are mistaken.

The very process of voting for the amendments took place most comically. Since it was not held in the form of a referendum, polling stations were not always used. There were cases when "voting" was carried out on stumps or car trunks. Of course, all this action took place during a pandemic, which, on the one hand, did not impede the holding of this circus at all, and on the other hand, the ban on meetings and rallies was still in effect.

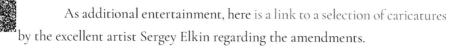

As additional entertainment, here is a link to a selection of caricatures by the excellent artist Sergey Elkin regarding the amendments.

However, the voting process itself was the icing on the cake.

We have already said that many of the amendments of 2020 directly contradict the rules specified in the first two chapters, which the authorities would like to change so much, but the Constitution itself prohibits. And if earlier I had questions about why there was such a tough procedure for changing the Constitution, now the question has disappeared. In principle, this was the purpose of the amendments (apart from zeroing out Putin): to turn the Constitution into a lump of contradictory rules. In this state, it loses its binding force.

How does it work? Let's say there are two articles: one says that something is forbidden for the authorities, and the other says it is acceptable. There are no collision rules (the rules on Articles' priorities) in the Constitution; thus, such contradicting articles have the same legal force. Accordingly, the authorities can refer either to one article or another, depending on how beneficial it is in the current situation.

However, the Constitutional Court, of course, did not see any violations.

In principle, with these amendments, we can confidently conclude that Russia no longer has a Constitution; it is dead. Russia, at the time of writing the book, is a feudal class state of the fascist type. It has nothing of a legal, social and democratic state. And that is how it became a zombie country, posing a significant threat to other countries.

In place of a conclusion

You probably think that I will now begin to give figures that so many articles of the Russian Constitution are in force, but so many are not. However, I will save time on this.

The fact is that the articles of the Constitution have a certain synergy. For example, if you have a right, but there is no mechanism for its protection, then anyone can violate such a right, and it disappears. Just like absolute protection will not help protect rights that you do not have. When the state violates both rights and at the same time does not allow these rights to be protected, then a person is reduced to the role of a slave, both in a figurative sense as deprived of his rights and in a literal one, which we saw in the analysis of the "right to work." And without civil rights, a person becomes dependent and poor, taking out his evil on anyone different from him and rejoicing that someone has been in trouble or lives worse than him. Such a state can only be returned by returning real rights.

But how do we determine that Russia has ceased to be a country of zombies?

Surgeons often remove cancerous or gangrene-affected organs to save a patient's life. Russia will need to follow a similar procedure.

If the Constitution is the brain, then Russia is a zombie country. It is ugly and terrible, sowing destruction and fear. It no longer has life, and it hates life in others. You can bring it back to life only if you remove the virus of Putinism, do not let it spread. Do not try to understand it, but only remove it, and then carry out gigantic and overwhelming work to restore human rights and the Constitution in Russia.

Before lifting sanctions, foreign states should consider the following changes and actions in Russia. If they don't exist, sooner or later, it will again take the path of fascism (especially in the face of humiliation from the inevitable defeat in the war with Ukraine):

1. Adoption of an entirely new Constitution. Even the Russian Constitution of 1993 had many significant flaws that helped Putin seize power and destroy civil society. His amendments to it turned the Constitution into a trash can—a tangle of vague, contradictory, and often wrongful rules. And I hope I was able to show and prove it.

2. A large open tribunal should be held over all persons involved in unleashing the war with Ukraine. Including propagandists (under articles 353 and 354 of the Criminal Code of the Russian Federation). The "list of 6,000" compiled by Navalny's team is the absolute minimum.

3. Lustration of all officials who held important positions under Putin. From judges of the Constitutional Court, and the Supreme Court, to parliamentarians, security officials, and even "ordinary" members of United Russia.

4. Complete liquidation of the FSB — the "worthy" successor of the bloody KGB — and with exactly the same concept of morality and attitude towards law and human rights.

5. Complete reform of all power institutions. The liquidation of the National Guard and the center-E, which has become, in fact, the political police.

6. Introduction of a complete ban on state funding of the media, political parties, and religious associations.

7. Conducting an audit of all existing regulations for compliance with the new Constitution.

Without all this, Russia will remain a zombie country and a threat to the entire free world.

How to determine that Russia has embarked on the path of correction? Whoever came to power in Russia after Putin, if he began to take the above seven steps, then Russia has a chance, and without them, the country will continue to pose a threat to everyone around.

In addition to these internal steps, Russia should be excluded from the UN Security Council, which slows down the already challenging and diplomatic work. Let me explain:

Russia retains permanent membership in the UN Security Council. Given the politics of chaos that Putin uses worldwide, this status must be reconsidered.

Russia occupies it because it self-proclaimed itself as the only successor to the USSR, which was a permanent member of the UN Security Council. However, the USSR no longer exists.

The USSR was included as a permanent member of UN security since it was in the camp of the victorious countries in the Second World War. But Russia did not participate in the Second World War. It was formed as a country in 1991, 50 years after it began and 46 years after it ended.

Second moment. The USSR broke up into the following countries: Azerbaijan, Armenia, Belarus, Georgia, Kazakhstan, Kyrgyzstan, Latvia, Lithuania, Moldova, Russia, Tajikistan, Turkmenistan, Uzbekistan, Ukraine, and Estonia, in addition, part of the territory went to China and even Norway. In terms of territory, Russia is also not identical to the USSR.

Russia is different from the USSR in terms of laws, formal state structure, and rulers.

The only way Russia argues why it should hold this post is because it accepted some of the debts of the USSR. However, along with the debts of the USSR itself, Russia also accepted the debts of other states to the USSR itself. Again, nowhere in international law are there any provisions on universal succession, that is, upon the collapse of a state, all rights and obligations pass to the country that assumed the old monetary debts.

Suppose Russia breaks up into several more countries: the Far East, Tatarstan, Chechnya, Moscow with the Region, and the Tver Region. In this case, why should Moscow have permanent membership? Because before the disintegration, the decision-making center was there? There is no logic in this.

In this regard, it is not at all clear why Russia considers itself the only state that should have permanent membership in the UN Security Council instead of the USSR. Therefore, Russia illegally uses the right of veto in the Security Council, which, as a result, made it extraordinarily ineffective and useless; the UN Security Council cannot decide on almost any issue because of Russia's dangerous position.

I want to emphasize separately that the concept of "succession" is not in the UN Charter. Each country must sign it, and the signed Charter is kept in the organization's archives. At one time, after the collapse of Yugoslavia, Serbia applied to the UN by way of succession, but it was refused and told to apply on a general basis. The Resolution of the United Nations Security Council No. S/RES/777 of September 19, 1992 and United Nations General Assembly Resolution No. A/47/RES/1 of September 22, 1992, was even issued on this.

I also need help finding documents confirming Russia's signing of the UN Charter. That may be why Putin doesn't follow it.

In any case, it is simply necessary to reconsider Russia's status in the Security Council and even in the UN and begin the long road of defashization of Russia and Russian society.